Dangerous Behaviour, th
and Mental Disorder

Dangerous Behaviour, the Law, and Mental Disorder

HERSCHEL PRINS

Tavistock Publications

London and New York

First published in 1986 by
Tavistock Publications Ltd
11 New Fetter Lane, London EC4P 4EE

Published in the USA by
Tavistock Publications
in association with Methuen, Inc.
29 West 35th Street, New York, NY 10001

Photoset by Rowland Phototypesetting Ltd,
Bury St Edmunds, Suffolk
Printed in Great Britain at the
University Press, Cambridge

British Library Cataloguing in Publication Data

Prins, Herschel A.
    Dangerous behaviour, the law, and mental
    disorder.—(Social science paperback; 333)
    1. Violence
    I. Title   II. Series
    303.6'2   HM281

    ISBN 0-422-79220-9

Library of Congress Cataloging in Publication Data

Prins, Herschel A.
    Dangerous behaviour, the law, and mental disorder.
    Includes bibliographies and index.
    1. Insane, Criminal and dangerous—Great Britain.
    2. Insane—Commitment and detention—Great Britain.
    3. Mentally ill—Care and treatment—Great Britain.
    4. Forensic psychiatry—Great Britain. 5. Criminal
    psychology. I. Title. [DNLM: 1. Counseling—methods.
    2. Forensic Psychiatry—methods. 3. Mental Disorders.
    HV8742.G72P73   1986   364.3'8   85-27923
    ISBN 0-422-79220-9 (pbk.)

Between the acting of a dreadful thing
And the first motion, all the interim is
Like a phantasma or a hideous dream.
SHAKESPEARE
Julius Caesar Act II, scene i

Contents

Acknowledgements

Few books appear without the help and encouragement of a good many people and this work is no exception. My thanks are due to a number of individuals: to the editorial staff at Tavistock Publications who have, as usual, been most encouraging and helpful; to various Home Office officials—Miss M. D. Samuels, Her Majesty's Assistant Chief Inspector, Probation Inspectorate; Mr L. Scudder and Mrs S. Murray, P2 Division; Mrs M. E. Bowden, C3 Division—for much helpful information and advice in connection with Chapter 3.

Some of the material in this book has been tried out over the past few years on a number of courses. I am grateful to the Probation Service Northern Region Staff Development Office (in particular to Mr George Best) for much help and encouragement in enabling me to experiment with a range of materials; my thanks are also due to Tony Walker, Sheila Kenyon, Jean Merchant, and Liz Hill for being such supportive colleagues on these courses. I have also used some of the material in this book on courses for 'approved social workers' and senior management staff employed by Leicestershire County Council Social Services Department. The authority has always been most supportive to me in my endeavours and I am particularly grateful to David Waddilove, formerly a training officer with the Department, for his help. In expressing my gratitude to all the above-mentioned, I must make it clear that they are in no way responsible for any errors or omissions in the book. In addition, the views expressed in the book are my own and should not be taken to be representative of any official body with which I am or have been associated.

Finally, my thanks once again to Janet Kirkwood for coping so willingly and cheerfully with my untidy scripts and to my wife, Norma, for doing her patient best to improve my written English. She, too, is not to be held responsible for any errors, omissions, or infelicities of style or grammar that remain; the final responsibility for these must rest with me.

HERSCHEL PRINS
Houghton-on-the Hill
Leicestershire
Summer 1985

Author's note—use of non-sexist language

In this book I have attempted wherever possible to use non-sexist language. In most instances, I have used the words 'he' and 'she' or the plural, 'they'. I have retained the *generic* use of the word 'he' where convention still seems to demand it—for example, in quotations from statutes—or when it would make communication excessively cumbersome or obtrusively ungrammatical.

Foreword

The world is steeped in the rhetoric of violence. The horror of international terrorism and the menacing aggression acted out between factions and adherents of religious and political ideologies feed the media and in time may dull our senses. Perhaps it is no worse now than at any other period of man's history but only seems so because modern communication has shrunk the world and the modern armoury has enormously increased the consequences of violence. Even if somehow we manage to distance ourselves from those horrors, however, they still provide a frightening backcloth to the violence and danger represented by some individuals in our society and expose the potential for devastating aggression in all of us.

We cannot establish that dangerous offending is on the increase in our own society, any more than we can prove this in the world as a whole, but however expressed—in robbery, assault, rape, affray, or football hooliganism—it rarely goes unnoticed and unreported. A Sutcliffe or a Nilsen will fill the papers and screens for days and the public's fear, as well as a mood of vengeance and sheer fascination with bizarre crime, is regularly re-awakened by the issue of possible parole for Myra Hindley; yet in neither medium does the good news attract much attention. We forget about the world's trouble spots of yesteryear as they return to something like normal; we hear little of the countless offenders once classified as dangerous who are successfully rehabilitated and go about their lives in the community. Of course, we may just tell ourselves that mankind has a remarkable capacity for survival and recovery yet it would be wrong to ignore the crucial outside intervention that may have brought about improvement and the continuing support that sustains it. Most of those whose behaviour has erupted in ways that have endangered others acquire the control or receive the medical or social work attention necessary to keep it within bounds. Our concern should centre on those whose dangerousness is altogether more threatening and persistent.

The increasing expense of institutional treatment, together with a disenchantment with its rehabilitative success and a concern not to deprive the mentally disordered of their liberty indefinitely, has led to a greater reliance on community provision. If, however, community provision is to offer the patient or offender the professional attention required and others the protection to which they are entitled, there must be more rigorous and extensive training for community supervisors, better collaboration between institution and community, and a less arbitrary division between medical/psychiatric and penal services.

In his highly respected practice, teaching, and writing, Herschel Prins has stood for professional thoroughness— examine all the evidence, assess the need, secure provision, co-ordinate support. Our state of knowledge about the causes and correction of dangerous behaviour may be limited but if we apply it methodically, review our practice, and show that there is careful management of potential danger, the public can be reassured that the risks are acceptable. The disciplined approach that Prins recommends is reflected in the presentation of this new book, which he has properly been encouraged to produce, giving more detailed attention to issues discussed in his earlier publication, *Offenders, Deviants, or Patients?* which has, over the years, amply proved its value to students and practitioners.

Herschel Prins does not claim to break fresh ground, nor to advocate new methods of treatment. He modestly refers to his work as 'other men's flowers' but that need not be taken as an apology. He has painstakingly selected his material from an extensive garden and presented it to great effect. As always, he directs his readers to a comprehensive bibliography on each aspect of his subject. This book will soon establish itself as an important reference work for those who share in the heavy responsibility of dealing with high-risk offenders in either the medical, social work, or criminal justice field. The writer has authority based on substantial and continuing experience of his subject in many capacities. He represents the true professional approach by exploring the body of available knowledge and theory and showing how this can be translated into the skills and methods of good practice.

MICHAEL DAY, OBE, MA
Chief Probation Officer
West Midlands Probation Service
June 1985

PART ONE
Legal and
Related Aspects

CHAPTER ONE

Rationale and outline

'A mighty maze! but not
Without a plan.'

POPE

In an earlier work (Prins 1980), I dealt in general terms with some of the problems presented by those offenders designated as mentally abnormal and potentially dangerous. The favourable reception given to that work and the views of helpful, discerning colleagues and critics led me to conclude that there was scope for a further contribution in this field. In addition, having taught various courses for local authority social workers, probation officers, psychologists, psychiatrists, magistrates, and others for the last five years, I have been struck by the continuing desire expressed by these workers and their colleagues for help in understanding and managing those offenders or offenders/patients regarded as dangerous. I have decided, therefore, that rather than merely providing a revision of my earlier book I could usefully take the opportunity to select for more detailed consideration some of the issues that could be touched upon only briefly in *Offenders, Deviants, or Patients?*, given the more general nature of that text. In the present book a major concern is the recognition not only of the multi-disciplinary nature of the task involved in handling dangerous and high-risk offenders but, in addition, of the wide range of knowledge required for effective practice in this area. It is also important to emphasize at this early stage that not all mentally disordered persons are dangerous and not all dangerous persons are mentally disordered. It is very unfortunate that the media sometimes tend to dramatize the singular case with the unfortunate result that the general public tend to associate mental disorder with violent and dangerous behaviour. As I shall demonstrate later in the text, such instances are fortunately rare, although their rarity should not lead us to avoid the means of managing and understanding them more competently.

Dangerous and high-risk offenders are dealt with either through the health care or penal systems, often in what appears to be a somewhat arbitrary fashion. In these two arenas there is ample room for confusion. Chiswick, McIsaac, and McClintock state the dilemmas very cogently.

> 'The criminal justice system is concerned with the mainten-
> ance of law and order and the administration of justice.
> Medical services are concerned with the delivery of health
> care. Though both systems meet a public need, they differ
> widely from each other in their disparate functions and their
> manner of operation. The two systems are required to over-
> lap in an area which for each system is a tiny fraction of their
> whole.'　　　(Chiswick, McIsaac, and McClintock 1984: 81)

The problem of which of the two systems should contain and care for the dangerous or potentially dangerous offender was graphically exemplified in the cases of Mawdsley and Williams, cited in *Offenders, Deviants, or Patients?* They are worth quoting again in the present context.

Case 1

Robert John Mawdsley, described by Mr Barry Mortimer, QC, prosecuting, as 'one of the most dangerous and determined killers held in prison in this country', pleaded guilty to murder-ing two prisoners at Wakefield Prison, and was sentenced to life imprisonment on each charge.

The killings took place when Mawdsley was already serving a sentence of life imprisonment for murder; the two victims had cells on the same landing. The motives for the killings were uncertain but about two months earlier, Mawdsley had told another prisoner that he was considering 'doing someone in' because he was sick of Wakefield and he would be certain to get moved to another prison.

On the morning in question, Mawdsley had obtained a fearsome weapon from somewhere unknown. It was a dagger made out of a piece of steel, which he tucked into his trousers. Sometime before exercise, (first victim) came into Mawdsley's cell. Mawdsley took the knife out and attacked (first victim), stabbing him about the back and head. During the course of the struggle (first victim) fell on to a bed and Mawdsley took a length of cord from his pocket and garrotted the man by tying a ligature tightly around his neck.

After exercise, Mawdsley was walking round the landing and saw (second victim) in a cell. He was on his bed and Mawdsley took out the knife and launched a terrifyingly violent attack on (second victim), stabbing and penetrating his skull, and stabbing his chest through to the stomach. He then caused some fearful damage to the side of (second victim)'s head, probably by banging his head against the wall.

In June 1974, Mawdsley had been convicted of manslaughter by reason of diminished responsibility after he had stabbed a man with whom he had a homosexual relationship. A hospital order had been made without time limit: Mawdsley was then held in Broadmoor Hospital.

On 26 February, 1977, Mawdsley and another prisoner took a fellow prisoner hostage in Broadmoor. After hours of negotiations with the staff, Mawdsley suggested that the hostage should be exchanged for a doctor. After torturing the victim, Mawdsley and another man strangled him by fastening a ligature around his neck. Mawdsley was convicted of murder, and remained in Broadmoor until his transfer to Wakefield.

At the trial for the Wakefield killings, Mr Mortimer said of Mawdsley that 'he is a man who may be said to have little to lose'. Mr Justice Cantley told Mawdsley: 'I make no recommendation about the minimum period of your detention because I see no point in doing so. At present, I see no reason why you should ever be released, but it may be that something will happen which will enable you to be released at some time.'

(Source: *Guardian* 17 March, 1979)

Case 2

Barry Williams, aged 34, armed with a gun in each hand, ran amok and killed three of his neighbours and two other people.

He was finally caught after a police chase through Derbyshire. At Stafford Crown Court on 26 March, 1979, he pleaded guilty to manslaughter on the grounds of diminished responsibility and was ordered to be detained indefinitely in Broadmoor. Williams, a foundry worker, was said to be an introvert, with an intense and irrational hatred of his allegedly noisy neighbours. He thought that they were against him and that they made noises deliberately to upset him. In October, 1978, after drinking nearly half a bottle of whisky, he launched an attack on them, shooting two male members of the Burkitt family, who were outside the house repairing a car. He then shot at Jill Burkitt as she came out of the house; when another neighbour came out to investigate the noise, she was shot in the chest and shoulder. Williams then drove off in his car, throwing a home-made bomb and firing six more shots at neighbouring houses. Later, in the course of his escape, he killed two members of staff at a nearby petrol station. When, after a long chase, he was subsequently overpowered by the police, he is alleged to have said: 'You don't understand. You would have shot them if you had been me. They were not human beings. They were just things.' At his trial, it was alleged that Williams was in legal possession of various firearms but enquiries subsequently re-vealed that he had been involved in a number of incidents which, had they been known to the issuing authorities, would most probably have prevented him from being granted a firearms certificate. Staff at one of the rifle clubs to which he belonged said that he was never interested in orthodox target shooting and had once been ordered off the range for dangerous behaviour. Other incidents included two occasions when Williams had made unprovoked attacks on persons he con-sidered to have been making a noise near his house. Seven days before the multiple killings, he is alleged to have threatened to exterminate his neighbours. Described as an introvert—'a shadowy figure', 'a mister nobody'—his phobia about noise was compounded by a sense of persecution. He is alleged to have told the police that he thought his neighbours had been laughing at him and that local people thought he was a 'poof' because he was quiet and had few girlfriends. It was suggested at his trial that he had also been contemplating his own death, for he had taken out an insurance policy which would have given his parents £6,000, had he died. Like Mawdsley, he may have considered that he had nothing to lose.

(Source: *Guardian* 27 March, 1979)

These two examples graphically illustrate the problems inherent in the choice of disposal referred to above but, perhaps even more importantly, they also illustrate some of the key issues to be addressed in this book; namely, the prediction, assessment, and management of dangerous behaviour. The satisfactory and humane disposal of those who may not only be a danger to others but to themselves is frequently hampered by lack of adequate resources.[1]

It is a well-established fact that many of the people who form the subject of this book are housed in prison when they should be in hospital (see, for example: Orr 1978; Chiswick, McIsaac, and McClintock 1984; Dell 1984; *Guardian* 15 October, 1984). The plight of such persons is very well illustrated by the case of Tina Evans, reported in the *Observer* on 14 October, 1984.

Case 3

'Tina Evans, 18, is a mentally disturbed girl who, her mother, doctors and court officials agree, should be in a special hospital.

'Instead, for four months she was incarcerated in the psychiatric wing of Holloway prison, London—because there was neither the money nor the resources to accommodate her elsewhere.

'Her plight was first described in the *Observer* last month when she attempted to mutilate herself by trying to gouge out an eye as a protest against her conditions.

'Her only "crime", for which she finished up in Holloway, was to set fire to the quilt of her hospital bed in the psychiatric ward of St John's Hospital, near Aylesbury, last June.

'These actions, said her mother, Mrs Sheila Evans, last week, were "a desperate cry for help".

'"Holloway terrified her and if she had been kept there much longer, she would have killed herself. It was only by breaking the law that she has received the help she needed."

'As a result of a judge's decision, Tina is to undergo three years' treatment at Moss Side Hospital, in Liverpool.

'At Aylesbury Crown Court Judge Lawrence Verney told her: "The purpose of the court in making the order is to help you." He said he was satisfied Tina suffered from a psychiatric disorder.

'Holloway's deputy governor, Mr Ivor Ward, commented after the case: "Of course mentally ill people should be dealt with elsewhere than a prison, but I have no control over who comes through my front door."

' "The prisons were never intended to be a depository for such cases. The courts have a terrible dilemma finding places for people they feel cannot be kept in the community."

'Her ordeal in Holloway began after Milton Keynes health authority said it could not afford the £31,000 a year needed in a private hospital for the girl's treatment. It could manage funding for only six months.

'Psychiatrist Dr Peter Grabbett said that Tina's treatment "could be a very long process. It could take a few years. It is terribly difficult to say."

'A twin, Tina has had a history of mental illness since she was three days old when she suffered a brain haemorrhage.

'Doctors said she would be a vegetable, but a loving family helped her to "walk, talk and do most things normal kids would do," her mother explained to the judge.

' "Two years ago Tina's grave mental problem surfaced. She started having fits and then slashing her wrists and taking overdoses," said Mrs Evans.

' "We didn't know what was the matter with her. We took her to doctors, social workers, psychiatrists—but nobody wanted to know," Mrs Evans explained.'

When an offence of grave harm has been committed either against persons or property we obviously try to seek for explanations of the occurrence. In general, the more horrific and bizarre the crime or the behaviour, the more we will be tempted to seek psychopathological explanations. The (understandable) lay response is likely to be 'he/she must have been mad to behave like that' but, as has been shown in numerous court cases, it is not always possible to provide psychiatric 'excuses', however humane the intentions of the courts and those proffering professional advice may have been. Cases such as Sutcliffe's and

Nilsen's illustrate the problems particularly graphically; more will be said about their particular cases and the issues they raise in Chapter 2.

As already stated, in cases where serious personal harm has been caused to others, often in bizarre and unusual circumstances, questions of explanation and exculpation arise. For this reason, it seems logical to begin this book with a brief consideration of the issues of responsibility for criminal behaviour and the situations in which an accused person seeks to demonstrate that his or her responsibility may have been diminished. Then follows an account of the main systems of disposal through the health care and penal systems of those adjudged to be mentally disordered and/or dangerous. These more general considerations form the substance of Part One of the book. In Part Two, I shall deal with more specific issues; here I shall be concerned with a consideration of dangerous behaviour, psychopathic personality disorder, serious sexual attack, alcohol, drugs and other substances as facilitators of dangerous behaviour, and arson. The comments on management of these more specific groups are intended to supplement and complement the more general consideration of dangerous behaviour in Chapter 4. In the final chapter I shall attempt to pull together some of the themes that have emerged from the foregoing material. Readers will have noted that homicide *per se* is not dealt with in a separate chapter. This is because homicidal behaviour will be referred to in the chapter on Issues of responsibility and at various places in Part Two. Neither do I cover in any detail the major problem of terrorist activity in its various manifestations, though as I draft these sentences (October 1984) this subject has a tragic topicality in the light of the IRA bomb attack at Brighton. I do not deal with the topic because it is highly complex and merits attention in its own right. However, those who wish to study the subject in more detail will find suggestions for further reading at the end of Chapter 4.

In concluding this introductory chapter, it is important to stress a number of points. First, we need to remember that in dealing with dangerous and high-risk offenders the borderline between those who are mentally disordered in a strictly clinical sense and those who may be regarded as just 'odd' is a very blurred one. Second, it is worth stressing that the number of persons who commit a second homicide or other serious crime against persons or property is, of course, very small. In acknowledging the comfort of this statement, it is nevertheless important for us to try to learn how to reduce the chance of repetition even further. Third, as we shall see in Chapters 2 and 5, it is very difficult to determine when behaviour is motivated by 'sickness' or when it is to be regarded as 'evil'. Fourth, following on from the third point, it is vitally important for all those working in this field not only to be 'open' in their communications with each other but also to be aware of the importance of the phenomenon of irrationality that underlies attitudes to those whom we often fail to understand. Dangerous, repellent, and incomprehensible behaviour not only requires a contextual understanding derived from the disciplines of psychiatry, psychology, biology, physiology, law, counselling, and ethics (to name but a few) but also needs to be understood against a broader, social anthropological background. As one distinguished anthropologist suggests:

'what kinds of antisocial or criminal behaviour fail to strike the slightest chord of sympathy, or even evoke your discomfort? To what extent do you spontaneously tend to describe such behaviour as 'inhuman', 'bestial' or 'fiendish'? . . . there are crimes which are within the range of our experience or potential experience, but there are others which go beyond the reach of our sympathy.'   (Pocock 1975: 189–90, 209)

In a comparatively short work of this kind it is possible only to introduce readers to the subject matter. However, the references cited and the suggestions for further reading should, in my view, enable those who wish to do so to acquire a very solid background of knowledge. I have found it necessary, for purposes of clarity and ease of presentation, to divide the material somewhat arbitrarily. However, the work is intended *to be viewed as a whole*; its central aims are to enhance understanding, to improve communication between disciplines and agencies, and to encourage the development of good practice. Finally, I hope that this book, like its predecessor, will appeal to a wide range of readers, specifically psychiatrists, psychologists, nursing staffs, probation officers, local authority social workers, staff of penal

institutions, lawyers, the police, and sentencers, both professional and lay.

References

Chiswick, D., McIsaac, M.W., and McClintock, F.M. (1984) *Prosecution of the Mentally Disturbed: Dilemmas of Identification and Discretion.*
Aberdeen: Aberdeen University Press.

Dell, S. (1984) *Murder Into Manslaughter: The Diminished Responsibility
Defence in Practice.* Institute of Psychiatry, Maudsley Monograph
No. 27. Oxford: Oxford University Press.

Orr, J.H. (1978) The Imprisonment of Mentally Disordered Offenders. *British Journal of Psychiatry* **133**: 194–99.

Pocock, D. (1975) *Understanding Social Anthropology.* Teach Yourself
Books. London: Hodder and Stoughton.

Prins, H. (1980) *Offenders, Deviants, or Patients? An Introduction to the Study
of Socio-Forensic Problems.* London: Tavistock.

FURTHER READING

*Contemporary issues concerning the management of the mentally abnormal
offender, including more particularly some of those who behave dangerously,
are well described and discussed in:*
Craft, M. and Craft, A. (eds) (1984) *Mentally Abnormal Offenders.*
London: Baillière Tindall.

*For those wishing to keep abreast of developments and issues at the interface of law
and psychiatry,* International Journal of Law and Psychiatry, *published
quarterly by Pergamon Press is recommended.*

Note

1 I should make it clear that in this book I am predominantly, though not
exclusively, concerned with dangerous behaviour towards *others* and not
with dangerous behaviour towards *self*. This is not to deny the very real
problems created by self-directed dangerous behaviour but merely to acknowledge that it is a topic better treated in its own right. Indeed, the
literature on the subject of self-harm and suicidal behaviour is vast.

CHAPTER TWO

Issues of responsibility

'The heart has its reasons
Which reason does not know.'
PASCAL

'And oftentimes excusing of a fault,
Doth make the fault worse by the excuse.'
SHAKESPEARE
King John Act IV, scene ii

As I indicated in Chapter 1, in cases where serious personal
harm may have been done to others (not infrequently in bizarre
or unusual circumstances), questions of exculpation from criminal responsibility may arise. It is therefore my intention in this
chapter to consider some of these matters. I make no attempt to
consider this complex subject in great detail. Those readers who
wish to obtain a general overview of the subject will find my
earlier work, *Offenders, Deviants, or Patients?* a useful guide
(notably Chapter 2). Those wishing to pursue this important
and fascinating topic in more detail should consult the works
suggested for further reading at the end of this chapter. Unless
stated otherwise, the legal framework referred to in this chapter
relates only to England and Wales.

Definition, meaning, and boundaries

Lay men and women are likely to use the term *responsibility* in a
rather less precise fashion than would lawyers or students of
jurisprudence; indeed, lawyers and legal philosophers have
argued for centuries over such questions as the interpretation to
be placed upon phrases such as *criminal responsibility*. The *Concise
Oxford Dictionary* defines 'responsible' as 'liable to be called to

account, answerable to, *morally accountable for actions*, capable of rational conduct'. The law, however, is not directly concerned with the words I have italicized and, as Finch says, 'clearly the spheres of law and morals do not necessarily coincide' (Finch 1974:4). For our particular purposes, the term *responsibility* merely means the liability to be dealt with by the criminal law and to be disposed of via the penal and health care systems (see Chapter 3 for details). As my colleague Professor Griew says, responsibility is a word 'so often bandied about; like a historical background it gives an air of learning to a discussion . . . it is a muddying word . . . liability is the better word as being less ambiguous' (Griew 1984a: 60). The confusions and ambiguities concerning the use of the word are also well set out in a stimulating paper by Kenny (1984). In this chapter, I shall not be concerned with wider aspects of the subject as, for example, whether or not people should be brought before the courts at all, or the extent to which they should be diverted from the judicial and penal systems altogether by the exercise of police or other discretion. Nor shall I be concerned with the question of the age at which people should be liable to prosecution, nor with the question of whether or not individuals should be prosecuted who have committed an offence of 'strict liability' in law (as, for example, when a butcher sells bad meat for public consumption but does not know that it is bad). I shall be only marginally concerned with the concept of *mens rea* (legal guilt) and then only in relation to the so-called 'insanity defence'. This chapter is more concerned with three specific areas in which liability to be dealt with by the law may be at issue. These are *Insanity as a defence (the special verdict); Unfitness to plead (disability); Diminished responsibility (including infanticide)*. More attention will be focused on the third topic than on the other two. The main intention of this chapter is to introduce readers to some key concepts and terms that are of importance in understanding the backgrounds and histories of those who have been adjudged to be serious or high-risk offenders.

Insanity as a defence (the special verdict)

It is a generally accepted view that men and women are to be held responsible (liable) for their actions and are capable of exercising control over them. (Those interested in examining some of the historical vicissitudes through which this notion has passed should consult Walker 1968, Jacobs 1971, and Clark 1975.)

It is reasonably safe to assume that in the sixteenth and seventeenth centuries only very serious mental disorder (so-called 'raving lunacy') would have been recognized as giving exculpation from liability for serious crime—in particular, homicide. However, contrary to general belief, issues relating to insanity were gradually being raised more frequently in respect of crimes less serious than homicide. As Eigen puts it, 'the jurisprudence of insanity appears to have arisen not out of sensationalistic murders or grotesque personal assaults, but from what were rather more routine "garden variety" crimes' (Eigen 1983: 426). In addition, broader interpretations of what might constitute mental disorder were being admitted; for example, in the case of Arnold in 1724, the judge suggested that 'if a man be deprived of his reason, and consequently of his intention, he cannot be guilty' (Jacobs 1971: 27). Similar views were expressed in the case of Lord Ferrers in 1760.

A subsequent case that brought the issue into sharper relief was that of Hadfield, who was tried in 1800 for shooting at George III. In Hadfield's case, his counsel (Erskine) obtained an acquittal on the basis of Hadfield's having sustained serious head injuries (sword wounds) during war service. These injuries had caused Hadfield to develop delusional ideas that impelled him to the belief that he had to sacrifice his life for the salvation of the world. Not wishing to be guilty of suicide, he chose to commit his crime for the sole purpose of being executed for it. The case is of interest for at least two reasons. First, it was probably the first time that brain damage (caused by injury) had been advanced as a relevant exculpatory factor. Second, Erskine, who was a brilliant advocate, was probably able more easily to secure an acquittal for Hadfield at a time when public interest in and sympathy towards the 'mad' had been fostered by the long-standing and intermittent malady suffered by the King (a malady of which the diagnosis has always been disputed). However, not all cases were brought to such a successful outcome as Hadfield's. A similar plea in the case of Bellingham (who in 1812 shot the Prime Minister, Spencer Perceval) was unsuccessful and he was condemned to death. As Walker (1968) reports, a similar fate befell a contemporary of Bellingham's —an epileptic farmer called Bowler, who had killed a neighbour. However, it is the case of Daniel M'Naghten[1] in 1843 that is of key interest from our point of view, for it was the outcome of M'Naghten's case that resulted in the formulation of a legal test of insanity, a test that is still in force today, though hardly ever used.

M'Naghten, a Scot, seems to have suffered from what we would describe today as paranoid delusions. As a result of these delusions, he attempted to kill the Prime Minister of the day, Sir Robert Peel, but not knowing what Peel looked like, M'Naghten shot and killed Peel's secretary, Drummond, by mistake. At his trial, a number of eminent medical men testified to his unsoundness of mind and he was found 'not guilty by reason of insanity'. Queen Victoria, who had been the object of several attempted assaults upon her person by various people alleged to be of unsound mind, was not pleased with the verdict. It may be that her displeasure, and the interest that she and her Consort took in this and other cases, was more than a little influential in the decision of the House of Lords to call the judges before them to answer certain questions arising from M'Naghten's case. Two of the answers given by the judges have come to be known as the 'M'Naghten test'. This states, in effect, that:

> 'the jurors ought to be told in all cases that every man is to be presumed sane and to possess a sufficient degree of reason to be responsible for his crimes, until the contrary be proved to their satisfaction; and that to establish a defence on the ground of insanity, it must be clearly proved that, at the time of committing the act, the party accused was labouring under such a defect of reason, from disease of the mind, as not to know the nature and quality of the act he was doing; or, if he did know it, that he did not know what he was doing was wrong.' (Quoted in Walker 1968: 100)

Once one has disentangled the somewhat archaic language, it is possible to see that there are two 'limbs' (as some lawyers call them) to the 'M'Naghten rules', as they have since (quite erroneously) been called. An accused has a defence, *first* if he or she did not know the nature and quality of their act, or, *second*, if they did not know that it was wrong. It is not hard to see why these so-called 'rules' have been the subject of continuous criticism almost from the day they were posited. In the first place, they were framed at a time when the disciplines of psychology and psychiatry were at an embryonic stage of development; a disproportionate degree of emphasis was given to the faculties of knowing, reasoning, and understanding (cognitive processes) to the exclusion of emotional and volitional factors (see also Bluglass 1979). Second, the 'rules' make use of such expressions as 'defect of reason', 'disease of the mind', 'nature and quality of his act'. These have caused numerous arguments concerning their precise legal interpretation. Third, the criteria for M'Naghten 'madness' are so tightly drawn that its use as a defence in homicide cases has always been fraught with difficulty. Since the implementation of the Homicide Act of 1957, with its defence of diminished responsibility (see later), the insanity defence has been used in a mere handful of cases each year. Its very rare use in non-homicide cases (for example, in cases of shoplifting) and the effects of its possible use in cases involving automatic behaviour (automatism) have been the subjects of interesting comment of late (see, for example, Cranston Low 1983, Mackay 1983, and Griew 1984b). As long ago as 1975, the *Committee on Mentally Abnormal Offenders* (chaired by the late Lord Butler of Saffron Walden) considered that the so-called M'Naghten 'rules' were unsatisfactory. They recommended a new formulation of the *special verdict*—namely, 'not guilty on evidence of mental disorder'. The grounds for this amended defence would consist of two elements.

(1) A *mens rea element*, approximating to the first 'limb' of the M'Naghten 'rules'; that is, the jury would find that the accused did the act but did not have the *mens rea*. The jury would then return a verdict of not guilty on evidence of mental disorder. There would have to be in such a case (as in the current M'Naghten rules) a clear *causal* connection between the mental disorder and the absence of *mens rea*.

(2) A *second element*, which would provide for specific exemption from conviction for defendants suffering from *severe* mental illness or *severe* subnormality (now 'impairment') at the

time of the act or omission charged. This element would need consequential changes in our existing mental health legislation (the 1983 Mental Health Act).

The Butler Committee also proposed a definition of *severe* mental illness which would be contained in a new or amending statute. Their definition is of interest and is worth quoting.

'A mental illness is severe when it has one or more of the following characteristics:

(a) Lasting impairment of intellectual functions shown by failure of memory, orientation, comprehension and learning capacity.
(b) Lasting alteration of mood of such degree as to give rise to delusional appraisal of the patient's situation, his past or his future, or that of others, or to lack of any appraisal.
(c) Delusional beliefs, persecutory, jealous or grandiose. Abnormal perceptions associated with delusional mis-interpretation of events.
(d) Thinking so disordered as to prevent reasonable appraisal of the patient's situation or reasonable communication with others.'

(Home Office and DHSS 1975: para. 18.35 and Appendix 10)

It is of interest to note the specificity of the criteria suggested —a far cry from the somewhat primitive concepts of 'disease of the mind' or 'defect of reason' of the M'Naghten formulation mentioned earlier. The Butler Committee's proposal in respect of the second 'limb' has been held to be somewhat controversial. It is clear that, unlike the M'Naghten requirement, there need be no *causal* connection between the mental disorder and the criminal behaviour; all that would need to be demonstrated was that the accused person was suffering from severe mental illness or severe mental impairment at the time that he or she committed the act in question. However, the Committee seemed to think that a causal connection could be assumed in view of the very stringent criteria contained in their proposed definition. Under the present law, if the court returns a 'special verdict' there is only one form of disposal available—namely, mandatory indefinite detention under the Criminal Procedure

(Insanity) Act of 1964. Such an order has the effect of a restriction order without limit of time, imposed under section 41 of the 1983 Mental Health Act (see Chapter 3). Under the Butler Committee's proposals, a court, in returning a mental disorder verdict, would be left with a wider range of sentencing options than exist at present. 'Instead the court would have flexible powers: in particular, it could make a hospital order with or without restriction order; or order out-patient treatment; or simply discharge the defendant' (Griew 1984a: 49). It was not intended by the Butler Committee that the courts would have the power to fine or imprison the defendant, as these courses were seen by them as punishment—as distinct from the treatment options that they wished to see implemented in such cases.

Unfitness to plead (being 'Under Disability')

As we have seen, the provisions and implementation of the 'special verdict' arise in cases where it has been shown that a defendant was very seriously mentally disordered *at the time of committing the offence*. But what if a defendant is considered to be suffering from mental disorder at the time of the trial? By tradition, a court has to be satisfied that an accused person can, first, understand the charges against them; second, exercise their right to challenge a juror; third, follow the evidence against them; fourth, instruct counsel. If the accused is considered to be unable to put the foregoing into effect, he or she has customarily been held to be 'unfit to plead' or, to use the term now favoured, to be 'under disability in relation to the trial' ('under disability', for short).[2] The issue of unfitness to plead is raised very infrequently, mainly because a person has to be very seriously disabled psychiatrically in order to satisfy the relevant criteria. I have, however, come across a few examples in my work.

The first concerned a man who was suffering from such serious psychotic delusions that in the course of them he killed his wife. He was still severely psychiatrically deluded at the time of his trial and subsequently. The second case concerned a young man who was found to be so impaired in intelligence and understanding that he, too, was found unfit to plead. A third case concerned a man who, while in the grip of severe psychotic delusions, attacked a near relative. His case raised the issue of disposal on return to normal mental functioning and I will deal with this later. In most cases, therefore, the defendant qualifying for a disability plea will be suffering from a very severe mental illness or severe mental impairment. An accused person alleged to be suffering from amnesia (as in the case of R. v. Podola 1959) or from 'persecution mania' (as in the case of R. v. Robertson 1968) would not normally satisfy the strict criteria laid down; with amnesia, for example, one could still be quite able to follow the trial itself. The consequences which flow from a finding of 'disability' can be very serious for the defendant; and, as the Butler Committee pointed out, are productive of some anxieties concerning civil liberties. If found to be 'under disability', the accused will currently be detained under the provisions of Section 4 of the Criminal Procedure (Insanity) Act of 1964. This has the effect of a restriction order under Section 41 of the 1983 Mental Health Act (see also Chapter 3). In practice, this means that the defendant may be detained in hospital without ever having had the chance to rebut the charges that have been brought and moreover, that he or she will have been sentenced to what some have regarded as custodial treatment for an indefinite period. The Butler Committee (Home Office and DHSS 1975) made certain recommendations in relation to both law and practice. They suggested that the existing criteria for determining whether a defendant was under disability should be brought up to date; in future they should consist of:

(a) Whether the accused can understand the course of the trial proceedings so that they can make a proper defence.
(b) Whether he or she can understand the substance of the evidence.
(c) Whether he or she can adequately instruct legal advisers.
(d) Whether he or she can plead with understanding to the indictment (charges).

The Committee went on to make a major proposal concerning procedure, which would help to obviate the injustice mentioned above. They recommended that the question of disability should be decided at the outset of the trial or as soon as it was raised as an issue. Where disability was found and where medical evidence suggested a prospect of early recovery, the judge would be given power to adjourn the trial for up to three months in the first instance, with renewal for a month at a time up to a maximum of six months. If the accused recovered within the six months' trial period, the normal trial should proceed immediately. A *trial of the facts* (that is, of the substance of the case) should take place either as soon as disability had been found and it was decided that there was no prospect of the accused recovering, or as soon during the six-month period as the accused might prove unresponsive to treatment or recover, as outlined above. If the accused *is found to be under disability*, there should be a trial of the facts at the appropriate time. If a finding of 'not guilty' cannot be returned, the jury should be directed to find that the 'defendant should be dealt with as a person under disability'.

This new form of verdict would not count as a conviction, nor, said the Butler Committee, should it be followed by custodial punishment; the court should have wide discretion as to what penalty should be imposed (cf. my earlier remarks concerning a finding of 'not guilty' on evidence of serious mental illness). The procedures outlined above and the Butler recommendations apply only to the Crown Court at present, but the Committee did suggest that the Magistrates' Courts should, in future, also have the power to determine and act upon the issue of disability. The implementation in October, 1984, of Section 36 of the Mental Health Act of 1983 goes some way towards meeting the Butler proposals, in that an accused person found to be suffering from *mental illness* or *severe mental impairment* may now be re-manded to hospital with a view to determining whether or not their condition is capable of remedy. (For further details of this and related provisions see Chapter 3 and Gostin 1984: 251–57.) Finally, we should note that a person currently found to be 'under disability' may be remitted to court for trial if, on medical advice, they are considered at any time no longer under disability. The third case to which I referred earlier is an illustration of this possibility. The accused, it will be recalled, had been found 'under disability' in relation to an indictment of assault on a close relative. The assault had occurred when the accused was very grossly deluded. Within a year, the hospital Responsible Medical Officer (RMO) in charge of his case was able to certify that he had recovered sufficiently to be able to plead. He was therefore remitted to court. The outcome was a Hospital Order *without restrictions* under Section 37 of the 1983 Mental Health Act and he was returned to the hospital in which he had been detained originally. The outcome for him was that his status had changed from restricted to unrestricted status. There is currently no limitation on the length of time during which a person may be remitted to stand trial following restoration of their mental health.

Diminished responsibility and infanticide

So far I have considered cases and situations in which only very serious and narrowly defined parameters of mental disorder may be put forward as limitations on full responsibility for action punishable by criminal law and the courts. As we shall see, the statutory notion of diminishment of responsibility, introduced in 1957, allows a more flexible approach to be taken, though, as we shall also see, the concept is not without its own considerable difficulties. In dealing with diminished responsibility, I shall also discuss two other matters that may arise in connection with it—namely, the defence of 'automatism' and the defence of being intoxicated through drink or other drugs. Their inclusion here is to some extent arbitrary, as they may also arise (but to a lesser extent) in relation to the exculpations from responsibility already discussed.

Some hundred years after the implementation of the M'Naghten 'rules', the law relating to murder was amended by the Homicide Act of 1957. The 'rules' were retained—contrary to the advice of the Royal Commission on Capital Punishment (Royal Commission Report 1953: 413)—and the ancient Scottish defence of diminished responsibility was introduced in England.

'The 1957 Act was essentially a compromise solution to the controversy over capital punishment. It appeased the retentionists by retaining as capital offences certain categories of murder, including murder by shooting and murder in the course of furtherance of theft; but the remainder, numerically more significant, carried a mandatory sentence of life imprisonment.'   (Jacobs 1971: 4)

Table 2(1) *Section 2 manslaughter convictions 1968–78*

1968	1969	1970	1971	1972	1973	1974	1975	1976	1977	1978
49	58	65	72	85	77	96	76	93	92	78

(Source: Home Office 1979: 176–77)

Subsequently, the Murder (Abolition of Death Penalty) Act of 1965 suspended capital punishment for five years; by later resolution of Parliament, capital punishment ceased to exist and all murders were made punishable by life imprisonment alone.[3]

For present purposes, the relevant part of the 1957 Homicide Act is Section 2. This states that:

'(1) Where a person kills or is party to the killing of another, he shall not be convicted of murder if he was suffering from such abnormality of mind (whether arising from a condition of arrested or retarded development of mind or any inherent causes or induced by disease or injury) as substantially impaired his mental responsibility for his acts or omissions in doing or being party to the killing.'

(Homicide Act 1957, Section 2)

Thus it will be seen that the section permits the recognition of a degree of partial responsibility. A plea of diminished responsibility may be raised by the accused, and if contested, will be decided by a jury 'on the balance of probabilities'. This test is somewhat less strict than the 'beyond all reasonable doubt' burden of proof required in most criminal trials. Upon a finding of manslaughter, the judge has an unfettered discretion in sentencing. The number of convictions for manslaughter under

Table 2(2) *Corresponding convictions for murder*

1968	1969	1970	1971	1972	1973	1974	1975	1976	1977	1978
76	78	99	91	85	83	135*	98	108	115	110

(Source: Home Office 1979: 176–77)
*This 'peak' figure of 135 is accounted for by convictions for increased terrorist activity in that year.

Table 2(3) *Infanticide cases*

1968	1969	1970	1971	1972	1973	1974	1975	1976	1977	1978
25	13	15	18	17	9	15	5	6	6	8

(Source: Home Office 1979: 176–77)

Section 2 of the Act for the years 1968–78 are shown in *Table 2(1)*. The corresponding convictions for murder are given in *Table 2(2)*. Comparative figures for conviction in cases of infanticide (see later discussion) are given in *Table 2(3)*. Note that there has been a steady decrease in recent years. A breakdown of the disposals for the Section 2 manslaughter cases for the year 1978 is given in *Table 2(4)*.

In recent years there has been a decline in the use of hospital order disposals for Section 2 cases; this has been studied in detail by Dell (1982, 1983, Dell and Smith 1983, Dell 1984). In a detailed discussion of the difficulties, Dell suggests three main reasons for the change in sentencing practice:

(1) Increasing difficulty in obtaining places for these particular offenders in the special hospitals, this difficulty being closely associated with an increase in the reluctance of

Table 2(4) *Disposal of section 2 manslaughter cases for year 1978*

life imprisonment	18
over 10 years' imprisonment	1
4–10 years' imprisonment	8
4 years' and under	16
*Section 65, 1959 Mental Health Act	18
*Section 60, 1959 Mental Health Act	4
probation and supervision orders	9
suspended sentence	3
other	1
	78

(Source: Home Office 1979: 176–77)
*Although hospital order disposals represent about 30 per cent of the total as indicated in the text, their use has declined.

psychiatric staff to consider those suffering from psycho-pathic disorders as treatable.

(2) A reluctance on the part of psychiatrists to recommend placement in an ordinary psychiatric hospital. It is suggested that, because of the factors outlined above, judges have had no alternative but to send those considered to be psychopathic to prison.

(3) For those suffering from other and more treatable conditions—such as depressive illness—Dell's research suggests that the decision to award custodial as distinct from hospital disposals is likely to have been due to retributive sentencing on the part of the judiciary (Dell 1984: 14–24).

A plea to diminished responsibility will be accepted by the judge on the basis of uncontested psychiatric evidence in a very high proportion of cases and without the issue having to be tried before a jury. In one of her studies, Dell looked at murder and manslaughter convictions for the years 1976 and 1977. She found that only 26 out of 194 cases went to trial by jury (Dell 1982). I shall say more about such contested cases later; however, at this stage it is useful to examine fairly closely some aspects of the wording of the 1957 Homicide Act and the difficulties that this wording has presented to the courts and others.

The first difficulty arises in relation to the term *impaired responsibility*. As Samuels has pointed out, 'the notion of impaired responsibility, substantially impaired responsibility, is difficult to grasp. Can there be degrees of responsibility?' (Samuels 1975: 198). Since the decision in the case of R. v. Byrne (1960), the issue of responsibility has clearly been one for the jury to decide; it is not an uncommon experience, however, for psychiatrists to be asked whether or not *they* consider responsibility to be impaired. In many instances, they have been prepared to answer such questions in an attempt to help the judiciary resolve difficult questions in sentencing. The question is not, however, psychiatric but fundamentally legal and moral. Moreover, it appears from a recent decision (R. v. Vernege 1982) that a jury is not bound to accept psychiatric evidence that responsibility is substantially diminished, even if there is unanimous psychiatric opinion to that effect; this was certainly the case in R. v. Sutcliffe (1981) as we shall see later (see also Hall Williams 1980, Prins 1983, and Spencer 1984).

Returning to our discussion of semantics we may ask ourselves, what meaning should be attached to the term 'abnormality of mind'? Two aspects of this question may be discerned. First, whether or not an abnormality of mind existed; second, whether it affected the defendant's 'mental responsibility' for his or her actions. Hamilton, a forensic psychiatrist and the Medical Director of Broadmoor Special Hospital, gives support to Samuels (1975) and indeed others when he asks 'What on earth does (mental responsibility) mean?' (Hamilton 1981: 434); and, as already suggested, are psychiatrists necessarily the most appropriate persons to give such opinions? Kahn poses the dilemma for psychiatrists in these matters very well.

'In deviation from the normal, particularly where behaviour is concerned, there may not necessarily be a medical contribution at all. The treatment may be purely legal or social action. The aim is to bring the behaviour into conformity . . . the psychiatrist comes into the study of some human problems only by invitation, and this invitation may not be wholehearted. It is as if the psychiatrist is expected to claim authority in every problem of living, only to have that claim challenged even while his help is being sought.'

(Kahn 1971: 230)

Thus, even before specific matters of motivation and its interpretation are raised and challenged under our adversarial system of justice, there seems to be a fundamental ambivalence to overcome. This ambivalence is well attested to in the paper by Kenny already referred to. Kenny begins his paper with an incisive discussion of the case of Hinckley, who attempted to assassinate President Reagan. He makes some trenchant observations about the role of expert witnesses, particularly psychiatrists.

'The law should be reformed by changing statutes which force expert witnesses to testify beyond their science, by taking the provision of expert evidence out of the adversarial context, and by removing from the courts the decisions whether a nascent discipline is or is not a science.'

(Kenny 1984: 291)

Before examing psychiatric and allied aspects of the problem more specifically, I shall deal briefly with the question of provocation, since this is a defence associated closely with the matters under discussion.

PROVOCATION

Section 3 of the Homicide Act of 1957 provides for a manslaughter verdict on the grounds of *provocation*. It is not normally possible to 'run' defences under both Sections 2 and 3. This is because Section 2 presupposes that a degree of mental derangement and abnormal behaviour will be established; in Section 3 a more 'normal' reaction will be presupposed. However, it is not hard to see that a person suffering from a degree of mental abnormality *might* be more easily provoked than the average person. Despite this, in cases where abnormality is not being pleaded psychiatric evidence has been held to be inadmissable (as, for example, in the cases of R. v. Chard 1971 and R. v. Turner 1975). In the latter case, Lord Justice Lawton said:

'trial by psychiatrists would be likely to take the place of trial by jury and magistrates.... Psychiatry has not yet become a satisfactory substitute for the common sense of juries and magistrates on matters within their experience of life.'

(Quoted in Hall Williams 1980: 279)

However, in many cases the dividing line between those behaviours that can be regarded as 'normal' and those that can be regarded as abnormal may not be quite as clear-cut as Lord Justice Lawton suggested. Some support for this contention is afforded by Dell's study; she found that 'in a few cases, the jury had found the defendant guilty on the grounds both of diminished responsibility and of provocation' (Dell 1984: 4).

I have already made brief mention of the problem of defining an 'abnormality of mind'; we must now consider this in a little more detail. In the case of R. v. Byrne (1960)—concerning a sexual psychopath—Lord Parker (LCJ) described abnormality of mind and its legal implications in the following terms:

'Inability to exercise will-power to control physical acts, provided that it is due to abnormality of mind from one of the causes specified . . . (i.e. in the Homicide Act) . . . is sufficient to entitle the accused to the benefit of the (defence); difficulty in controlling his physical acts depending on the degree of difficulty may be. *It is for the jury to decide on the whole of the evidence* whether such inability or difficulty has, not as a matter of scientific certainty, *but on the balance of probabilities* been established, and in the case of difficulty is so great as to amount in their view to *substantial* impairment of the accused's mental responsibility for his acts.'

(R. v. Byrne 1960; italics not in the original judgement)

Some further points emerge from this statement. First, such a definition reinforces the much wider interpretation of mental disorder than that within the narrow confines of the M'Naghten 'rules' referred to earlier. Second, it seems to acknowledge that will-power can be impaired and it introduces a notion akin to the American concept of the 'irresistible impulse'—a notion not popular hitherto with English jurists. Third, we can draw the inference that the judiciary could permit the view that the mind can be answerable for behaviour. Other points that arise out of this important judgement are that the question of *substantial* impairment was a matter for the jury to decide, but *how* it arose and its *causes* were questions for the doctors. As to the meaning of *substantial*, it has been held subsequently that 'substantial does not mean total. . . . The mental responsibility need not be totally impaired, destroyed altogether. At the other end of the scale substantial does not mean trivial or minimal' (R. v. Lloyd 1967). In order to illustrate further some of the problems already alluded to, I shall use the cases of Sutcliffe, Nilsen, and Telling but, as already indicated, two other issues need to be considered in relation to the question of an accused's liability to be dealt with for his or her alleged criminal acts. These are the defences of automatism and intoxication.

AUTOMATISM

Automatism is a phenomenon that may occur in situations where loss of consciousness is the cause of an *involuntary* (unintentional) act, which may in certain circumstances nevertheless be held to constitute a crime. For legal purposes, then, automatism means being in a state capable of action but not being conscious of that action. In certain cases, it has been held that such a state can be offered as a defence because:

'the act . . . is done by the muscles without any control by the mind, such as a spasm, a reflex action or a convulsion; or an act, done by a person who is not conscious of what he is doing, such as an act done whilst suffering from concussion or whilst sleep-walking.'   (Jacobs 1971: 119–20)

The automatism defence is a comparatively recent one in English criminal law and reported cases go back only to the early 1950s. Hall Williams points out that 'the way the law has developed is to recognise two kinds of automatism; sane automatism and insane automatism' (Hall Williams 1980: 279). If all the evidence in the case points towards mental abnormality, then the court has available the Insanity (Special) Verdict (see earlier discussion) or, in the case of homicide, a verdict of diminished responsibility. In exceptional circumstances, a blow on the head, a cerebral tumour (as in the case of R. v. Charlson 1955), or sleep-walking (somnambulism) *may* be a justification for pleading sane automatism—in which case, a complete acquittal may be possible. It is worth pointing out that the courts have, on the whole, been reluctant to accept pleas of automatism. This reluctance, as Maher, Pearson, and Frier suggest, may stem

'from the fact that . . . (the criminal courts) . . . can ensure future control over an individual in order to prevent the repetition of possible dangerous behaviour . . . in only one of two ways; either by convicting him of a crime or by acquitting on the grounds of insanity (which leads to committal to a mental hospital). The courts have adopted two tactics to restrict the automatism defence to ensure control over categories of persons with conditions which can give rise to states of automatism.'   (Maher, Pearson, and Frier 1984: 95)

The first has already been referred to, namely, to treat the case as one of insanity with consequent indefinite hospitalization (as in the cases of R. v. Kemp 1957, Bratty v. Attorney-General for Northern Ireland 1963, and more recently in the

House of Lords decision in the case of R. v. Sullivan 1984). In Sullivan's case, as in some others, the issue concerned the question of what constitutes a proper defence for an accused who had assaulted someone during the course of a seizure caused by psychomotor epilepsy. (The possibility that certain epileptic conditions may be associated with violent behaviour will be examined in some detail in Chapter 4.) The House of Lords, though obviously unhappy about attaching a label of 'insanity' to cases of epilepsy, held none the less that only a defence of insanity and not one of (sane) automatism was open to the accused. An important point that arises from this judgement is that the idea of 'disease of the mind' (see earlier discussion) was to be given a very broad definition, so that society 'would be protected against recurrence of dangerous conduct' (Maher, Pearson, and Frier 1984: 96). The second tactic adopted by the courts to restrict the automatism defence is to hold that being in a state of automatism is not a defence if the accused is in some way to blame or is at fault for getting into that condition; for example, through getting into a state of acute intoxication (see also later discussion). A review of some of the relevant case law reveals that it has been held that a person is responsible for the consequences of his decision either to do something (such as ingest drink or drugs) or not to stop some activity (such as continuing to drive while beginning to feel overcome by the need to sleep); for example, in the well-known motoring case of Kay v. Butterworth (1945), the court held that if a defendant knew that drowsiness was overcoming him then he should have stopped driving and averted an accident. It will no doubt have occurred to the reader that there may well be a number of medical and mental conditions that are likely to be associated with automatism: epilepsy is one and diabetes mellitus another. (Those wishing to explore in particular the relationship between epilepsy and serious crime, within the context of this chapter, will find the work of Fenton (1975, 1984) helpful. In addition, useful accounts providing guide-lines as to whether a crime has been committed after an epileptic attack or in a state of epileptic confusion may be found in Blair (1977) and, more briefly, in Lishman (1978). A discussion of the legal issues in three well-known cases in which diabetes has featured in relation to pleas of automatism (Watmore v. Jenkins 1962,

R. v. Quick 1973, and R. v. Bailey 1983) may be found in Maher, Pearson, and Frier (1984).

Most observers seem to agree that the consequences that can flow from a plea of automatism not only seem to be somewhat arbitrary but are also drastic (for example, detention in a psychiatric hospital without limit of time). As a result of the 1984 case of R. v. Sullivan, 'all people who have transient episodes of impaired awareness are, at least temporarily, insane' (Fenton 1984: 197). The legal issues that arise from this and other decisions have recently been reviewed in a comprehensive paper by Mackay (1983).

INTOXICATION

I now turn to the allied and closely connected problem of intoxication. It is not uncommon in cases involving serious violence against persons or property for a plea to be made by or on behalf of the accused that their responsibility should be diminished because of the effects of taking alcohol and/or other drugs. In general, the law holds that being in a state of intoxication is no defence to crime but if the offence requires what lawyers call a specific intent (such as that which would be required for a finding of guilt on a charge of murder) the fact that the accused had been drinking might help to negate that intent and thus might provide a defence. (Other examples of crimes requiring specific intent are theft, fraud, and burglary.) However, various legal decisions and interpretations on this matter appear to suggest some conflict of opinion. For example, in the case of Bratty (1963) already referred to, it was held that in crimes such as murder, where proof of a specific intent was required, the intent might be negated by drunkenness and the accused might thus be convicted of a lesser charge, for example, manslaughter or even unlawful wounding. However, the issue is not always quite so clear-cut. In the recent and as yet not fully reported case of R. v. Gittens (*Law Society Gazette* 5 September, 1984), the appellant had been tried on counts of the murder of his wife and the rape and murder of his fifteen-year-old stepdaughter. An issue arose as to whether his admitted abnormality of mind, which substantially impaired his mental responsibility, was caused by the drink or the drugs he had taken, as the prosecution contended, or whether it was due to *inherent* causes *coupled with the ingestion of drugs and drink*, as the defence contended. The jury had been directed to decide whether it was, on the one hand, the *drink and drugs*, or, on the other, *the inherent causes* that were the main factors that caused him to act as he did (my italics). He was convicted of murder but appealed on the grounds that the jury had been misdirected, in that the proper question for them to decide was whether or not the abnormality arising from the inherent causes substantially impaired his responsibility for his actions. His appeal was upheld and a Section 2 conviction for manslaughter substituted for his conviction for murder. Lord Lane (LCJ), giving judgement, said that it was improper in *any circumstances* to invite the jury to decide the question of diminished responsibility on the basis of 'what was the substantial cause of the defendant's behaviour?' The jury were to be directed, first, to disregard what they thought the effect on the defendant of the alcohol- and drug-induced mental abnormality was, since such abnormality was *not* within Section 2(1). They were *then* to go on to consider whether the combined effect of *other matters*, which *did* fall within Section 2(1), amounted to such abnormality of mind as substantially impaired his mental responsibility within the meaning of 'substantial' as set out in R. v. Lloyd (1967). This being so in this case, said Lord Lane, the jury had been misdirected.[4] (My italics.)

In the case of R. v. Lipman (1970), the accused claimed successfully that he was under the influence of lysergic acid diethylamide (LSD) when he killed the girl he was sleeping with. Part of Lipman's defence consisted of the claim that as a result of his being in a drug-induced state he thought that he was being attacked by snakes; the immediate cause of his unlucky companion's death was asphyxia caused by having part of a sheet stuffed into her mouth. However, in the case of R. v. Majewski (1977) the House of Lords held that in the case of an impulsive act such as an assault, intoxication of itself would not constitute a defence. It was alleged that Majewski had been a drug addict and that he also had a personality disorder. He had been drinking heavily on the day in question and had mixed alcohol with quantities of sodium nembutal and dexadrine. Having ingested what must have amounted to a highly potent cocktail, Majewski became involved in a fracas in a pub, in the course of which he assaulted the landlord and another customer. Having been removed from the premises, he returned brandishing a piece of broken glass (Hall Williams 1980). The case of Majewski tends to support the view that the law sees the ingestion of alcohol and other drugs as an aggravating rather than as a mitigating factor and that voluntary intoxication is no defence.

If, however, an accused person can show that he or she was in a state of *involuntary* intoxication—where, for example, the accused had been deliberately drugged or had consumed intoxicants mixed into a non-intoxicating beverage without his or her knowledge—then he or she may have a defence. Such a form of defence will not be likely to succeed if an accused takes alcohol against medical advice after using prescribed drugs, or if they fail to take insulin for a diabetic condition (that is, in crimes requiring evidence of specific intent—as in the cases of R. v. Burns 1973, R. v. Quick 1973, and R. v. Stephenson 1979). In order to resolve some of these difficulties, the Butler Committee suggested—as have others (see, for example, Samuels 1975)—that a new offence be created: namely, being voluntarily drunk and dangerous. Thus it would be an offence for a person whilst voluntarily intoxicated to commit an act or make an omission that would amount to a dangerous offence if it was done or made with the requisite state of mind (intent) for such an offence. The new offence of being 'drunk and dangerous' would not be charged in the first instance but the jury would be directed to return a verdict on this offence if intoxication was being raised successfully as a defence. The Butler Committee also included a definition of a 'dangerous offence': an offence involving injury to the person or consisting of a sexual attack on another, or involving the destruction of or causing damage to property so as to endanger life—as, for example, in the case of arson (Home Office and DHSS 1975: paras 18.53–9).

CASES INVOLVING PROBLEMS OF RESPONSIBILITY

Following this brief but important digression, we can now return to an elaboration of some further issues involved in determining responsibility and the degree to which it may be eroded by mental disorder. Many of these issues are graphically illustrated in the recent cases of Peter Sutcliffe, Dennis Nilsen, and Michael Telling.

The case of Peter Sutcliffe

The case of Peter Sutcliffe attracted such notoriety that some of the key issues concerning the diminishment or otherwise of his mental responsibility for his acts have tended to be over-shadowed by the horrendous nature of his crimes and the furore surrounding the circumstances of his detection and eventual arrest (see, for example, Prins 1983 and Burn 1984). However, Sutcliffe's case—and to a somewhat less dramatic extent those of Dennis Nilsen and Michael Telling—highlights in compelling fashion many of the issues I have sought to address in the latter pages of this chapter. I have already indicated that a court frequently accepts a plea of diminished responsibility on the basis of agreed and uncontested psychiatric evidence—that is, the psychiatrists for the prosecution and for the defence are all agreed on the diagnosis.[5] It will be recalled that the issue of diminished responsibility is raised by and rests with the defence and that proof is on the *balance of probabilities*. And, as already indicated, if such a plea is accepted by the judge (in a non-contested case), or by a jury (after a trial of the issue), a person who would otherwise have been liable to conviction for murder will be convicted of manslaughter with a wide range of options available as to sentence. As is now well known, the trial judge in Sutcliffe's case—Mr Justice Boreham—refused (as was his right) to accept the agreed views of both prosecution and defence and decided to put the issue of Sutcliffe's mental responsibility to a jury. It is important to ask why this very experienced judge embarked upon this particular course of action when four highly experienced psychiatrists were all agreed on Sutcliffe's mental state. We can consider a number of possibilities. First, although a plea of Section 2 diminished responsibility is only available in a murder case, the judge may have been very conscious of the fact that the public might have considered it to be a somewhat contradictory and idiosyncratic state of affairs that allowed Sutcliffe to plead *guilty* to the *attempted murder* of seven women and *not guilty* to the murder of thirteen (when the fact that he had actually *committed* the murders was not being disputed—merely his criminal responsibility for so doing). To the general public (but not of course to the legally informed) it might also have seemed somewhat disturbing that such pleas were acceptable when, presumably, only good fortune saved the lives of seven of his victims. Hence, the judge might well have considered that 'public interest' demanded that the issues involved be made absolutely clear. Second, the judge would no doubt have been very conscious of the public's more general concern about the case and the notoriety attaching to it. It might have seemed to him to have been doing both the case and the public less than full justice to have disposed of it without a full public enquiry into the defendant's alleged motivation and mental state. Third, the judge, having read all the papers beforehand, might well have wondered at the apparent discrepancies between what Sutcliffe was alleged to have told the police in the course of their prolonged interviews with him, what he was alleged to have confided to the prison officers, and what he told the four psychiatrists who examined him. (See Spencer 1984: 106–13 for a full discussion of some of these issues.) Fourth, the judge would no doubt have considered the possibility of putting the case to a jury in the knowledge that, following a finding of guilty to *murder*, he could not only pass a life sentence but could also add *a recommendation as to what the minimum sentence should be*.[6] This possibility would not be available to him in a finding of Section 2 manslaughter. For all these reasons, the judge's decision seems very understandable, though the final outcome of almost certainly indefinite detention in hospital or prison could have been predicted.

According to media accounts of the trial, we had the somewhat unusual (some would say undignified) spectacle of all the psychiatric witnesses being cross-examined by the prosecution —including their own witness—when, only a few hours before, all parties in the case had been agreed on the course of action that should be taken. The manner in which the psychiatric evidence was received and commented upon in the media (notably the press) during the trial revealed very clearly the ambivalence of society that I referred to earlier towards the intervention of psychiatry in matters of behaviour. This ambivalence is, of course, compounded by the fact that our adversarial system of justice does not lend itself comfortably to discussion and deliberation of complex and finely drawn issues of intent and motivation. Psychiatrists, in their day-to-day practice, are accustomed to dealing with grey areas of motivation and far less with the black-and-white issues of fact demanded by the constraints of our system of criminal law. Some people have suggested that the psychiatrists could have made a better showing in court. They were certainly subjected to a good deal of criticism, if not ridicule. On going over the various press accounts of the case, much of this appears to have been ill-founded, given the constraints already referred to and the fact that press reporting can be highly selective. It is quite likely that some of the statements attributed to the psychiatric witnesses, like 'he had diagnosed schizophrenia in a quarter of an hour', were more than likely made within the context of more detailed statements and further qualified in some way. (See Prins 1983 and in particular the notes referred to therein for reference to the press accounts.)

Although I shall be considering the relationship between mental disorder and dangerous offending in Chapter 4, it is appropriate at this point to make brief comment about the relationship between some forms of schizophrenia and crime, since schizophrenia was the diagnosis that the psychiatrists gave in Sutcliffe's case. We can say that the relationship between schizophrenia and crime in general is very slight and not often *causally* associated (for a detailed discussion see Prins 1980 and 1983). However, the *particular* diagnosis given for Sutcliffe's disorder was *paranoid* schizophrenia. This disorder is characterized to a large extent (but not exclusively) by delusions. There are a number of well-documented cases concerning persons who have committed homicide and other serious offences whilst under the influence of such delusions, the most well known probably being the case of Daniel M'Naghten, referred to at the beginning of this chapter. In more recent times, John Ley, a former senior Australian Law Officer, was convicted of involvement in the murder of a man he deludedly believed to have seduced his wife. Following the trial and death sentence for murder he was found to be suffering from paranoid illness, reprieved, and sent to Broadmoor (Special Hospital), where he died soon afterwards. In more recent times, Ian Ball was ordered to be detained in a special hospital following his conviction for attempting to kidnap Princess Anne in London's Mall. Ball was suffering from a highly delusional system of beliefs that led him to execute a most elaborate and well-thought-out kidnap plot. In a recent work, Schreiber (1984) has graphically and in horrifying detail traced the history of such psychotic beliefs in the murderer and rapist Joseph Kallinger.

Another type of more narrowly focused form of paranoid disorder is that of morbid or pathological jealousy—sometimes referred to as the 'Othello Syndrome' because its essential features are so graphically depicted in Shakespeare's play of that name. This almost exclusively male condition is character-ized by a fixed and irrational belief that the spouse or partner is being systematically unfaithful. The person concerned will go to the most elaborate lengths to find proof of the alleged infidelity. Occasionally, a spouse or other partner will be attacked in the course of the pursuit of these beliefs; if she is lucky enough to escape with her life, she may be very seriously injured.

The most important point to remember about the paranoid disorders (and their variants) is that the individual is quite likely to appear sane, purposive, and intelligent in all other aspects of their lives. It is only when the actual subject matter of their delusional belief is touched upon that their symptoms may emerge with unexpected impact. It is not altogether surprising, therefore, that Sutcliffe was able to cover his tracks because one can be highly paranoid yet also highly evasive and cunning. As already indicated, the individual's delusional system may be so well encapsulated that it may not emerge until and unless the matters upon which the system has fastened are explored in a detailed and systematic examination by a skilled psychiatric assessor (see, for example, the work by Schreiber (1984) re-ferred to above). It is hardly to be wondered at that the police and prison officers obtained one impression of Sutcliffe and the psychiatrists another; much depends upon the questions one asks and the manner and skill with which one asks them.

At the time of his trial, other diagnoses of Sutcliffe's disorder seem to have been ruled out. We know that he is alleged to have suggested a head injury at some point. In some instances, if head injuries are serious enough to result in brain damage, they can produce delusional symptoms (as in the case of Hadfield referred to at the beginning of this chapter). Neither does a diagnosis of psychopathic disorder appear to have been entertained, though given his past history and background and apparent long-standing paranoid ideation such a diagnosis would seem unlikely (see also Burn 1984 and Chapter 5). A clear-cut diagnosis of paranoid schizophrenia does not seem to be without its difficulties either, given Sutcliffe's conflicting statements and his apparent capacity for acting with insight in order to avoid detection. Spencer suggests that 'in his *apparent* simulation of insanity, his alleged and God-inspired delusions and the sadistic undertones of his killings, Sutcliffe falls exactly halfway between the murderers John George Haigh and Neville Heath' (Spencer 1984: 112–13; my italics).[7] Spencer also suggests that a better defence for Sutcliffe might have been that he suffered

> 'from a clear-cut abnormality of mind of a strangely paranoid type. Starting in 1969 with an unexplained attack on a prostitute and enhanced in 1979 by trivial humiliation, it developed into a bizarre, homicidal hatred of women, particularly prostitutes or alleged prostitutes. It continued with a strongly sadistic overtone and possibly—perhaps probably—as the result of a low-grade schizophrenic process. Whether or not the basis was schizophrenic, there was surely substantially more than minimal or trivial diminishment of responsibility?'   (Spencer 1984: 113)

The rest of the story is well known. The jury, with its 10–2 majority verdict, found Sutcliffe guilty of murder. It is important to emphasize that in doing so they did not necessarily reject the argument that Sutcliffe was suffering from paranoid schizophrenia, only that it was *not of sufficient degree substantially to impair his mental responsibility*. He was sentenced to life imprisonment and Mr Justice Boreham made a recommendation that he serve a minimum of thirty years. Almost exactly a year later, on 25 May, 1982, he was refused leave to appeal. However, subsequent events have vindicated the views of the psychiatrists to some extent. Sutcliffe's mental condition deteriorated steadily in prison; not only did his delusions become much more severe but he was also the victim of a serious assault by a fellow prisoner. Despite the increasing severity of his symptoms, his vulnerability to attack, and the difficulty his management posed for the prison medical authorities, it was not until the end of *March 1984* that the Home Secretary signed the necessary papers to give effect to Sutcliffe's transfer to a special hospital. Such a transfer order had been supported by the statutorily required psychiatric evidence of two very experienced doctors as long ago as 1982! (*Guardian* 28 March, 1984). No doubt the Home Secretary of the day considered that the public had now had its pound of flesh and that such a move—although three years too late—was not now likely to be politically embarrassing.

The outcome of the Sutcliffe case demonstrates very clearly the unsatisfactory nature of the diminished responsibility defence. It supports the arguments of those who wish to see the abolition of the mandatory life sentence for murder; it also demonstrates the establishment's quite unnecessary caution and apparent lack of courage in effecting humane disposals unless they are considered to be politically expedient.

The case of Dennis Nilsen

In 1983, similar problems emerged in the almost equally notorious case of Dennis Nilsen. Nilsen admitted to killing fifteen men and dissecting, boiling, and burning their bodies. He was sentenced to life imprisonment, the judge adding a minimum recommendation that he serve twenty-five years. The jury had convicted him of murder by a majority verdict of 10–2 on all but one of the counts against him; in the latter case, they reached a unanimous verdict. In arguing for a manslaughter verdict, Nilsen's counsel had tried to convince the jury that 'anybody guilty of such horrific acts must be out of his mind' (*The Times* 5 November, 1983). In Nilsen's case, unlike that of Sutcliffe, there had been no unanimous prior agreement by the psychiatrists, nor was Nilsen's alleged mental disorder as floridly psychotic or akin to the lay person's notion of madness as was Sutcliffe's. Nilsen was said to be suffering from a personality disorder (see Chapter 5); he was also said to have suffered because of abnormal sexual development. The psychiatrists disagreed not only as to the nature of the diagnosis in this case but also as to whether it constituted an abnormality of mind within the meaning of the Homicide Act. However, no one reading the press accounts of Nilsen's life history, his crimes, and his attitudes towards his victims, would fail to agree that his behaviour was decidedly abnormal by any standards (*The Times* 5 November, 1983; *Guardian* 5 November, 1983). (For a sensitive attempt to explore Nilsen's motivation and background, see Masters 1985.)

One of the key issues that emerges from Nilsen's case is similar to that which emerged in Sutcliffe's—namely, the difficulty in fitting the inherently imprecise concepts used in psychiatry into the confining strait-jacket of the present law. However, there is an important difference between the two cases. Sutcliffe's disorder was one that can be improved by treatment, even if not completely cured. The most florid and intrusive features of his delusions can be treated and abated, to some extent, by medication. In Nilsen's case, his personality disorder—even if it had constituted an abnormality of mind —was considered to be largely untreatable, so that a penal as opposed to a hospital disposal may seem only marginally less helpful. As I shall show in Chapter 5, some personality disorders *can* be minimally improved, given the right approach and environment. It could be argued, at least hypothetically, that under current conditions of prison overcrowding and lack of resources, the penal disposal in Nilsen's case might not have been particularly helpful.

The case of Michael Telling

Finally, to complete the picture, it will be useful to make brief reference to the case of Michael Telling. On 29 June, 1984, Telling was gaoled for life for the manslaughter of his second wife, Monika. Following a nine-day trial, he had been found guilty of manslaughter but not of murder by a *unanimous* jury verdict. It is of interest to note that the jury took only two-and-a-half hours to reach its verdict. It was alleged that Telling had not really matured from the days when he was an extremely disturbed boy and that he had demonstrated a marked lack of ability to control his impulses and emotions. (This description of lack of impulse control has much in common with that in the case of R. v. Byrne, quoted earlier.) The facts in Telling's case are, to some extent, only minimally less bizarre than those in Sutcliffe's and Nilsen's. Admittedly, he had only committed one murder, but the circumstances of that single killing seem both gruesome and highly pathological. According to the press reports (*Guardian* 30 June, 1984), Telling shot his wife after she had allegedly taunted him beyond endurance with details concerning her sexual exploits with members of both sexes. After killing her, he moved her body around the house for a week or so, calling in occasionally to kiss and talk to the corpse as it lay on a camp-bed. He then placed the body in a half-built sauna in the house. *Five months* later he decided to take the body to Devon. Having tried unsuccessfully to bury the body (the ground being too hard for digging because of the prolonged summer drought), he dumped it in some bracken overlooking the River Exe. He cut off the head and took it with him. It was subsequently found in the boot of his car. In Telling's case, *two* psychiatrists testified that Telling's responsibility was diminished and *one* testified against that view. It is difficult to tell whether the jury was more influenced by the opinions of the *two* psychiatrists, who viewed him as suffering from a disorder that would diminish his responsibility, or by his bizarre activities following the killing when they took the view that he 'must have been mad' to have behaved in that fashion. Samuels has some very apt words on this latter point.

> 'If a defendant just kills his victim for what appears to be a very ordinary motive such as greed or jealousy, diminished responsibility stands little chance of being established, but if the defendant has a history of mental trouble, goes in for perverted sexual practices with the victim before and after death, *mutilates the body, cuts it up . . .* (or) . . . sends it through the post . . . then the more horrible the killing, the more likely diminished responsibility will be established, because *the further removed from normal behaviour the behaviour of the defendant, the more he appears to be mentally ill*, or so the submission runs.'
>
> (Samuels 1975: 199–200; my italics)

In the light of the foregoing accounts, it is somewhat difficult to reconcile the conflict of evidence and verdicts in the three cases. There are, of course, other and somewhat less notorious cases that have posed the same dilemmas and questions. I shall refer to some of these inconsistencies in my concluding observations, but before doing so I must make brief reference to the offence of infanticide.

INFANTICIDE

Apart from the Homicide Act, the law makes *specific* provision for the erosion of responsibility in one other way. This is through the Infanticide Act of 1938. This enactment (which amended an earlier act of 1922) was introduced in order to relieve women from the death sentence for murder who, under certain specific circumstances, had caused the death of their children. In the context of this chapter, its creation is of interest in that it gave statutory recognition to a *specific state of mind* in a woman who caused, by any wilful act or omission, the death of her child *under the age of twelve months* when the balance of her mind was disturbed by reason of her not having fully recovered from the *effect of giving birth to a child, or by reason of the effect of lactation consequent upon that birth*. The act was passed at a time when more emphasis was placed upon what were thought to be the adverse effects of childbirth on a woman's mental state than would be considered relevant today. When one examines these comparatively rare cases (see *Table 2(3)*), there are nearly always significant factors operating other than, or in addition to, psychiatric disorder following the birth—for example, adverse social conditions or a severely stressful and complex personal situation—that would most probably enable the case to be dealt with under the provisions of the Homicide Act. A recently reported case illustrates these points well.

A woman killed her four-year-old daughter shortly after the latter had witnessed her mother killing her seventeen-month-old baby brother by strangulation. In this case, the prosecution accepted pleas of diminished responsibility and the woman was discharged on condition that she receive hospital treatment. Defending counsel said that the woman had experienced a slow build-up of pressure and had suffered a depressive disorder from the birth of her son. In theory, had she killed this child within the first twelve months of his life instead of at seventeen months, she could have been charged with infanticide, as well as being charged with the murder of the four-year-old (*Guardian* 27 November, 1984). This case highlights the somewhat outmoded and arbitrary nature of the infanticide defence. The Butler Committee proposed that the offence itself could be subsumed under the defence of diminished responsibility and this seems sound (Home Office and DHSS 1975: paras 19–26) but the Criminal Law Revision Committee favoured its retention (CLRC Report 1980: paras 100–04, 114:1). It seems to me that the fewer unnecessary special defences there are the better; the special offence of infanticide could quite readily be subsumed within some of the proposals for reforming the present law.

Conclusions

I have tried to illustrate, in this inevitably discursive chapter, a number of cases and situations in which those accused of serious crimes against persons or property may proffer a disturbed or abnormal mental state as mitigation of liability to be dealt with as an ordinary offender, i.e. as absolving them wholly or partly from criminal responsibility. In making this attempt, I have had to take a number of short cuts and to give insufficiently detailed attention to some important legal, ethical, philosophical, and psychiatric concepts. The law is complicated not only because it has evolved slowly over time in relation to a wide range of cases but also because concepts of mind, of disease, and of culpability have not evolved in a natural and uniform sequence. Developments in medicine, neurology, and psychiatry, for example, have affected the way in which personal responsibility for behaviour has to be viewed differently today from how it was regarded 150 years ago. In addition, public attitudes to those who practise the art and science of medicine, particularly psychiatry, affect the climate of opinion in which these practitioners, judges, and lawyers play out their roles within the arena of the court.

To some, the law appears to be unnecessarily complicated and proposals to adopt the French concept of *demence* (as in the Code Napoléon) find favour with some critics (see, for example, Fitzgerald 1981). The adoption of this concept would provide quite simply that where an accused person was suffering from *demence*, he or she should be deemed to be not capable of crime and exculpated from all liability. (This would apply in particular to cases now dealt with under the M'Naghten ruling and those found to be 'under disability'. Those interested in examining the concept of *demence* and its derivatives should consult Foucault 1979: 19–23.) The Butler Committee made a not wholly dissimilar proposal in relation to diminished responsibility. They suggested that if the mandatory life sentence for murder was to be abolished, the defence of diminished responsibility (with all the complexities and contradictions and ambiguities illustrated in the Sutcliffe, Nilsen, and Telling cases) would be obsolete; the judge could then exercise the widest possible discretion in sentencing. Failing abolition, the Committee recommended a rewording of Section 2 of the Homicide Act. This would be to the effect that if the defendant was found to have a mental disorder (as defined by the (then) Mental Health Act of 1959) that was such as to be an extenuating circumstance, then the charge could be reduced to manslaughter. However the Criminal Law Revision Committee (1980) and Bluglass (1980) have pointed out that offences currently dealt with as cases of diminished responsibility would be excluded unless a wider interpretation of mental illness (undefined in the current Mental Health Act) was to be allowed. Dell has put the case for change very powerfully.

> 'if the mandatory life sentence for murder was abolished, there would be an end to the stretching and manoeuvres which have now to be undertaken in order to give homicides suitable, instead of unsuitable sentences. Not only the defendant, but judges, doctors and lawyers would benefit from the change.' (Dell 1984: 60)

Zeegers has highlighted some of the more positive elements in notions of diminished responsibility.

> 'Our far from perfect society, with imperfect laws, imperfect courts, imperfect ways of handling drop-outs, imperfect social care, imperfect people and imperfect knowledge of the human mind should be very careful and reserved in its verdict. Applying penal law means an appeal to us all, to acknowledge *our* responsibility. A healthy society ought to accept responsibility, and ought to show concern towards its

members, especially to those who prove to be not mentally able to cope.'   (Zeegers 1981: 444; italics in original)

It seems to me that some of the reforms I have suggested would go some way towards establishing that sense of community responsibility and humaneness that Zeegers evokes in the above passage.

With this important message in mind we can now proceed to Chapter 3, in which I shall examine the main disposals available to the courts for those adjudged to be serious and high-risk offenders and the methods by which these disposals are implemented. The remaining chapters are concerned almost exclusively with specific classes of high-risk and serious offenders and with how they may best be managed. It is important to emphasize yet again the need to view the information presented in this book *as a whole*.

References

CASES AND AUTHORITIES FOR CITATIONS

Bratty v. Attorney-General of Northern Ireland (1963) AC 386
Kay v. Butterworth (1945) 173 LT 191
R. v. Bailey (1983) 1 WLR 760
R. v. Burns (1973) 58 Cr. App. R. 364
R. v. Byrne (1960) 2 QB 396–455
R. v. Chard (1971) 56 Cr. App. R. (268)
R. v. Charlson (1955) 1 ALL ER 859
R. v. Kemp (1957) 1 QB 399
R. v. Lipman (1970) 1 QB 152
R. v. Lloyd (1967) 1 QB 175–181
R. v. Majewski (1977) AC 443
R. v. Matheson (1958) 42 Cr. App. R. (154) 1 WLR 474
R. v. Podola (1959) 3 ALL ER 418
R. v. Quick (1973) QB 910 and 3 WLR 26
R. v. Robertson (1968) 3 ALL ER 557
R. v. Stephenson (1979) 3 WLR 193
R. v. Sullivan (1984) 3 WLR 123
R. v. Sutcliffe (*The Times* and *Guardian*, various days in May 1981)
R. v. Turner (1975) 2 WLR 56
R. v. Vernege (1982) Crim. Law Rev. 598–600
Watmore v. Jenkins (1962) 3 WLR 463

TEXT REFERENCES

Bartholomew, A.A. (1983) R. v. Sutcliffe, Letter. *Medicine, Science and the Law* **23**: 222–23.

Blair, D. (1977) The Medico-Legal Aspects of Automatism. *Medicine, Science and the Law* **17**: 167–82.

Bluglass, R. (1979) The Psychiatric Assessment of Homicide. *British Journal of Hospital Medicine* **October**: 366–77.

—— (1980) *Psychiatry, The Law and The Offender—Present Dilemmas and Future Prospects*. Seventh Denis Carroll Memorial Lecture. Croydon: Institute for the Study and Treatment of Delinquency.

Burn, G. (1984) *'Somebody's Husband, Somebody's Son': The Story of Peter Sutcliffe*. London: Heinemann.

Clark, M.J. (1975) The Impact of Social Science on Conceptions of Responsibility. *British Journal of Law and Society* **2**: 32–44.

Cranston Low, N. (1983) Neither Guilty Nor Insane. *Medicine, Science and the Law* **23**: 275–78.

Criminal Law Revision Committee (1980) *Offences Against The Person*. Cmnd. 7844. London: HMSO.

Dell, S. (1982) Diminished Responsibility Reconsidered. *Criminal Law Review* **December**: 809–18.

—— (1983) The Detention of Diminished Responsibility Homicide Offenders. *British Journal of Criminology* **23**: 50–60.

—— (1984) *Murder into Manslaughter: The Diminished Responsibility Defence in Practice*. Institute of Psychiatry, Maudsley Monograph No. 27. Oxford: Oxford University Press.

Dell, S. and Smith, A. (1983) Changes in the Sentencing of Diminished Responsibility Homicides. *British Journal of Psychiatry* **142**: 20–34.

Eigen, J.P. (1983) Historical Developments in Psychiatric Forensic Evidence: The British Experience. *International Journal of Law and Psychiatry* **6**: 423–29.

Fenton, G.W. (1975) Epilepsy and Automatism. In T. Silverstone and B. Barraclough (eds) *Contemporary Psychiatry*. Ashford: Headley Brothers. (For Royal College of Psychiatrists.)

—— (1984) Epilepsy, Mental Abnormality and Criminal Behaviour. In M. and A. Craft (eds) *Mentally Abnormal Offenders*. London: Baillière Tindall.

Finch, J. (1974) *Introduction to Legal Theory* (second edition). London: Sweet and Maxwell.

Fitzgerald, E. (1981) Is the System Fair to the Likes of Peter Sutcliffe? *Guardian* 25 May.

Foucault, M. (1979) *Discipline and Punish: The Birth of the Prison*. Harmondsworth: Penguin.

Gostin, L. (1984) Mental Health Law in England and Wales: An

Exposition and Leads for the Future. In M. and A. Craft (eds) *Mentally Abnormal Offenders*. London: Baillière Tindall.

Griew, E. (1984a) Let's Implement Butler on Mental Disorder and Crime. In University College, London *Current Legal Problems*. London: Sweet and Maxwell.

—— (1984b) Another Nail for M'Naghten's Coffin? *New Law Journal* **134**: 935–36.

Hall Williams, J.E. (1980) Legal Views of Psychiatric Evidence. *Medicine, Science and the Law* **20**: 276–82.

Hamilton, J (1981) Diminished Responsibility. *British Journal of Psychiatry* **138**: 434–36.

Home Office (1979) *Criminal Statistics for England and Wales, 1978*. London: HMSO.

Home Office and DHSS (1975) *Report of the Committee on Mentally Abnormal Offenders (Butler Committee)*. Cmnd. 6244. London: HMSO.

Jacobs, F.G. (1971) *Criminal Responsibility*. London: Weidenfeld and Nicolson.

Kahn, J.H. (1971) Uses and Abuses of Child Psychiatry: Problems of Diagnosis and Treatment of Psychiatric Disorder. *British Journal of Medical Psychology* **44**: 229–38.

Kenny, A. (1984) The Psychiatric Expert in Court. *Psychological Medicine* **14**: 291–302.

Lishman, W.A. (1978) *Organic Psychiatry: The Psychological Consequences of Cerebral Disorder* (p. 346). Oxford: Blackwell Scientific.

Mackay, R.D. (1983) The Automatism Defence—What Price Rejection? *Northern Ireland Law Quarterly* **34**: 81–105.

Maher, G., Pearson, J., and Frier, B.M. (1984) Diabetes Mellitus and Criminal Responsibility. *Medicine, Science and the Law* **24**: 95–101.

Masters, B. (1985) *Killing for Company*. London: Cape.

Neustatter, W.L. (1957) *The Mind of the Murderer*. London: Christopher Johnson.

Prins, H. (1980) *Offenders, Deviants, or Patients? An Introduction to the Study of Socio-Forensic Problems*. London: Tavistock.

—— (1983) Diminished Responsibility and the Sutcliffe Case: Legal, Psychiatric and Social Aspects. *Medicine, Science and the Law* **23**: 17–24.

Royal Commission on Capital Punishment (1953) *Report* Cmnd. 8932. London: HMSO.

Samuels, A. (1975) Mental Illness and Criminal Liability. *Medicine, Science and the Law* **15**: 198–204.

Schreiber, F.R. (1984) *The Shoemaker: The Anatomy of a Psychotic*. Harmondsworth: Penguin.

Spencer, S. (1984) Homicide, Mental Abnormality and Offence. In M.

and A. Craft (eds) *Mentally Abnormal Offenders*. London: Baillière Tindall.

Walker, N. (1968) *Crime and Insanity in England, Volume I*. Edinburgh: Edinburgh University Press.

Zeegers, M. (1981) Diminished Responsibility—A Logical, Workable and Essential Concept. *International Journal of Law and Psychiatry* **4**: 433–44.

FURTHER READING: BOOKS

Items marked with an asterisk are focused rather more on American problems and attitudes but they also contain material highly relevant to UK practice.

On the relationship between psychiatry and the law:

* Bromberg, W. (1979) *The Uses of Psychiatry in the Law: A Clinical View of Forensic Psychiatry*. London: Quorum.
* Fersch, E.A. (1980) *Psychology and Psychiatry in Courts and Corrections: Controversy and Change*. New York: Wiley.
* Fingarette, M. and Hasse, A.F. (1979) *Mental Disabilities and Criminal Responsibility*. London: University of California Press.

Flew, A. (1973) *Crime or Disease?* London: Macmillan.

* Guttmacher, M. (1968) *The Role of Psychiatry in Law*. Illinois: Charles C Thomas

* Jeffery, C.R. (1977) *Criminal Responsibility and Mental Disease*. Illinois: Charles C Thomas.

Moore, M.S. (1984) *Law and Psychiatry: Rethinking the Relationship*. Cambridge: Cambridge University Press.

Morris, N. (1982) *Madness and the Criminal Law*. London: University of Chicago Press.

—— (1983) Mental Illness and the Criminal Law. In P. Bean (ed.) *Mental Illness: Changes and Trends*. Chichester: Wiley.

* Slovenko, R. (1973) *Psychiatry and Law*. Boston: Little Brown.

West, D.J. and Walk, A. (1977) *Daniel MacNaughton: His Trial and the Aftermath*. Kent: Gaskell. (For Royal College of Psychiatrists.)

On forensic psychiatry:

Craft, M. and Craft, A. (1984) *Mentally Abnormal Offenders*. London: Baillière Tindall.

* Halleck, S.L. (1967) *Psychiatry and the Dilemmas of Crime*. New York: Harper and Row.

Macdonald, J.M. (1969) *Psychiatry and the Criminal* (second edition). Illinois: Charles C Thomas.

Power, D.J. (1979) *Principles of Forensic Psychiatry*. London: Edsall.

* Sadoff, R.L. (1975) *Forensic Psychiatry: A Practical Guide for Lawyers and Psychiatrists*. Illinois: Charles C. Thomas.

Trick, K.L.K. and Tennent, T.G. (1981) *Forensic Psychiatry: An Introductory Text*. London: Pitman.

Whitty, C.W.M. and Zangwill, O. (1977) *Amnesia: Clinical, Psychological and Medico-Legal Aspects* (second edition). London: Butterworths.

On forensic psychology:

Green, R.K. and Schaefer, A.B. (1984) *Forensic Psychology: A Primer for Mental Health Professionals*. Illinois: Charles C Thomas.

Havard, L.R.C. (1981) *Forensic Psychology*. London: Batsford.

Lloyd-Bostock, S.M.A. (1981) (ed.) *Psychology in Legal Contexts: Applications and Limitations*. London: Macmillan.

Wright, F., Bahn, C., and Reiber, R.W. (1980) *Forensic Psychology and Psychiatry*. (Volume 347 of the Annals of The Academy.) New York: New York Academy of Sciences.

FURTHER READING: ARTICLES

Briscoe, O.V. (1975) Assessment of Intent—An Approach to the Preparation of Court Reports. *British Journal of Psychiatry* **127**: 461–65.

Chiswick, D. (1978) Insanity in Bar of Trial in Scotland: A State Hospital Study. *British Journal of Psychiatry* **132**: 598–601.

Eagle, M. (1983) Responsibility, Unconscious Motivation and Social Order. *International Journal of Law and Psychiatry* **6**: 263–91.

McLean, A.M. and Harland, W.A. (1978) The Brennan Case: Medico-Legal Insanity? *Medicine, Science and the Law* **18**: 124–27.

Moore, M.S. (1979) Responsibility for Unconsciously Motivated Action. *International Journal of Law and Psychiatry* **2**: 323–47.

—— (1983) The Relevance of Philosophy to Law and Psychiatry. *International Journal of Law and Psychiatry* **6**: 177–92.

Morse, S.J. (1979) Diminished Capacity: A Moral and Legal Conundrum. *International Journal of Law and Psychiatry* **2**: 271–98.

Pond, D. (1980) Responsibility. *Bulletin of Royal College of Psychiatrists* **January**: 10–13.

Smith, R. (1980) Scientific Thought and the Boundary of Insanity and Criminal Responsibility. *Psychological Medicine* **10**: 15–23.

Wootton, B. (1980) Psychiatry, Ethics and the Criminal Law. *British Journal of Psychiatry* **136**: 525–32.

Notes

1 The spelling of his name has varied over the years. I have used that currently favoured.
2 Cases of deaf-mutism may also rarely occur, and very occasionally a person may be deemed to be 'mute of malice'. I am not considering such cases here.
3 There are two, virtually obsolete, exceptions: theoretically, it would still be possible to face the death penalty for Piracy with Violence or High Treason.
4 I am grateful to my daughter, Miss Helen E. Prins, LLB, Solicitor, for kindly bringing this case to my attention.
5 Acceptance by the courts of pleas of diminished responsibility on agreed psychiatric evidence has occurred only since 1962. Between 1957 and 1962 (following the decision in R. v. Matheson in 1958) the issue had to be put to a jury in *all* cases (Bartholomew 1983).
6 By virtue of Section 1(2) of the Murder (Abolition of Death Penalty) Act of 1965.
7 Haigh was the so-called 'acid bath murderer' and Heath the sadistic, sexual psychopathic killer of two women. Both were executed. (For accounts of psychiatric aspects of their cases see Neustatter 1957: Chapters 10 and 11.)

CHAPTER THREE

Systems of disposal

'The greater the power, the more dangerous the abuse.'

EDMUND BURKE

In this chapter I shall describe the main systems of disposal for those who have committed grave offences against persons or property—for example, homicide and cognate offences, other serious violence against the person, serious sexual attack, and arson. In order to keep the material within reasonable bounds, I shall give only an outline description of methods of disposal through the mental health care and penal systems. This is preceded by a short account of the methods available for making enquiry into an accused person's mental state and certain allied matters. In this chapter, the main emphasis is upon hospital orders with restrictions and the implementation of the life sentence. It should be read in close conjunction with Chapter 4, in which the reader will find a more detailed consideration of some of the more practical matters only touched upon here.

Readers will also observe that I concentrate exclusively upon the adult offender. The number of children and young persons under sixteen sentenced and currently held in institutions for homicide and other grave crimes is very small (about twenty). Despite their small number, the problems they present really merit treatment in their own right and it has not been possible to do this within the confines of this book. Many of the observations I shall make concerning general principles of assessment and management can also be applied to juveniles. A few words are in order, however, concerning the law and practice in their case. A person convicted of murder who was less then eighteen years old at the time the offence was committed will be ordered to be detained 'during Her Majesty's pleasure' (Children and Young Person's Act 1933: Section 53(1)). To all intents and purposes, this is similar to a life sentence, except that the offender may be detained 'in such place and under such conditions as the Secretary of State may direct'. The places chosen for such detention will vary according to the age of the offender and his or her circumstances, which may change over time. Thus, the youthful offender may start his or her sentence in a local authority residential establishment (such as a community home with education—formerly called an Approved School) or a Special Youth Treatment Centre controlled by the DHSS. (There are currently two—St Charles, at Brentwood in Essex, and Glenthorne in Birmingham. Both centres cater for the very highly disturbed young person.) The youthful offender may also be detained in a Special Hospital, a Youth Custody Centre (formerly known as Borstal), or, if detained for long enough, he or she may be transferred to an adult prison. Persons who are under *seventeen* and convicted of crimes other than murder for which a sentence of life imprisonment may be passed on an adult, may be sentenced to detention for life under Section 53(2) of the Children and Young Person's Act of 1933. Such a sentence has virtually the same effect as one of Detention During Her Majesty's Pleasure. The oversight of the care and control of children and young persons subject to the sentences just outlined rests jointly with the Home Office and with the DHSS (the latter is the central government department having overall responsibility for the care and control given by local authorities and others to all children and young persons). Children and young persons discharged into the community from such sentences will be supervised by the probation service, working in close co-operation with local authority social services departments.

The material that follows is divided into three sections. Section A is concerned with *Enquiries into Mental State and Allied Matters*; Section B deals with *Mental Health Care Disposals*; and Section C covers *Penal Disposals*. In order to achieve some degree of clarity, the three sections are also divided into a number of subsections.

Section A: Enquiries into mental state and allied matters

In Chapter 2 we were much concerned with the state of mind of those accused of grave offences. We must now briefly consider the procedures available for causing enquiry to be made into the mental state of such a defendant. In murder cases, reports are prepared *automatically* by the prison medical officer. The history of the practice of preparing these reports is outlined in the *Report of the Royal Commission on Capital Punishment* (1953: Chapter 6). The practice seems to have arisen mainly because of the importance attached to the need to secure detailed psychiatric evidence in cases where the death penalty could still be imposed and because of the seriousness with which all accusations of murder were (and still are) treated. It is also important to note here that the probation and after-care service has an *obligation* to provide a pre-sentence report in murder cases if asked to do so by the court and if the defendant consents. The service also has an obligation to provide a detailed post-trial and post-sentence report on the prisoner's social background and circumstances (Home Office 1984a: paras 15/16). Other reports into the accused's mental and physical state may be prepared at the instigation of the Director of Public Prosecutions (DPP) or by the accused's legal advisers. In almost all cases of alleged murder, the reports will be prepared in custody; however, in certain exceptional cases in recent years, an accused has been allowed bail with a condition that he or she remain in a psychiatric hospital in order for reports to be prepared. In murder and some other cases, where the accused's mental condition gives rise to doubts as to diagnosis or the case is problematic in other ways, the psychiatric investigations will always include very thorough physical, neurological, and haematological investigations. (The need for these will be apparent in the light of some of the cases and examples discussed in Chapter 2.)

STATUTORY AUTHORITY FOR OBTAINING REPORTS

In cases other than murder (where, as I have indicated, reports are obtained automatically), the courts may remand a convicted offender for the specific purpose of obtaining reports. This will be for three weeks at a time if in custody and for four weeks if on bail (Criminal Justice Act 1967: Section 30). It is important to note that courts remand only rarely for psychiatric reports—various studies give a remand rate of something in the order of 2 to 4 per cent. However, as already indicated, murder cases will always be investigated, as will certain other crimes, such as arson, and some sexual offences. In addition, any oddness on the part of the accused whilst held in custody or during appearance in court may prompt a remand for psychiatric opinion. Such remands may arise at the request of the sentencer, defence lawyers, the police, or the probation and after-care service. Probation officers play a highly significant part not only in acting as primary screeners but in providing very valuable background information both to the court and to the examining psychiatrist, should a report be requested. The Butler Committee wished to see an extention of this screening role (Home Office and DHSS 1975: 2.46). For reviews of current practices in obtaining reports and of the relevant literature, see Prins 1980, Chapter 4; Campbell 1981; Donovan and O'Brien 1981; Quinsey and Maguire 1983; Schaffer 1983; Soothill *et al.* 1983; Craft 1984, Chapter 19.

REMANDS TO HOSPITAL[1]

Remands for reports

As from 1 October, 1984, Section 35(1) of the Mental Health Act of 1983 empowers courts to order the remand of an accused person *to hospital* for the preparation of a report into his or her mental condition. This provides an alternative to remanding an accused person in custody in situations where it would not be practicable to obtain the report if they were remanded on bail—for example, if a defendant decided to breach a *bail* requirement that they reside in hospital for examination, the hospital would be unable to prevent them from leaving; the *remand to hospital* under Section 35 gives the hospital power to *detain* the accused. This power to remand to hospital applies to any person *awaiting trial* by the Crown Court for any offence punishable with imprisonment, or any person who has been convicted but not yet sentenced, but excludes persons convicted of murder. The power may be exercised only if an appropriately authorized medical practitioner (see below) reports orally or in writing that there is reason to believe that the accused is suffering from mental illness, psychopathic disorder, severe mental impairment, or mental impairment. In the first instance, a remand may be for up to twenty-eight days; after this initial period, the accused may be remanded for periods of up to twenty-eight days up to a maximum of twelve weeks. It should be noted that the criteria for *remands to hospital* are more limited than those which obtain for *remands on bail*. In the case of remands to hospital, the court must be satisfied that the accused is suffering from one of the four forms of mental disorder listed above and for which a hospital order may be made (see below).

Remands for treatment

Section 36 of the Act empowers the Crown Court to remand an accused person to hospital for treatment. The court must be satisfied on the written or oral evidence of *two* authorized medical practitioners that the accused is suffering from *mental illness or severe mental impairment* of a nature or degree which makes it appropriate for them to be detained in hospital for medical treatment. In the first instance, the remands may be for up to twenty-eight days. The remand may be renewed at twenty-eight day intervals for a period of up to twelve weeks. The court is also empowered to terminate the remand for treatment at any time; for example, in the event of the accused recovering or in the event of the court hearing that no effective treatment is possible. This new provision (effective from 1 October, 1984) gives courts an additional option for those found to be 'under disability' (see Chapter 2).

INTERIM HOSPITAL ORDERS

In addition to their powers under Sections 37 and 41 of the Act (see below), courts now have the power under Section 38 of the Act to make interim hospital orders in all cases other than murder. This provision also came into effect on 1 October, 1984.

As with the preceding provisions, the court has to be satisfied on duly approved medical evidence that this is the most appropriate course of action and that the accused is suffering from one of the four categories of mental disorder defined in the Act. The provision is likely to be of use in those cases where the court and the hospital wish to make some evaluation of an accused's likely response to treatment without irrevocable commitment on either side. An interim hospital order may be made in the first instance for a period of up to twelve weeks; it may be renewed for periods for up to twenty-eight days to a maximum of six months. The court may also terminate an interim hospital order after considering the written or oral evidence of the hospital Responsible Medical Officer (RMO), or if it makes a full hospital order (see below), or if it decides to deal with the offender in some alternative fashion.[2]

Section B: Mental health care disposals

HOSPITAL ORDERS

Section 37 of the Mental Health Act enables a crown court to make a hospital order. In order to make such an order, the court must be satisfied:

(a) that, having regard to all the circumstances, including the nature of the offence and the antecedents of the offender, other methods of disposal are not suitable and that a hospital order is the most suitable method of dealing with the case;

(b) that the accused has been convicted of an offence punishable with imprisonment (other than murder);

(c) that two doctors (at least one of whom is approved for the purpose by a local health authority under the provisions of Section 12 of the Act) state that the offender is suffering from mental illness, psychopathic disorder, mental impairment, or severe mental impairment of a nature or degree *that it is appropriate for the offender to be detained in hospital for medical treatment* and, in the case of mental impairment or psychopathic disorder, that the medical treatment *is likely to alleviate or prevent a deterioration in the patient's condition.*

It should be stressed here that the condition *must* be one that merits compulsory detention in hospital and is not one that could be treated by other means; for example, by a requirement for mental treatment under a probation order—this requires the consent of the offender and the stay in hospital is on an informal basis. It should also be noted that the 1983 Act now requires, in cases of mental impairment and psychopathic disorder, an indication that treatment will alleviate or prevent a deterioration in the condition. Before making such an order, the court must be satisfied that arrangements have been made for the offender's admission to hospital.

A court is, of course, not *obliged* to make a hospital order merely because two doctors recommend it. In practice, courts will usually follow recommendations for psychiatric disposal in almost all cases.[3] A hospital order lasts initially for six months and is renewable for a further six months and then at annual intervals. An offender/patient may be discharged by the Responsible Medical Officer (RMO) at any time. The patient, or his or her nearest relative, may also make an application for discharge from the order to a Mental Health Review Tribunal (MHRT) in the period between the expiration of six months and the expiration of twelve months beginning with the date of the order and in any *subsequent* period of twelve months. Under Section 117 of the Act, after-care must now be provided by the District Health Authority and the Local Authority Social Services Department for those who cease to be compulsorily detained under Section 37 and who leave hospital. This Section clarifies the previous somewhat uncertain powers provided under previous health service legislation. Most of the cases we are considering, however, will be of sufficient gravity to merit the imposition of a restriction order.

RESTRICTION ORDERS

Section 41 of the Act enables a Crown Court (but *not* a Magistrates' Court) to make a restriction order. The criteria for making such an order are as follows:

(1) that following conviction it appears to the court, having regard to:

(a) the nature of the offence,

(b) the offender's antecedents, and

(c) the risk of the offender committing further offences if discharged,

that a restriction order is necessary *for the protection of the public from serious harm*;

(2) that at least one of the medical practitioners authorized under Section 12 of the Act, whose written evidence is before the court, has also given that evidence orally.

The criterion I have italicized was not in the 1959 Mental Health Act and has been inserted to ensure that only those offenders/patients who are considered likely to constitute a real threat to the public would be subjected to the serious restrictions on liberty that follow the making of such an order.

A restriction order may be made either for a specific period or without limit of time, the latter being the course most frequently adopted. The effects of a restriction order may be summarized as follows:

(1) The offender/patient cannot be given leave of absence from the hospital, be transferred elsewhere, or be discharged by the RMO without the consent of the Home Secretary.

(2) The Home Secretary may remove the restrictions if he considers they are no longer required to protect the public from serious harm.[4] Should the order remain in force without the restriction clause, it has the same effect as an order made under Section 37 of the Act (see 'Hospital orders', above).

(3) The Home Secretary may at any time discharge the offender/patient, absolutely or subject to conditions.

In considering restricted cases which:

(1) are considered to be particularly problematic,

(2) need special care in assessment and

(3) involve a fear of possible future risk to the public,

the Home Secretary will seek the advice of his Advisory Board on Restricted Patients (known customarily as the Aarvold Board). This body was set up following the recommendation of a committee chaired by Sir (Judge) Carl Aarvold. The Committee had examined the circumstances in which an offender/

patient (Graham Young) had come to re-offend shortly after his discharge into the community from Broadmoor (Home Office and DHSS 1973). The Aarvold Board is quite independent of the MHRT and its main concern is with proffering advice to the Home Secretary about the likely risk to the public of releasing the more problematic restricted offender/patient back into the community; it is not concerned with the patient's rights. It should be stressed that the Aarvold Board does not deal with every restricted case but only with those 'cases needing special care in assessment' (Home Office and DHSS 1973: 9).

Under Section 73 of the Act a *Mental Health Review Tribunal* (MHRT) may exercise *its* powers concerning restricted patients in the following fashion:

(1) If the Tribunal is satisfied that:
   (a) the offender/patient is not now suffering from one of the forms of mental disorder specified in the Act which make it appropriate for them to be detained in hospital for medical treatment; *or,*
   (b) it is not necessary for the health and safety of the offender/patient or for the protection of other persons that he or she should receive such treatment; *and,*
   (c) it is not appropriate for the offender/patient to remain liable to be recalled to hospital for further treatment,

   the Tribunal *must* order the patient's *absolute* discharge.

(2) If the Tribunal is satisfied as to the criteria contained in (a) and (b) above but *not* as to (c), they *must* order the patient's *conditional* discharge. An offender/patient so discharged may be recalled to hospital by the Home Secretary at any time during the duration of the restriction order. An order for conditional discharge may contain a range of requirements held to be conducive to the welfare of the offender/patient and, more importantly, for the protection of the public. Examples of such requirements might be that the offender/patient should live at a specified place, should not contact certain individuals, or should be under the supervision of a social worker and/or a psychiatrist. The latter are required to make reports to the Home Secretary at regular intervals concerning not only the offender/patient's

general progress, but more specifically on any matters giving rise to immediate concern.

Under the Mental Health Act of 1959, Tribunals could only *advise* the Home Secretary on the discharge of restricted patients. They now have the power themselves to order discharge in the manner described above. In order to exercise these new powers, Tribunals (which consist of legal, psychiatric, and lay members) must be chaired by a senior legal practitioner approved by the Lord Chancellor—currently a Circuit Judge or person of equivalent status.

TRANSFER OF PRISONERS FOUND TO BE MENTALLY DISORDERED

Sections 47–53 of the Act enable the Home Secretary to transfer sentenced or unconvicted prisoners from prison to hospital if they are found to be suffering from mental disorder as defined in the Act. We saw how this could come about in the discussion of the case of Peter Sutcliffe in Chapter 2. Under the provisions of Section 47, an order in respect of a sentenced prisoner *may* be made without restrictions but, as for example in Sutcliffe's case, it will be much more likely to be made with restrictions under the provisions of Section 49. If the Home Secretary is notified by the RMO or an MHRT that such a person no longer needs treatment for mental disorder he has two possibilities open to him:

(1) If the offender/patient has become eligible for parole or has earned statutory remission, he can order his discharge.
(2) Alternatively, he can order that the patient be remitted to prison to serve the remainder of his sentence. If, for example, Sutcliffe recovers sufficiently from his mental disorder to no longer need treatment or detention in hospital, he will automatically be returned to prison, as he was given a life sentence with a minimum recommendation as to how long he should serve. Sections 48, 51, 52, and 53 of the Act apply to various categories of unsentenced prisoners. (For more detailed discussion of these provisions see Bluglass 1983: 64–71 and Gostin 1984: 259–66.)

The various disposals are summarized in *Figure 3(1)*.

Figure 3(1)   Disposal of serious offenders through the mental health
care and penal systems

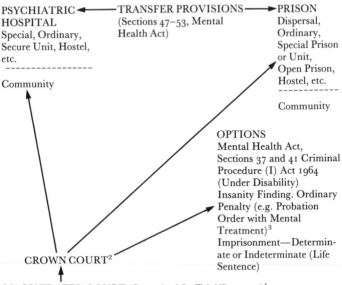

MAGISTRATES' COURT (Committal for Trial/Sentence)[1]

Notes to Figure 3(1)
1 All grave offences will be sent for trial from the Magistrates' Court to the
Crown Court. A Magistrates' Court may also commit to the Crown Court
with a view to a hospital order being made *with restrictions*. Committal for trial
may be in custody, on bail, or, as we have seen earlier, by *remand* to hospital.
2 The powers available to the Crown Court are also exercisable on appeal by
the Court of Appeal.
3 See Chapter 2 for discussion of procedure in cases found to be 'under
disability'. Courts also have the general option of making a probation order
with a requirement for mental treatment as an in-patient under the terms of
Section 3 of the 1973 Powers of Criminal Courts Act. However, such powers
are likely to be used only exceptionally in the types of cases discussed in this
book.

HOSPITAL PROVISIONS[5]

The majority of offenders/patients subject to restriction orders
will be detained, at least in the first phase of their detention, in
one or other of the Special Hospitals (see below). They may
occasionally be detained from the outset in an ordinary

psychiatric or subnormality hospital. More often than not, their stay in a local hospital will be part of a plan for a phased return to the community. In recent years, local open psychiatric hospitals have, for a variety of reasons, been very reluctant to accept difficult, potentially dangerous restricted offenders/ patients. Their reasons include a concern that such patients cannot be detained easily on 'open' wards, may prove to be too disruptive for staff to manage, and may upset other patients. This reluctance has resulted not only in an accumulation of such patients in the Special Hospitals, but also in consequent delays in initiating their return to the community. The Butler Committee became so concerned about the overcrowding in the Special Hospitals, delays in discharge, and the numbers of mentally disordered persons being held in the prisons, that they issued an Interim Report in 1974 (Home Office and DHSS 1974). They strongly recommended that urgent priority be given to the establishment of regional secure units. The government of the day gave rapid acceptance to these proposals and earmarked large sums of central government money for the purpose. Unfortunately, administrative delays at regional level and an attitude of general obstructiveness and lack of co-operation characterized developments over the next few years. Currently there are nine secure units in operation and four under construction (1984/85). In addition, there are some 300 places available in other facilities (such as interim secure units) and some beds in other types of accommodation, such as special care units (Mason 1984: 14–15).

Constraints of space preclude a detailed discussion of this particular topic but the historical background, objectives, and the regimes suggested for secure units are well described by Bluglass 1978, Faulk and Taylor 1984, and Higgins 1984a and b. It is important, however, to note that secure units are best seen as forming an integral part of a network of hospital, penal, and community services—a point well made by Higgins (1984a). As already indicated, most restricted offenders/ patients will be detained in one of the Special Hospitals. About 140 restriction orders are made by the courts annually (Home Office 1982b: 56). There are approximately 2,000 restricted patients in hospital at any one time and about 140 restricted patients are discharged subject to conditions each year (Home

Office 1985: personal communication). About the same number leave the system in various ways; for example, through absolute discharge, through remaining in hospital after the restrictions have expired, through remission to prison, or through death.

SPECIAL HOSPITALS

There are four Special Hospitals in England (Broadmoor, Rampton, Moss Side, and Park Lane), one in Scotland (Carstairs), and none in Wales. Their history and evolving patterns and changes in management are interesting and reflect changes in attitudes not only towards mentally disordered offenders but also towards the mentally disordered more generally. Those readers interested in pursuing the history of these hospitals and some of the social policy implications should consult Greenland 1969, Walker and McCabe 1973, Gostin 1977, Department of Health and Social Security 1980, Cohen 1981, Black 1984, and Mason 1984.

Under Section 4 of the National Health Service Act of 1977, the Secretary of State for Social Services is required to provide and maintain such institutions as are necessary for persons subject to detention under the mental health legislation who, in his or her opinion, require treatment of special security because of their dangerous, violent, or criminal propensities. It should be noted that about one-third of all Special Hospital patients are *not* offenders but have been admitted because of their difficult or disruptive behaviour in ordinary psychiatric or subnormality hospitals.

Broadmoor

This is the oldest of the Special Hospitals and is in Berkshire. It currently has a population of some 500 patients; during the 1950s and late 1960s it had become increasingly overcrowded. Some relief has now been afforded by the construction of Park Lane Hospital. Broadmoor admits mainly those patients suffering from mental illness and psychopathic disorder.

Rampton

This hospital in Nottinghamshire has also suffered from over-crowding in the past; unfortunately, it has also suffered from a degree of notoriety brought about by allegations of ill-treatment by staff. These resulted in the prosecution of some staff members, a government enquiry, the institution of a Review Body, and the re-establishment of the post of Medical Director (a post that had lapsed some years earlier). Rampton is now considerably less overcrowded (currently housing some 600 patients) and is trying hard to improve its image. It caters predominantly for those who are suffering from psychopathic disorder and from mental impairment. Like Broadmoor, it suffers from some degree of geographical isolation; this has tended to create a certain amount of insularity and a trend towards complacency in the use of old-fashioned treatment regimes. This has been particularly the case at Rampton, which was described in the report of the government enquiry as 'a backwater . . . the main currents of thought about the care of mental patients have passed it by' (Department of Health and Social Security 1980: iii).

Moss Side

This Liverpool hospital takes mentally impaired, mentally ill, and psychopathically disordered patients. It does not appear to have suffered from the same degree of overcrowding experienced at Broadmoor and Rampton. Currently, it has a population of about 250.

Park Lane

Built next to Moss Side, is the newest of the Special Hospitals. It was opened in 1979 with the aim of reducing overcrowding at Broadmoor. It will eventually cater for some 400 patients, mainly those suffering from mental illness and psychopathic disorder. Built with the advantages of modern and sophisticated security devices, it enables maximum movement to take place within the hospital perimeter in the knowledge that, from the public's point of view, it is probably one of the most secure institutions in the United Kingdom.

Although the Special Hospitals have at various times all come in for a good deal of criticism, even their severest critics have acknowledged that these institutions have to undertake a tremendously difficult task in attempting to combine contain-ment, clinical treatment, and rehabilitation in a climate of opinion that places the 'mad and the bad' at the bottom of the economic priority list. They also have to function in a society that prefers not to know or to care too much about its more highly disturbed and deviant members. The community usually shows concern, and then only negatively, when pro-fessional efforts fail and the very occasional disaster occurs (see also Chapter 4).

SUPERVISION IN THE COMMUNITY

As already indicated, a conditionally discharged, restricted offender/patient may be supervised in the community by a probation officer, a local authority social worker, or, in theory, by any other person appointed to undertake the task. The probation service derives its authority for this supervision from paragraph 32(3) of the 1984 Probation Rules; the authority for social workers to carry out these functions is contained in health service legislation concerned with the general duties of local authorities to provide care and after-care of psychiatric patients, as now further clarified in Section 117 of the Mental Health Act of 1983. About 500 such cases may be under active supervision in the community in any one year (Home Office 1985: personal communication). Of these, about one-third are supervised by the probation service: the figures for the years 1978, 1979, 1980, and 1981 were 160, 170, 180, and 210 respectively (Home Office 1984b: 71). Of forty-six offenders/ patients discharged in the early part of 1985, eight were to be supervised by probation officers and thirty-five by local auth-ority social workers; three were conditionally discharged to go abroad (Home Office 1985: personal communication).

In addition to supervision by a social worker, the offender/ patient is also likely to be placed under the care and treatment of a local psychiatrist. It will be remembered that release may also be conditional upon compliance with certain other re-quirements, such as living in a specified place, under certain conditions, or refraining from certain employments or from contacting named individuals. The Aarvold Committee considered that the choice of supervisor should normally be made by those who knew the offender/patient, his or her history and social background best. The Committee also considered that where there was

'no clear-cut indication, or where it is especially important to ensure that supervision and support will be thorough, the responsible medical officer . . . might approach both the Principal Probation Officer and the Director of Social Services . . . asking them to consult and consider how supervision could best be handled.'

(Home Office and DHSS 1973: 17)

Support for these views was echoed by the Butler Committee. They considered that

'supervision should be undertaken by the person who can bring most to the case in the way of knowledge, expertise and resources in the particular circumstances of the case. The arrangements may need to take particular account of the needs of public safety.'

(Home Office and DHSS 1975: 124)

In my experience, local authority social workers are rather less enthusiastic about taking on these cases than are probation officers. I believe this to be partly because local authority social workers are less familiar with work with adult offenders and the control element that is often required. They also have to give priority to a more diverse range of statutory duties (particularly concerning child care) than do members of the probation service. However, now that there are much more well-defined obligations laid upon those local authority social workers who will act as 'Approved Social Workers' under the Mental Health Act of 1983 and their roles have also been more clearly set out, it may well be that they will begin to feel less reluctant to embrace work with this admittedly small but very challenging group of clients. In my own local authority area, the very comprehensive course of training undertaken by potential Approved Social Workers contains a proportionately high input on work with offenders/patients. As the Butler Committee indicated, concern for public safety is of paramount importance. It is essential that there is open and constructive liaison with the psychiatrist concerned with the case. Clear procedures for such liaison should be established, set out, and acknowledged. Not infrequently, decisions may have to be made at a time of crisis; for example, an offender/patient's behaviour may have deteriorated to the extent that recall to hospital may need to be considered. In each area where restricted cases are being carried, the worker with the day-to-day responsibility for managing the case should have direct access not only to the psychiatrist involved in treating the offender/patient but also to senior management. This system not only enhances accountability but also provides moral and practical support for the worker. In cases of emergency, Home Office officials are available for consultation—if necessary, after normal office hours. The names and telephone numbers of these officials should be made known to the workers responsible for the day-to-day supervision of the case as a matter of routine. In situations other than those requiring recourse to *immediate* advice, the officer supervising the case should make a report to the Home Office (with copies if necessary to the local psychiatric consultant responsible for the case and to the hospital RMO). Cases in which such advice might be sought would include those where there appears to be an actual or potential risk to the public, where contact with the offender/patient has been lost, where there has been a substantial breach of the conditions of discharge, where the offender/patient's behaviour suggests a need for recall for further in-patient treatment, or where the offender/patient has been charged with or convicted of a further offence.

If the offender/patient is recalled by order of the Home Secretary, the latter is obliged under Section 75 of the Act to refer the offender/patient's case to a MHRT within one month of his or her recall. In deciding whether or not to issue a warrant for recall, the Home Secretary will treat every case on its merits. If an offender/patient has been hospitalized in the past for very serious violence or for homicide, comparatively minor irregularities of conduct or failure to co-operate with the terms of the conditional discharge might well be sufficient to merit the consideration of recall. Similar issues arise in relation to prisoners released from life sentences on parole, and these are discussed below. The factors that may indicate that all is not well in the offender's or the offender/patient's social and environmental situation and the danger signals that demand recognition are discussed in Chapter 4.

Section C: Penal disposals

Although our main concern in this section is with the imposition and consequences of the life sentence, it should be noted that dangerous and high-risk offenders will often be subject to determinate sentences and their release into the community will present similar problems to those already discussed in connection with restricted offenders/patients. However, the imposition of the life sentence and its consequences provide a useful illustration of the parole system, from which readers may make their own more general extrapolations. As we saw in Chapter 2, a life sentence *must* be imposed on a finding, or plea, of guilty to a charge of murder. It *may* also be imposed in other homicide cases; for example, for manslaughter under the Homicide Act of 1957. It is also available and sometimes used as a maximum sentence for certain other grave crimes, such as armed robbery, arson, serious sexual assault, kidnapping, and certain offences concerned with causing explosions. In the autumn of 1983, the Home Secretary indicated, as a result of what he considered was a growing degree of public anxiety about the increase in crimes of violence, that he would exercise his executive discretion to ensure that prisoners serving sentences of over five years for offences of violence (for example, those listed above) and trafficking in drugs would not be granted early parole. (A prisoner becomes eligible for parole when he or she has served not less than six months or one-third of their sentence, whichever is the longer.) Under this new edict, parole would be contemplated only when release under supervision for a few months before the end of the sentence was likely to reduce the long-term risk to the public or in circumstances that were genuinely exceptional (Home Secretary, in response to a parliamentary question, Hansard, 30 November, 1983). In addition, the Home Secretary went on to state that, in respect of the release of life-sentence prisoners, he would also exercise his executive discretion so that 'murderers of police or prison officers, terrorist murders, sexual or sadistic murders of children and murders by firearm in the course of robbery . . . (could) . . . normally expect to serve at least 20 years in custody; and there will be cases where the gravity of the offence requires a still longer period. Other murders, outside these categories, may merit no less punishment to mark the seriousness of the offence.'

(Continuation of answer to parliamentary question, Hansard, 30 November, 1983)

The Home Secretary's statement and his apparent interference in what had long been regarded as the executive functions of the Parole Board caused a very great deal of disquiet. Following the determination of cases brought by four prisoners through the High Court and subsequently the Court of Appeal, the House of Lords finally ruled that it *was* within the Home Secretary's discretion to exercise his functions in this way (House of Lords written judgement given 15 November, 1983). It is important to note that the Parole Board for England and Wales and the Board for Scotland, unlike their counterparts in Canada, the United States, and some European countries, are not *judicial* bodies; they merely *advise* the Home Secretary (and his Scottish counterpart) on the release of prisoners who *apply* for parole. The Home Secretary may, in fact, choose to reject the Board's advice to release, though this is a comparatively rare occurrence. He is not at liberty to reject the Board's advice *not* to release. Those who wish to study the parole system and some of the recent deliberations as to its future, should consult Nuttall *et al.* 1977, *Reports of the Parole Board* (Home Office 1981a, 1982a, and 1983, particularly the Appendices), *Review of Parole in England and Wales* (Home Office 1981b), Hawkins 1983, and Bottomley 1984. With regard to the Home Secretary's recent decision to restrict the discharge of life-sentence prisoners in the categories described above, when I served on the Parole Board it was my experience that the offenders he specified did, in fact, serve very long sentences indeed; occasionally even in excess of the terms he set out in his statement of intent. It is important to emphasize that the Home Secretary has always had sole responsibility for the release of life-sentence prisoners, though since the introduction of parole in 1968 the Parole Board has been given the task of advising him in the exercise of these functions.

Currently there are about 2,000 men and about 60 women serving life sentences. It is anticipated that these numbers will not diminish in the years ahead and are likely to rise. As already indicated, the Home Secretary may grant release on licence to those sentenced to life imprisonment, if recommended to do so by the Parole Board. However, under Section 61(1) of the Criminal Justice Act of 1967, the Home Secretary *must* consult the Lord Chief Justice and the trial judge (if available) before release on licence is granted. In exercising his functions concerning release on licence, the Home Secretary will customarily be advised not only by the Parole Board but by his own departmental officials having special responsibility for life-sentence prisoners. These will include senior officials of the Prison Department and the Prison Medical Service. The prison department keeps very thorough records on all life-sentence prisoners and of their progress through the prison system. Such records will include detailed reports on the offence itself, the prisoner's circumstances at the time of the offence, social, medical, and other background information and on-going reports from within prison establishments from the governor grades, uniformed officers, medical staff (including visiting psychotherapists), education officers, chaplains, and probation officers, amongst others. During my service on the Board, I came to be very impressed with the care and concern exercised by the Prison Department in respect of life-sentence prisoners, both for the prisoner himself or herself and for the public's protection. (The same concern was also evident in respect of other offenders serving long sentences for very serious offences.) To give effect to the new criteria for determining life-sentence cases, the Home Secretary now obtains the *initial* views of the Lord Chief Justice and the trial judge (if available) on the period of custody necessary to meet the requirement of retribution and deterrence. This first consultation will normally occur when the prisoner has been detained for about three years. Following this, the Home Secretary will set a date for the first review of the case through the usual parole machinery. At each formal review, the case will be considered first by the Local Review Committee (LRC) at the prison; this committee comprises representatives of the Board of Visitors at the prison, the probation service, independent persons, and the prison governor. The LRC's recommendation is then forwarded to the Home Office, where, after examination by Home Office professional advisers, the case will be put for consideration to a panel of the Parole Board. In considering life-sentence cases, the panel of the Board *must*, by statute, include a High Court judge and a psychiatrist. In my view it is preferable that the panel should also include a senior representative of the probation service and/or a person experienced in the causes of crime and the management of offenders. If it seems likely to the Home Office that the panel might consider early release, the Lord Chief Justice and the trial judge (if available) will be consulted, whether or not they have already given a view as to the period of detention required to meet the requirements of deterrence and retribution. This further consultation is required to meet the precise requirements of Section 61 of the Criminal Justice Act of 1967. The Board may recommend that the prisoner be given a provisional date for release or that the case should be reviewed again after a specified period of time. (Those readers wishing to obtain a detailed account of the complex procedures involved in these reviews will find an excellent account in Maguire, Pinter, and Collins 1984.)

If, as is inevitable in some cases, release is not likely to be contemplated for many years ahead, the case will be reviewed regularly within the prison system—usually at about three-yearly intervals. It will be obvious that the increase in the size of the prison population generally, and of the life-sentence population in particular, has presented the prison service with management problems of some magnitude. This is particularly so in the case of those prisoners who show by their behaviour that they are actually or potentially dangerously disruptive. These problems have been the subject of two recent Prison Department reports. The first is a report by a working party set up by the Chaplain General's Department (Prison Department 1983); the second is a wider review of the problems of management in the long-term prison system (Home Office 1984c). Apart from the wider considerations of management, there is the serious problem that the impact of life and other very long sentences poses in purely personal terms for both inmates and staff. Such research evidence as is available suggests that emotional and physical deterioration may not in fact be as severe as had once been supposed; of far greater importance is the impact of broken family and similar ties. The characteristics of life-sentence prisoners are usefully described in Smith (1979); the results of various researches into the effects of imprisonment upon life-sentence and long-term prisoners has been usefully discussed by Sapsford (1979, 1983), Flanagan (1980), Rasch (1981), and Worth *et al.* (1981).

Life-sentence prisoners do not remain in any one establishment for the whole of their sentence. Initially, they are likely to be held at a local or remand prison. Following conviction and sentence they will normally be transferred to a prison offering maximum security, where they may remain for some years; examples of such prisons are Gartree in Leicestershire, Hull, Albany on the Isle of Wight, Wakefield in Yorkshire, and Long Lartin in Worcestershire. Those considered likely to benefit from psychiatric intervention but who are not sufficiently disordered to merit transfer to hospital under the Mental Health Act may be sent to a prison offering special psychiatric facilities; examples are Parkhurst on the Isle of Wight and the special psychiatric prison at Grendon Underwood in Buckinghamshire. Male lifers who have been involved in what are often described as 'domestic' killings may be sent to Kingston prison in Hampshire; this is a small prison catering specifically for life-sentence prisoners in this category. A year or two prior to release, lifers will normally be transferred to an open prison, such as Leyhill in Gloucestershire, Sudbury in Derbyshire, or Acclington in Northumberland. As part of this allocation, the prisoner will probably spend some time on the Pre-Release Employment Scheme (PRES); this may include residence in a hostel attached to the prison or work in the outside community with a return to the prison each night. In this way, some attempt can be made to monitor the prisoner's responses to near normal living conditions. This is vital if one considers the artificiality of the prison environment and its lack of provision for placing prisoners under the kind of stressful conditions they are likely to meet outside. The system operates in much the same way for women sentenced to life imprisonment, except that the range of institutions available is inevitably smaller and the problems associated with family ties may be even more acute than they are for men.

RELEASE AND AFTER-CARE

A life licence remains in force for the remainder of the individual's life and the licensee may be recalled to prison at any time if their conduct gives rise for concern. (This is unlike the situation of those released from determinate sentences on parole; their licences will end at a specified time.) If all goes well, the conditions of a life licence—such as the requirements to live in a specified place, to report to the probation officer, to receive visits, or not to take specific employments—may be cancelled, usually after some four or five years have elapsed. Currently, there are some 400 life-sentence prisoners being actively supervised by the probation service (Home Office 1984: personal communication). It will have become obvious from what has already been said about the supervision of restricted cases that this is a very difficult area of work. As with the supervision of restricted offenders/patients, the probation officer will have a dual concern for the welfare of the licensee and the protection of the public; in some instances, the latter may well have to take precedence over the former (Home Office 1984a). The supervision of life licensees and similar cases requires skills and commitment of a very high order. There are some who consider that the supervision of such cases should be undertaken only by very experienced probation officers or those of senior officer status (see, for example, Floud and Young 1981: 142). The probation service itself takes the supervision of such cases very seriously indeed. This is attested to by the number of working party reports prepared by the service that have appeared in recent years: two examples are a report by the Conference of Chief Probation Officers 1980 and a report by the Devon Probation and After-Care Committee on *Serious Offenders* 1981.

Conclusions

In this chapter, I have attempted to provide an outline account of the methods available for enquiry into a defendant's mental state, the major means of disposal for those sentenced to a mental health care disposal, and of disposal through the penal system. Such an account must inevitably be brief, and the reader wishing to secure further information will be able to do so by following up the references and the works suggested for further reading. In the next chapter, I shall consider in some detail how supervision and care in the community may best be effected, both in the interests of the supervisee and the public. In order to do so I shall examine some concepts of dangerousness, the nature of violence and its precipitants, and the manner in which all the parties involved may best be protected from the commission of further acts of grave harm.

References

Black, T. (1984) Treatment in Maximum Security Settings. In M. and A. Craft (eds) *Mentally Abnormal Offenders*. London: Baillière Tindall.

Bluglass, R. (1978) Regional Secure Units and Interim Security for Psychiatric Patients. *British Medical Journal* **1**: 489–93.

—— (1983) *A Guide to the Mental Health Act, 1983*. Edinburgh: Churchill Livingstone.

Bottomley, A.K. (1984) Dilemmas of Parole in a Penal Crisis. *Howard Journal of Criminal Justice* **23**: 24–40.

Campbell, I.G. (1981) The Influence of Psychiatric Pre-sentence Reports. *International Journal of Law and Psychiatry* **4**: 89–106.

Cohen, D. (1981) *Broadmoor*. London: Psychology News Press.

Conference of Chief Probation Officers (1980) *Through Care Sub-Committee Report of the Life-Sentence Working Group*. Lawefield Lane, Wakefield: Yorkshire.

Craft, M. (1984) Psychiatric Reports for the Courts. In M. and A. Craft (eds) *Mentally Abnormal Offenders*. London: Baillière Tindall.

Department of Health and Social Security (1980) *Report of the Review of Rampton Hospital (Boynton Report)*. Cmnd. 8073. London: HMSO.

Devon Probation and After-Care Committee (1981) *Report of the Working Party on Serious Offenders*. Queen Street, Exeter: Devon.

Donovan, W.M. and O'Brien, K.P. (1981) Psychiatric Court Reports —Too Many or Too Few? *Medicine, Science and the Law* **21**: 153–58.

Faulk, M. and Taylor, J. (1984) The Wessex Regional Secure Unit. In T. Williams, E. Alves, and J. Shapland (eds) *Options for the Mentally Abnormal Offender*. Issues in Criminological and Legal Psychology No. 6. Leicester: British Psychological Society.

Flanagan, T.J. (1980) The Pains of Long-Term Imprisonment. *British Journal of Criminology* **20**: 148–56.

Floud, J. and Young, W. (1981) *Dangerousness and Criminal Justice*. London: Heinemann Educational.

Gostin, L. (1977) *A Human Condition, Volume II*. London: MIND (NAMH).

—— (1984) Mental Health Law in England and Wales: An Exposition and Leads for the Future. In M. and A. Craft (eds) *Mentally Abnormal Offenders*. London: Baillière Tindall.

—— (ed.) (1985) *Secure Provision*. London: Tavistock.

Greenland, C. (1969) The Three Special Hospitals in England and Wales and Patients with Dangerous, Violent or Criminal Propensities. *Medicine, Science and the Law* **9**: 253–64.

Hawkins, K. (1983) Assessing Evil: Decision Behaviour and Parole Board Justice. *British Journal of Criminology* **23**: 101–27.

Higgins, J. (1984a) An Ideal Forensic Psychiatry Service. In T. Williams, E. Alves, and J. Shapland (eds) *Options for the Mentally Abnormal Offender*. Issues in Criminological and Legal Psychology No. 6. Leicester: British Psychological Society.

—— (1984b) The Regional Secure Unit. In M. and A. Craft (eds) *Mentally Abnormal Offenders*. London: Baillière Tindall.

Home Office (1981a) *Report of the Parole Board*. London: HMSO.

—— (1981b) *Review of Parole in England and Wales*. London: Home Office.

—— (1982a) *Report of the Parole Board*. London: HMSO.

—— (1982b) *Criminal Statistics, England and Wales: Supplementary Tables, 1982 (Volume IV)*. London: HMSO.

—— (1983) *Report of the Parole Board*. London: HMSO.

—— (1984a) *Home Office Circular No. 55*. London: Home Office.

—— (1984b) *Probation Statistics, England and Wales, 1982*. London: Home Office.

—— (1984c) *Managing the Long-Term Prison System: The Report of the Central Review Committee*. London: HMSO.

Home Office and DHSS (1973) *Report on the Review of Procedures for the Discharge and Supervision of Psychiatric Patients Subject to Special Restrictions (Aarvold Report)*. Cmnd. 5191. London: HMSO.

—— (1974) *Interim Report of the Committee on Mentally Abnormal Offenders*. Cmnd. 5698. London: HMSO.

—— (1975) *Report of the Committee on Mentally Abnormal Offenders (Butler Committee)* Cmnd. 6244. London: HMSO.

Maguire, M., Pinter, F., and Collins, C. (1984) Dangerousness and the Tariff. *British Journal of Criminology* **24**: 250–68.

Mason, P. (1984) Services for the Mentally Abnormal Offender—An Over-view. In T. Williams, E. Alves, and J. Shapland (eds) *Options for the Mentally Abnormal Offender*. Issues in Criminological and Legal Psychology No. 6. Leicester: British Psychological Society.

Nuttall, C.P., Barnard, E.E., Fowles, A.J., Frost, A., Hammond, W.H., Mayhew, P., Pease, K., Tarling, R., and Weatheritt, M.J. (1977) *Parole in England and Wales*. Home Office Research Unit, Research Study No. 38. London: HMSO.

Prins, H. (1980) *Offenders, Deviants or Patients? An Introduction to the Study of Socio-Forensic Problems*. London: Tavistock.

Prison Department (Chaplain-General's Office) (1983) *Report of Working Party on Regimes For Dangerously Disruptive Prisoners*. London: Home Office.

Quinsey, V.L. and Maguire, A. (1983) Offenders Remanded for Psychiatric Examination: Perceived Treatability and Disposition. *International Journal of Law and Psychiatry* **6**: 193–205.

Rasch, W. (1981) The Effects of Indeterminate Detention: A Study of Men Sentenced to Life Imprisonment. *International Journal of Law and Psychiatry* **4**: 417–31.

Royal Commission on Capital Punishment (1953) *Report*. Cmnd. 8932. London: HMSO.

Sapsford, R.J. (1979) *Life Sentence Prisoners: Detention and Coping*. Milton Keynes: Open University Press.

—— (1983) *Life Sentence Prisoners—Reactions, Response and Change*. Milton Keynes: Open University Press.

Schaffer, E. (1983) A Study of Post-Conviction Psychiatric Reports in Glasgow Sheriff Court. *Medicine, Science and the Law* **23**: 283–89.

Smith, D. (ed.) (1979) *Life Sentence Prisoners*. Home Office Research Unit, Research Study No. 51. London: HMSO.

Soothill, K.L., Adserballe, J., Bernheim, T., Dasananjali, T.W., Harding, T., Thomas, T., Reinhold, F., and Ghali, H. (1983) Psychiatric Reports Requested by Courts in Six Countries. *Medicine, Science and the Law* **23**: 231–41.

Walker, N. and McCabe, S. (1973) *Crime and Insanity in England and Wales Volume II*. Edinburgh: Edinburgh University Press.

Worth, J., Staples, J., Bingham, H.B., Scriven, P., and Gibbs, P. (1981) Collection of papers in issue of *Prison Service Journal* devoted to Life-sentence Prisoners. **42**: 2–15.

FURTHER READING

On mental health care systems:

Department of Health and Social Security (1981) *Review of Leave Arrangements for Special Hospital Patients*. London: DHSS.

DHSS (1983) *Mental Health Act, 1983—Memorandum.* Part III. London: HMSO.

Gostin, L. (1983) *A Practical Guide to Mental Health Law.* Chapters 5 and 6. London: MIND (NAMH).

Gunn, J. and Farrington, D.P. (1982) *Abnormal Offenders, Delinquency and the Criminal Justice System.* Part III. Chichester: Wiley.

Hamilton, J.R. (1983) Observations on the Mental Health Act, 1983. *International Journal of Law and Psychiatry* **6**: 351–70.

Home Office (1980) *Mentally Disordered Persons: The Giving of Reasons to a Person Recalled to Hospital.* Circular No. 117/80. London: Home Office.

—— (1983) *Mental Health Act, 1983, Implementation.* Circular dated 19 August, 1983. London: Home Office.

—— (1984a) *Implementation of Sections 35, 36, 38 and 40(3) of the Mental Health Act, 1983.* Circular dated 11 October, 1984. London: Home Office.

—— (1984b) *Treatment of Mentally Disordered Offenders Who are Subject to the Special Restrictions Set Out in Section 41 of the Mental Health Act, 1983.* Draft memorandum. London: Home Office.

Kittrie, N.N. (1971) *The Right to be Different: Deviance and Enforced Therapy.* (On general aspects of enforced treatments.) Baltimore: Johns Hopkins Press.

Lawson, W.K. (1984) Mentally Abnormal Offenders in Prison. In M. and A. Craft (eds) *Mentally Abnormal Offenders.* London: Baillière Tindall.

Prins, H. (1984) Attitudes to the Mentally Disordered. *Medicine, Science and the Law* **24**: 181–91.

Shapland, J. and Williams, T. (1983a) Legalism Revisited: New Mental Health Legislation in England. *International Journal of Law and Psychiatry* **6**: 351–70.

—— (eds) (1983b) *Mental Disorder and the Law: Effects of the New Legislation.* Issues in Criminological and Legal Psychology No. 4. Leicester: British Psychological Society.

On penal disposals:

Boyle, J. (1984) *The Pain of Confinement: Prison Diaries.* (Describes the work of the Special Unit for Violent and Disruptive Inmates at Barlinnie Prison in Scotland.) Edinburgh: Canongate Press.

CIBA Foundation (1973) *Medical Care of Prisoners and Detainees.* Symposium 16 (New Series). Amsterdam: Associated Scientific Publishers.

Cohen, S. and Taylor, L. (1972) *Psychological Survival: The Experience of Long-Term Imprisonment.* Harmondsworth: Penguin.

Coker, J. B. and Martin, J. P. (1985) *Licensed to Live*. (An account of research into the supervision of life-sentence prisoners.) Oxford: Basil Blackwell.

Gunn, J., Robertson, G., Dell, S., and Way, C. (1978) *Psychiatric Aspects of Imprisonment*. (On Grendon Psychiatric Prison and other special psychiatric facilities in prison.) London: Academic Press.

Jones, K. and Fowles, J. (1984) *Ideas on Institutions: Analysis of the Literature on Long-Term Care and Custody*. Especially Chapters 10, 11, and 12. London: Routledge and Kegan Paul.

King's Fund Centre (1978) *Medical Services for Prisoners: Report of a Day Conference*. London: King's Fund Centre.

Smith, R. (1984) *Prison Health Care*. (Papers originally published in the *British Medical Journal*.) Especially Chapters 5 and 8. London: British Medical Association.

Williams, M. (1984) Reflections on Data Collected in the Prison System. In T. Williams, E. Alves and J. Shapland (eds) *Options for the Mentally Abnormal Offender*. Issues in Criminological and Legal Psychology No. 6. Leicester: British Psychological Society.

Notes

1 The decision to include the provision for remand to hospital here rather than under Section B has been made, somewhat arbitrarily, on the basis that it is a temporary, rather than a long-term, measure.

2 Some of the provisions outlined above may also be applied by Magistrates' Courts. However, as we are mainly concerned here with high-risk and grave cases, I have confined my account to Crown Court procedures (see *Figure 3(1)* for the system as a whole). For an excellent summary of all the legal provisions relating to mentally disordered offenders, see Bluglass 1983, especially Chapter 11.

3 Courts also have the power to make Guardianship Orders under the Act; the same criteria apply as for the making of hospital orders. In practice, very few such orders are made and they would not be implemented in the type of cases we are considering in this book.

4 *Serious harm* does not appear to be defined in the legislation. We may take it to mean the types of serious offences against persons or property that are the subject of this book.

5 The provision of secure accommodation for mentally ill and mentally handicapped people has recently been extensively reviewed by Gostin (ed.) (1985).

PART TWO
Management

CHAPTER FOUR

Dangerous behaviour

'*Nemo repente fuit turpissimus*
(No-one ever became thoroughly bad in one step)'
JUVENAL

'All tragedy is the failure of communication'
JOHN WILSON

With the benefit of hindsight?

In July, 1962, Graham Young, then just under fifteen years of
age, was made the subject of an order under the Mental Health
Act 1959, requiring him to be detained in Broadmoor with
restrictions on his discharge for a period of fifteen years. He had
been convicted of three charges of causing grievous bodily harm
by administering poison to his sister, his father, and to a school
friend. Happily, all three survived; however, they had suffered
the most severe pains and discomfort as a result of his activities
and Young's father was never able to bring himself to forgive
him. Some of the psychiatric evidence given at his trial indicated that his long-standing interest in, and obsession with,
poisons, his apparent lack of remorse, and the calculated nature
of his activities, would render him a potentially highly dangerous individual for a very long time to come (Greenland 1978a).
According to Anthony Holden's account of Young's life and
career, his stay in Broadmoor appears to have not been without
incident; the staff (particularly the nurses) appear to have been
divided in their opinions as to his progress and potential for
causing further grave harm to others (Holden 1974). Despite
whatever reservations there may have been, Young was
eventually considered fit for release. In February, 1971, he was
conditionally discharged into the community and placed under

the supervision of the probation and psychiatric services. It is of interest to note that, prior to his release, Young had made two interesting (but unsuccessful) applications for jobs: one was to a forensic science laboratory and the other to a pharmaceutical training school! It is not clear from Holden's account whether or not the Broadmoor authorities were aware of these applications —probably not. Young found employment quickly with a firm of optical and photographic equipment manufacturers and accommodation was found for him in lodgings. By April, 1971 (only two months after his release), a number of Young's workmates began to be taken seriously ill and two of them subsequently died. Even then, a not inconsiderable time appears to have elapsed before it dawned on the authorities that Young might be involved. Had it not been for the perceptiveness of Young's employer and a local general practitioner, his nefarious activities might have continued unchecked. Eventually, in July, 1972, at St Albans Crown Court, Young was found guilty on two counts of murder and two counts of attempted murder. He was sentenced to life imprisonment. On two further charges of administering poisonous substances, he was sentenced to five years' imprisonment, to run concurrently with the life sentence. No attempt was made at this court appearance to secure a mental health disposal for Young. The rest of the sorry saga has already been referred to in Chapter 3 (see page 58).

Following Young's conviction and the public concern it created, the Home Secretary of the day set up the Aarvold Committee to enquire specifically into cases such as Young's (Home Office and DHSS 1973). He also set up the more wide-ranging enquiry into the disposal of mentally abnormal offenders under the chairmanship of the late Lord Butler (Home Office and DHSS 1975). Young's case exemplifies most graphically the subject matter of this chapter. With hindsight, could his highly dangerous behaviour after discharge from Broadmoor have been predicted and perhaps prevented? In view of his past history, was sufficient control exercised over his post-release activities—including not only his particularly ominous choice of employment but also the physical circumstances of his day-to-day living? These latter aspects raise important questions concerning the liberty of the individual and the degree to which freedom to live in the community in such cases can or should ever be without intensive and sometimes highly intrusive oversight.

The recent case of Colin Evans (*Guardian* 18 and 20 December, 1984), jailed for life with a minimum recommendation that he serve thirty years, provides a further tragic illustration of this dilemma. Evans, a known and previously convicted child molester, was able to involve himself in voluntary work with highly vulnerable small children. It is alleged that those who gave him this opportunity had not been made aware of his criminal background as a persistent sexual assaulter of small children. Hindsight would dictate that Evans should perhaps have been subject to more rigorous screening and oversight. Some would argue (erroneously, in my view) that even society's paramount regard for the welfare of children should not necessarily infringe personal liberties, even if the subject has a past record of serious sexual assaults on children or crimes of a similar nature. I believe that these subjects sometimes need to be protected from placing themselves in situations where they may be highly likely to offend because of their distorted and misdirected sexual drives. In connection with Young's case and the question of vulnerability and prevention, it is of interest to record the scene that greeted the police when they eventually entered his room at his lodgings.

> 'The walls were festooned with pictures of Hitler and other Nazi leaders, decorated with swastikas. The window sill, table and shelves were lined with bottles, phials and tubes containing substances of various colours . . . just inside the door . . . (were) . . . crude drawings of graveyards and tombstones, spidery men clutching their throats, and wielding hypodermic syringes and bottles marked "Poison". Many were bald, some were pictured with their hair falling out. There were skulls and cross-bones everywhere.'
>
> (Holden 1974: 107)

In connection with the drawings, it is pertinent to point out that Young had used thallium to poison his victims. This is a tasteless but highly virulent poison, which not only causes intense pain but produces the loss of hair and even baldness depicted in Young's drawings. With hindsight, one must wonder at the ease with which Young gained further access to the means of causing serious injury to others. Some words in Shakespeare's *King John* come readily to mind: 'How oft the sight of means to do ill deeds makes deeds ill done' (Act IV, scene ii). It is important to stress that cases such as Young's are fortunately extremely rare in penal and forensic practice. The re-conviction rate for further homicide on the part of those already detained for a similar crime and subsequently released into the community is something in the order of 1 per cent (Tidmarsh 1982). The re-conviction rate for other, less serious, offences appears to be less than for those discharged from penal institutions. Nevertheless, we must always be prepared to improve our skills so that the chance of the rare tragedy may be reduced to a minimum. It is one of the main aims of this book to make some small contribution to this process.

Can dangerousness be defined?

In recent years, there has been a great deal of interest shown in the concept of dangerous behaviour and its definition. (For a review of some of these aspects see Bottoms 1977; Prins 1975, 1980a and b, 1981, 1983a, b, and c; Webb 1976; Hepworth 1982.) In defining terms, it is always useful to look at their etymological origins. It may come as a surprise to some readers (as it once did to me) to find that the word danger is in fact derived from the Latin *dominiarium* which means lordship or sovereignty. This derivation has strong connotations of power relationships and Sarbin (1967) has stressed the importance of this derivation because of these relationship elements. The term 'dangerous' itself has little meaning from our point of view. It is only when it is infused with the relationship elements described by Sarbin that it takes on a special significance. Walker has pointed out that

> 'dangerousness is not an objective quality, but an ascribed quality like trustworthiness. We feel justified in talking about a person as dangerous if he has indicated by word or deed that he is more likely than most people to do serious harm, or act in a way that is likely to result in serious harm.'

> (Walker 1978: 37)

Steadman has also made the important point that the notion of dangerousness implies a *prediction*—a concern with *future* conduct. 'It is the fear of the shadowy stranger attacking in the night that elicits public fear and reaction' (Steadman 1976: 53). Apart from a *very small* group of individuals who may be intrinsically dangerous because of some inherent physical or other defect, which may render them particularly explosive, our concern is with the *situation* in which the combination of the *vulnerable* individual and a *provoking* situation may spark off explosive and dangerous behaviour. As the Butler Committee pointed out,

> 'the individual who spontaneously "looks for a fight" or feels a need to inflict pain or who searches for an unknown sexual victim is fortunately rare, although such people undoubtedly exist. Only this last category can be justifiably called "unconditionally dangerous".'
>
> (Home Office and DHSS 1975: 58)

For the purposes of this book, we are mainly concerned with those people who have a history of inflicting serious personal harm on others, or who are considered to be likely to do so. In order to place this concern in context, it is as well to ask ourselves who is the more dangerous—the armed bank robber, the terrorist, the zealot, the individual who deliberately and knowingly drinks too much before driving, the person who fails to disclose a serious disabling disorder that makes them unfit to drive, the person who fails to inform the medical and other authorities that they have a dangerous and highly contagious communicable disease, or the pedlar of dangerous drugs, such as heroin? A case illustrating the last category was that involving Richard Catherwood, a London supply teacher who received a sentence of seven years' imprisonment for supplying the drug LSD to teenagers. A further interesting aspect of this case is that Catherwood obtained work as a teacher despite five previous court appearances for drugs offences (*Guardian* 18 December, 1984; cf. the Evans case discussed above).

In the United Kingdom, dangerous individuals and dangerous behaviour are not *specifically* defined by statute. However, as we saw in Chapter 3, the special hospitals exist to deal, *inter alia*, with those patients showing dangerous propensities. The provisions of the Mental Health Act of 1983 also enable compulsory powers to be used in the interest of a patient's own safety or *for the protection of other persons*. As shown in Chapter 3, an important criterion when making a restriction order is the *protection of the public from serious harm*. The law does, of course, make some provision for certain specific offences that may be held to imply dangerous conduct: for example, dangerous or reckless driving, endangering the lives of passengers, or, as noted above, being in possession of, or distributing, dangerous drugs. Dangerous behaviour may, of course, be implied in prosecutions for criminal negligence. In addition, a small group of offenders who persist in criminal activities—not necessarily of a dangerous, seriously assaultive type—may be liable to a sentence of extended imprisonment (formerly called preventive detention). The court must be satisfied on the basis of previous criminal record and current offence that they are eligible for such a disposal. The criteria for the imposition of such sentences are very strict and the penalty is rarely used these days. As already indicated, the word 'dangerous' has strong emotive connotations: for example, the history of the English Poor Law from the time of Elizabeth I onwards shows a fervent concern that the poor were not only idle but dangerous. As Rennie points out, 'for nearly four hundred years, from the thirteenth through the sixteenth centuries, the English criminal law was obsessed with vagrants and beggars, who were viewed as a great danger to society' (Rennie 1978: 5). (They were thought to be not only dangerous to others, but dangerous also in that they threatened the social and economic structure.) Foucault (1978) has suggested that from the nineteenth century onwards psychiatrists have been employed to delineate individuals who were considered dangerous and to deal with their incomprehensible behaviour.

I now return to the problem of definition. The Butler Committee considered that, for their purposes, dangerousness was 'a propensity to cause serious physical injury or lasting psychological harm. Physical violence is, we think, what the public are most worried about, but the psychological damage which may be suffered by some victims of other crimes is not to be underrated' (Home Office and DHSS 1975: 59). Scott defines dangerousness as 'an unpredictable and untreatable tendency to inflict or risk irreversible injury or destruction, or to induce others to do so' (Scott 1977: 128). He also stressed that the social context was extremely important. By way of illustration, he cites the case of the man who smokes on an oil tanker as being the creator of a *potentially* dangerous hazard because of the nature of the explosive material around him. If he persistently refuses to 'douse that glim' it is likely to be assumed that he has dangerous intentions rather than that he is merely careless or feckless (Scott 1977). Some readers may find that Scott's definition is somewhat over-pessimistic with its emphasis upon untreatability; however, his emphasis on the *predictive* aspect is of paramount importance. As already suggested, one of the central elements of considering dangerous behaviour is the threat of repetition and the steps that might be taken to prevent that threat.

Can dangerous behaviour be predicted?

In recent years, there has been a vast outpouring of material on the assessment of risk and the prediction of dangerous behaviour. (For some examples, see: Tong and Mackay 1959; Gathercole *et al.* 1968; Sheppard 1971; Kozol, Boucher, and Garofalo 1972; Payne, McCabe, and Walker 1974; Quinsey, Pruesse, and Fernley 1975; Megargee 1976; Steadman 1976, 1983; Greenland 1978b, 1980; Berger and Dietrich 1979; Pfohl 1979; Quinsey 1979; Dowie and Lefrere (eds) 1980; Soothill, Way, and Gibbens 1980; Monahan 1981; Shah 1981; Brearley 1982; Petrunik 1982; Tidmarsh 1982; Harding and Adserballe 1983; Conrad 1984; Crawford 1984; Montanden and Harding 1984.) Despite a vast literature (and the selection of papers just cited is but a tiny fraction of this), one has to conclude that there are no reliable actuarial and statistical devices as yet that can predict with any degree of certainty the likelihood of dangerous behaviour. Moreover, many of the published studies suffer from serious methodological weakness (for example, inadequate sampling and follow-up). Some of the research evidence does show that most professional workers in this field tend to err on the side of caution when invited to make predictions about the future dangerousness of others. In a very well-known study,

Steadman and Cocozza (1974) examined a group of allegedly dangerous mentally abnormal offenders, who had been ordered to be freed from detention as a result of a famous American court decision, the case of Baxstrom. It had been held that Baxstrom had been detained unconstitutionally. As a result of the court's finding in his case, a large number of other offenders/patients had to be discharged into the community. These offenders/ patients (who had been detained because of their so-called criminal and dangerous propensities) were followed up by Steadman and Cocozza. At the end of a large-scale and careful survey, they concluded that mental health professionals were over-cautious in their predictions and that prolonged incarceration was not required for the majority of such offenders/ patients. However, it is important to stress that a large number of the offenders/patients in their sample were over the age of fifty when released. Had their research involved a younger and potentially more aggressive age group, their findings might have been different.

A later study by Thornberry and Jacoby (1979) gives some support for Steadman and Cocozza's findings. They followed up a fairly similar group of American offenders/patients, who had also been released in 1971 as a result of a court decision (the Dixon case). At many points, the results obtained by Thornberry and Jacoby are very similar to those of Steadman and Cocozza. Psychiatrists have often been criticized for their interventions and for their over-cautiousness in this field (see, for example, Pfohl 1979). It is only fair to say, however, that these clinicians have often undertaken tasks in this field because others have been unwilling to do so. Greenland (who is not a psychiatrist) goes so far as to suggest that 'until more efficient and humane methods are developed and sanctioned by society, clinical psychiatrists should stop being apologetic and defensive and accept these difficult, and often thankless tasks as part of their professional and legal mandate' (Greenland 1980: 102).

In summary, we lack accurate statistical and similar devices for the prediction of future dangerous behaviour. To make matters worse, those concerned with making judgements about the future dangerous behaviour of others will tend to produce what statisticians describe as false positives (at the risk of over-simplification, decisions that too many people should be detained). In view of this sad state of affairs, are we left with *any* indicators of the probability of *future* dangerous behaviour? There is no doubt that *past* violent conduct is likely to be the best predictor of *future* violent conduct. People with several previous convictions for violence are considerably more likely to be convicted of violence in the future than those not so convicted. Those inclined to cynicism might agree that nothing predicts behaviour like behaviour. (As an illustration, we may take the case of men who indecently expose themselves. Such offenders tend to repeat their offences but, fortunately, they seldom go on to engage in more serious sexual criminality. It is worth noting, however, that where acts of indecent exposure are associated with minor assaultive or verbally threatening behaviour, the likelihood of engagement in later serious sexual criminality is quite strong (Bluglass 1980).) It is therefore very important to study the circumstances of the behaviour or offence *in considerable detail*, for these can often provide very important diagnostic and prognostic clues—a matter to which I shall return later.

The components of dangerous behaviour

As already indicated, our concern with dangerous behaviour is fundamentally a concern about actual or likely displays of aggression and violence. It is, therefore, appropriate to begin this section with a brief discussion of these two phenomena. The terms aggression and violence are often used synonymously. This is not strictly correct, since we can be aggressive without necessarily being violent. Aggression is best regarded as denoting *assertive* behaviour, which may express itself physically or verbally. There have been long-standing debates concerning the true nature of aggression; those readers who would like to explore this topic in detail should consult the suggestions for further reading listed at the end of this chapter. Violence is frequently regarded as destructive aggression—that is, aggression harnessed for *harmful* purposes. Scott describes it as 'aggression concentrated into brief time'. It is also useful to note that he went on to suggest that it was 'not necessarily more destructive than continued aggression of lesser intensity' (Scott 1977: 128). It would appear, then, that the difference between aggression and violence may sometimes be a matter of degree. In this book, I am mainly concerned with those behaviours that are marked by great ferocity, force, threats, and, in most instances, a degree of premeditation. The event or incident will usually occur over a short time-span but not necessarily so. The debate as to whether aggression and a propensity for violence are all pervasive, innate, or acquired, has continued over the centuries. As Storr states, 'that man is an aggressive creature will hardly be disputed. With the exception of certain rodents, no other vertebrate *habitually destroys members of his own species. No other animal takes positive pleasure in the exercise of cruelty upon another of his own kind* . . . there is no parallel in nature to our savage treatment of each other' (Storr 1975: 9; my italics).

In view of the acknowledged universality of the phenomenon of aggression, it is of considerable interest to note that its overt expression appears to be determined quite markedly by cultural conditions. In their studies of so-called primitive societies, anthropologists (such as Mead, Benedict, Murdock, and Turnbull) demonstrated the great variety that exists in the display of aggressive behaviour. Fromm (1977) has attempted to synthesize some of their work. He found that three different and clearly delineated forms of society could be discerned: *Life-Affirmative Societies*; *Non-destructive-Aggressive Societies*; *Destructive Societies*. In *Life-Affirmative Societies*, the main emphasis is upon the preservation and growth of life in all forms. 'There is a minimum of hostility, violence or cruelty among people, no harsh punishment, hardly any crime, and the institution of war is absent or plays an exceedingly small role' (Fromm 1977: 229). In *Non-destructive-Aggressive Societies*, 'aggressiveness and war, although not central, are normal occurrences, and . . . competition, hierarchy and individualism are present' (Fromm 1977: 230). *Destructive Societies* are 'characterised by much interpersonal violence, destructiveness, aggression and cruelty . . . pleasure in war, maliciousness and treachery' (Fromm 1977: 231). Readers may reach the sombre conclusion that this last form of social structure seems all too familiar in our so-called modern, advanced Western society.

Whatever view we may take about the causes of aggression and display of violence, the following points would possibly find general acceptance:

(1) Violence when shown by non-human animals is usually purposive, self-protective, and conforms to certain ritualized patterns (see, for example, Lorenz 1966).

(2) In the *human* species, violence may be sanctioned by a community and be culturally determined (see above and the detailed analysis provided by Fromm (1977)).

(3) It takes little to disinhibit violence in human societies. It seems likely that men and women have always had the potential for the commission of a great deal of violence but that this is normally kept in check by society's sanctions. These sanctions can, however, change over time—witness the enormity of the atrocities against millions of people during the Nazi regime in Germany in the 1930s and 1940s. Internal control is also exercised by certain psychological 'defence mechanisms', such as denial, repression, and projection. Some psychoanalysts—in particular the late Melanie Klein (1963)—claim, on the basis of not inconsiderable clinical data, that even very small infants possess highly destructive and violent urges. These may come to the fore in the face of hunger and frustration (see Segal 1964 and Williams 1982). Such urges normally find appeasement but in the event of failure in this respect, serious distortions of personality may occur, as in the case of some psychopathically disordered individuals (see Chapter 5).

Whichever framework we choose to espouse for understanding aggression and violence—be it psychoanalytic, anthropological, or psychological (in terms of learned responses or reactions to frustration)—we can at least agree that aggressive and violent behaviour are highly pervasive in most human societies. Such behaviour is often very frightening but, if handled judiciously, it can also be harnessed and used in a positive fashion. Steadman provides us with a useful summary statement of the essence of the matter: 'Aggression is assertive behaviour. Violence is destructive aggression and *dangerousness is an estimation of the probability of dangerous behaviour*' (Steadman 1976: 50; italics in original).

The rest of this chapter is concerned with the following matters. *First*, the relationship between dangerous behaviour and mental and allied disorders. *Second*, other factors in the facilitation of dangerous behaviour. *Third*, its assessment and management. In discussing the third topic, I shall be particularly concerned with the feelings and attitudes of those who have the task of managing and controlling those adjudged to be dangerous.

Dangerous behaviour, violence, and mental disorder

As noted in Chapter 2, the relationship between mental disorder and crime in general is, at best, equivocal. Even in the highly selected populations of prisons and remand centres, the proportion of offenders considered to be suffering from a formal psychiatric disorder is something in the order of 10 to 15 per cent. Within that percentage, the majority will be stated to be suffering from that ill-defined and much disputed condition —personality disorder. (Useful summaries of some of the major epidemiological studies may be found in Prins 1980b, Chapter 3, and 1980c; Taylor 1982; Howells 1982; Monahan and Steadman 1983, Chapter 4.) A basic problem is that we are attempting to compare two phenomena that are not directly comparable. Definitions of crime and criminals are by no means universally agreed upon and there are also disputes about the nature, definition, and classification of mental disorder. In addition, as we saw in Chapter 2, there are few instances in which an absolute causal connection can be discerned between an allegedly disordered mental state and a criminal act. Tennent has usefully clarified the relationship in the following way.

> 'There are, theoretically, three types of relationship that can exist between aberrant and dangerous behaviour and mental disorder. Dangerous behaviour can occur as a result of mental illness. . . . In individuals within this category successful treatment of the illness will also be expected to alter behaviour. . . . Secondly, patterns of aberrant and dangerous behaviour may occur in those with mental illness, but in whom successful treatment of the mental illness will have no effect on the pattern of behaviour. . . . Finally, dangerous behaviour will be found in individuals without any evidence of mental disorder. In practice, these categories, especially the first two, merge into one another.'

> (Tennent 1975: 311)

Although the relationship between mental disorder and the commission of a violent crime is tenuous, there are certain disorders which appear to be important in individual cases (as, for example, in the case of Sutcliffe, discussed in Chapter 2). It is particularly important to stress that very few people suffering from mental disorder are violent or dangerous. It is sad that the media so often quite erroneously equate the two phenomena. The importance of some of these disorders is not always recognized, however, so brief consideration will be given to some of them. (For more detailed accounts of the general relationship between mental disorder and crime, see Prins 1980b, Chapter 3, and 1980c.)

FUNCTIONAL PSYCHOSES

The functional psychoses include the affective (depressive) disorders and the schizophrenias. Both are severely disabling psychiatric illnesses of uncertain aetiology. (For detailed accounts of these and the disorders to be discussed later see Prins 1980b, Chapter 3.)

(1) Depressive disorder, violent behaviour, and crime

Occasionally, an individual suffering from a severe (psychotic) form of depression will believe that the world has become such a dreadful place that they must kill their loved ones to save them from it and then kill themselves. West, in his study *Murder Followed by Suicide*, describes the condition graphically. Such people may

'become so convinced of the utter hopelessness of their misery that death becomes a happy escape. Sometimes before committing suicide, they first kill their children or other members of the family. . . . Under the delusion of a future without hope and the inevitability of catastrophe overtaking their nearest and dearest as well as themselves, they decide to kill in order to spare their loved ones suffering.'
(West 1965: 6)

Such beliefs have a delusional and irrational quality. Schipkowensky comments upon the importance of the patterns and depths of the delusional beliefs in such cases: 'the patient feels his personality is without value (delusion of inferiority). His life is without sense, it is only . . . (one) . . . of everlasting suffering . . . and that he deserves to be punished for his imaginary crimes' (Schipkowensky 1969: 64–7; see also Lawson 1984).

Fortunately, the condition just described is reasonably amenable to help by physical means, such as drugs or electro-convulsive therapy (ECT), although such treatment invariably needs to be linked with skilled personal counselling and support. This is vital, in order not only to monitor the effects of the physical treatment itself but also to spot early signs of possible relapse. The time when potentially dangerous behaviour is most likely to occur is when the person who has hitherto been so severely depressed as to be incapable of all activity begins, with the help of treatment, to emerge from a phase of withdrawal and apathy. It is at this point that suicidal or homicidal intentions may well be put into effect (see, for example, MacDonald 1968). The task of estimating the cause, extent, and duration of a depressive illness and its relevance to serious offending may be a very difficult one. Gunn *et al.* suggest that

'it is very difficult to establish *unless several helpful informants are available* whether a depressed murderer is depressed because he has been imprisoned for life, depressed because of the conditions under which he has been imprisoned, depressed by the enormity of his crime, or whether he committed the crime because he was depressed in the first place.'

(Gunn *et al.* 1978: 35; my italics)

These comments highlight the importance of obtaining a comprehensive history not only of the offender but also of his or her wider social background. As we shall see later, very full details of the actual offence or dangerous behaviour are vital if their true meaning and implications are to be understood.

The importance of the social context is stressed (albeit by implication) by Woddis (1957, 1964) in his attempt to classify three groups of cases in which depressive disorder seemed important:

(1) Those cases in which depressive illness had not been recognized because its possibility had never, at any time, been considered.

(2) A handful of cases in which a tendency to repeated crime had been alleviated by treating the depressive illness.

(3) A very small number of cases of depressive disorder in which violence had been shown. Following the violence, all the clinical features of depression tended to disappear as if the explosive act had produced its own cure for the illness.

(2) Manic episodes

Mania or, far more often, hypomania, lies at the other end of the spectrum of depressive disorders. In mania and hypomania, we see the reverse of the symptoms found in depression: the mood is highly elated, there is gross over-activity, and the sufferer may think himself or herself to be omnipotent. He or she may become convinced that the wild and grandiose ideas typical of manic and hypomanic states are very practical. This euphoric, arrogant, and restless behaviour may lead to reckless and dangerous behaviour because, being utterly convinced that what he or she is doing is right, the sufferer will countenance no interference. Those unwise enough to interfere may well find themselves the subject of an attack of serious personal violence. The following case illustrates some of these points.

'A twenty-three-year-old car salesman initially impressed his employer with his energy and enthusiasm. However, it was not long before his ideas and activities took on the grandiose and highly unrealistic qualities of the person suffering from hypomania. For example, he sent dramatic and exaggerated letters daily to a wide range of motor manufacturers. His social behaviour began to deteriorate rapidly; he lost weight through not eating (he 'never had time') and he rarely slept. (Both of these behaviours are characteristic of the condition.) One night, in a fit of anger directed towards his "ungrateful" employer, he returned to the garage showrooms, smashed the windows and also caused extensive damage to a number of cars. He was charged with criminal damage and when he appeared at the crown court he was made the subject of a Hospital Order.'   (McCulloch and Prins 1978)

Such individuals can, therefore, be highly dangerous. Because their memory is unimpaired, they are capable of giving rational arguments and explanations to support their proposed actions. In some cases, the person may actually suffer from hallucinations. In the case just described, for example, the young man claimed that he 'saw' the motor manufacturers reading his letters to them. Occasionally, the hypomanic episode will be followed by a swing into a depressive state. It is very difficult to persuade manic and hypomanic persons to accept the need for treatment and compulsory admission may be needed.

In summary, sufferers from mania and hypomania resist the notion that there is anything wrong with them, they lack insight, and yet are often deceptively lucid and rational. As already indicated, when the illness is at its height, and they feel that they are being thwarted, they can be hostile and extremely aggressive; hence the need for hospital admission (Armond 1982). Medication, particularly the use of the drug lithium, seems to control the disorder quite well but follow-up and social support are essential if long-term benefits are to be achieved.

(3) Schizophrenic and associated illnesses

The schizophrenic disorders do not feature significantly from a numerical point of view in the causation or explanation of criminality (see Woddis 1964, West 1965, Kloek 1969, Faulk 1976, Taylor 1982, and Spry 1984). Very occasionally, a person suffering from what is known as catatonic schizophrenia may erupt into an unpredictable outburst of violence. This illness is characterized by lack of response to stimulation, negativism, muteness, and a strange rigidity of the limbs that enables the sufferer to hold them in strange poses for long periods of time without any apparent discomfort. In Chapter 2, we saw the part that paranoid schizophrenia might play in relation to violent crime; some well-known cases were cited by way of illustration. It is very important to emphasize yet again that the seriously paranoid individual may be highly likely to appear to be sane and intelligent in all other respects. The illness is usually so well encapsulated (contained) that the unwary or unskilled interviewer may be easily misled. It is only when the matters which the delusional system has fastened upon are referred to that the severity of the illness may be revealed. The psychotically or morbidly jealous individual can be a very dangerous person indeed. Such individuals, usually men, often develop a fixed and unshakeable belief that their spouse or partner is being unfaithful to them. What may have begun, perhaps, as a belief in a minor transgression, rooted in reality, develops into florid and unshakeable irrationality. The partner will be followed and confronted with accusations of sexual infidelity. The person suffering from the disorder will go to the most extraordinary and unpleasant lengths to substantiate and rationalize their beliefs; for example, he or she will examine the partner's underclothing for signs of seminal staining, in order to prove that intercourse has taken place with another partner. Occasionally, the innocent partner will be so terrified and cowed by the accusations that they may 'confess' to behaviour of which they are not guilty. Such 'confession' serves only to feed the morbid jealousy of the disordered partner even further (i.e. it provides confirmatory sanction for mayhem). As a result, the partner may be violently assaulted or even killed.

The irrational nature of this disorder has been well described in the mythology of Greece and Rome and the world's great literature. There are examples in *The Decameron* and in the work of Tolstoy. There is probably no more graphic illustration of the syndrome than that to be found in Shakespeare's *Othello*.

> 'But jealous souls will not be answered so;
> They are not ever jealous for the cause,
> But jealous for they're jealous; 'tis a monster
> Begot upon itself, born on itself'
> > (Act III, scene iv)

> 'O, beware, my lord, of jealousy;
> It is the green-eyed monster, which doth mock
> The meat it feeds on.'
> > (Act III, scene iii)

Shakespeare provides us with a further description of the pathological nature of extreme and dangerous jealousy through his characterization of Leontes in *The Winter's Tale*.

> 'were my wife's liver
> Infected, as her life, she would not live
> The running of one glass.'
> > (Act I, scene ii)

So graphically does Shakespeare describe the condition in *Othello* that it has been called the *Othello Syndrome* (Enoch and Trethowan 1979, Chapter 3). The management of the disorder is extremely difficult, as no wholly effective treatment has yet been found for it. 'The prognosis is very doubtful ... the symptoms often fade with chemotherapy, returning when this is discontinued. Psychotherapy can be of help in some cases and *usually must continue for a long time, i.e. a period of years*' (Enoch and Trethowan 1979: 46–7; my italics). These authors quote Clouston, a nineteenth-century physician, with graphic effect.

> 'I now have in an asylum two quite rational-looking men, whose chief delusion is that their wives, both women of undoubted good character, have been unfaithful to them. Keep them off that subject and they are rational. But on that subject they are utterly delusional and insane.'
>
> (Enoch and Trethowan 1979: 47)

(For a more recent account of the relationship between pathological jealousy and aggression, see Mullen and Maack 1985.)

In view of the intractable nature of this disorder and its often disastrous outcome, the best advice to the partner—if she survives an attack—may be that she should remove herself from the vicinity and endeavour to change her identity. When the time comes for such an offender/patient to be discharged into the community under supervision, it may, of course, be possible to insert into the licence conditions a requirement that they do not go near or make contact with their partner. Infringement of such a requirement or an early warning of its likelihood could lead to immediate recall if danger seemed imminent (see Chapter 3).

(4) Schizophrenic disorder and bizarre and violent crimes

Occasionally, a crime, because of its ferocity or depravity, shocks not only the public but even the most dispassionate of professionals. Such offences may well be committed by individuals who seem to have behaved with senseless and quite appalling cruelty. They show a lack of feeling for their victims which seems quite incomprehensible to most of us. In such (very rare) cases, it is sometimes found that a schizophrenic illness of insidious onset has been developing but that its presence has been overlooked. It seems probable that *some* cases of particularly sadistic murder may be committed by someone suffering in this way. It may, however, be difficult to differentiate the diagnosis in such a case from a similar crime committed by the cold and callous psychopath. (An example of this kind of difficulty can be found in the case of Neville Heath, who was hanged for killing two women and savagely mutilating them during a state of sexual frenzy.) The severe lack of feeling that may accompany this type of schizophrenic disorder may also help us to understand how those who immolate themselves by fire are able to destroy themselves in this way because they have been able to split off feeling from consciousness (see Topp 1973).

NEUROTIC AND STRESS CONDITIONS

Unless we choose to include psychopathic personality disorder, the neuroses (psychoneuroses) do not figure extensively in the aetiology of violent and dangerous behaviour. I will exclude psychopathic personality disorder here, since I deal with it separately in Chapter 5. Occasionally, a person suffering from a state of chronic anxiety or stress may find the build-up of tension so unbearable that even a minor and quite unrelated degree of frustration may result in an explosive outburst. Scott (1977) describes the case of a man of forty-seven, who asked the female storekeeper at his place of work for an item. She failed to produce it and, furthermore, failed to treat him with the respect he considered was his due. He beat her about the head with a spanner and nearly killed her. On psychiatric examination, he was not found to be formally mentally ill but was seen to be very disturbed about his present predicament. A *carefully elicited history* revealed that he was married to a dominant lady who nagged him and frequently expressed lack of satisfaction with his earnings. He had not had a holiday away from home for twenty years and in the last few weeks had been suffering from chest trouble that had kept him awake at night. At the time of the offence, he had been feeling unwell and taking a medicine containing codeine. When one examines all the background factors *and* the circumstances of the provoking incident that led to the offence, it seems reasonable to conclude that he behaved as he did because of mounting tension. He then vented all his suppressed resentment towards his unsympathetic spouse on his unfortunate victim (Scott 1977: 133). Such offences seem particularly likely to occur in males who, for whatever reason, feel that their self-image and masculinity have been impugned or threatened. Such instances may also occur in individuals in whom an anxiety state is accompanied by, or associated with, an obsessional or perfectionist personality. I know of a young man who made an unprovoked and quite serious attack upon an innocent passer-by in the street. As the defendant put it, 'I just exploded. I don't know why; the tension I'd been feeling recently just became unbearable.' During therapy, which lasted many months, he revealed a very vulnerable personality. This was coupled with a marked lack of self-esteem and a compulsive need to work in order to keep hitherto unrecognized anxieties at bay. Much later on, as therapy proceeded, he was able to reveal that his problems were associated with feelings towards his father that bordered on hatred. On the day in question, the innocent passer-by *happened* to look like his father. The assault was therefore no mere 'accident'. Both cases indicate the need for careful elicitation of all the facts in the past and present situation, including the offence itself.

HYSTERICAL REACTIONS

As discussed in Chapter 2, some individuals charged with very serious offences may claim amnesia for the event and try to establish that the crime was committed whilst in a state of dissociation or fugue. Hysterical symptoms can be grouped as follows:

(1) Those associated with the senses—for example, deafness or blindness.
(2) Those associated with motor symptoms—paralysis, spasms, tremors.
(3) Those in which the mental symptoms manifest themselves, such as in a fugue or wandering state. Strictly speaking, amnesia and fugue states are not synonymous. Amnesia may cover a much broader spectrum of behaviour and events. A fugue state is more likely to occur as a single and

specific incident. (See Lasky 1982, especially Chapter 7, for an interesting psychoanalytical interpretation and classification of these behaviours.) Other features include pseudo-dementia, the Ganser syndrome, stupor, and hysterical phobias (see Prins 1980b for discussion of these).

It is often very difficult to distinguish between a genuine hysterical disorder, a disorder due to organic factors (see later) or malingering. Most authorities agree that there is a large degree of overlap. Very careful elicitation of the facts may be required, but the following points may be found helpful.

(1) In malingering, the motivation is more or less at a conscious level; the symptoms are usually of sudden onset and have some connection with situations that the malingerer is keen to avoid (see Neustatter 1953).
(2) The malingerer's symptoms are usually over-acted and exaggerated, as in the case of Haigh, the 'acid-bath murderer'. Haigh produced bizarre symptoms in support of his claim to insanity. He stated that at various times he had drunk blood and urine. (For a critical account of this aspect of Haigh's case, see Prins 1984.) Malingerers charged with serious offences against the person tend to present the kind of symptoms they *believe* an insane person would present.
(3) The symptoms may only be present when the malingerer is being observed. Close observation by a number of people over a prolonged period of time is therefore essential.
(4) The symptoms tend to be made to order. If the examiner suggests that a certain symptom of the illness being feigned is missing in the individual's presentation, the malingerer will sometimes try to produce it.

By now, readers will have deduced that the presence or absence of malingering may well be of considerable importance in determining the genuineness or otherwise of a claim to amnesia for an offence involving serious violence, notably homicide (Gibbens and Hall Williams 1977). On the basis of a fairly extensive review of the literature, O'Connell concluded that the difference between malingered and hysterical amnesia was more likely to be one of *degree* than of kind (O'Connell 1960).

(Support for this view may be found in Neustatter 1953 and Hays 1961.) In fact, both conditions may co-exist in the same individual and serve a common purpose—namely, loss of memory for an alleged grave offence (see later discussion of the problems of estimating the degree of guilt or remorse shown by the offender). Power (1977) suggests the following further aids to distinguishing between genuine (hysterical) and feigned amnesia.

(1) Study the character of the alleged amnesia itself. An amnesic episode of sudden onset and termination is highly suggestive of feigned memory loss.
(2) Study the details and character of the crime itself. Motiveless crimes may be committed impulsively without premeditation or concealment and be accompanied by needless violence. They may even be committed in the presence of witnesses. (In this connection, one is reminded of the (no doubt apocryphal) account of one judge, who used to ask in cases of alleged insanity, 'Would the defendant have committed the offence with a policeman standing at his elbow?').
(3) Endeavour to detect inconsistencies in the current account given by the accused with that originally given to the police.
(4) Attempt to assess whether the accused seems, in general terms, to be a person of honesty. To some degree this can be achieved by reference to past social history and by paying careful attention to any past amnesic episodes.

Organic and allied disorders

Because of their comparative rarity, organic and allied disorders or malfunctions are often overlooked in discussions of the aetiology and precipitation of violent and dangerous behaviour. Most non-medically qualified personnel (particularly local authority social workers, probation officers, and other lay counsellors) are understandably more likely to look for causal factors in terms of psychopathology and social environment. It is, therefore, important to correct this tendency by paying some attention to 'physical' factors, for it is the under- or non-investigated case that may result in a tragedy. Before doing so, however, something needs to be said in more general terms about the biological aspects of violent and dangerous behaviour.

BIOLOGICAL ASPECTS OF VIOLENT AND DANGEROUS BEHAVIOUR

As I am neither a professional biologist nor a neurochemist, I shall not attempt a sophisticated presentation of this topic. Those who wish to take the matter further would do well to consult the specialist literature that I have listed at the end of this chapter. What follows is a very simplified statement of some important facts—stripped, however, of a good deal of qualifying and amplifying data.

Neurobiology

Advances in medical technology (made possible by progress in physics, biochemistry, and optics) have opened up for exploration new areas of biophysical systems. There has been a large amount of work carried out on the physiology of violence in recent years (particularly in the United States). The area of the brain that is considered to be influential in the aetiology of violent behaviour is known as the 'limbic' system—an area nearest the brain stem. It is important to note that part of the cortex associated with the limbic system is especially susceptible to injury, circulatory insufficiency, and infectious processes. Damage to this region in humans often results in epileptiform discharges that produce the same effects as artificially induced stimulation of this region in animals. There is a growing body of experimental evidence (both in animals and in humans) that shows a degree of correlation between aggressive behaviour and gross structural lesions in parts of the limbic system; for example, lesions in the *hypothalamus* in animals induce symptoms of rage and, in humans, such lesions (caused by tumours) may produce the progressive development of uncontrollable rage behaviour. Lesions in those parts of the brain known as the *hippocampus* and the *amygdala* may produce similar results. One of the problems in establishing *certain* evidence is that it is not normally possible to identify and record disturbances much below the level of the cortex (simply put, the outer covering of the brain) and this is usually the site for EEG (electroencephalography) procedures.

Neurochemistry

Much of neurochemistry is concerned with the transmission of chemical substances between nerves. The neurochemistry of aggression is concerned with what occurs at the junctions between these nerves and with trying to distinguish the different types of substances transmitted. The secretion of some of these neurochemical substances more than others has been shown (under experimental conditions) to facilitate aggression.

Hormones

Hormones (conveyors of chemical messages) are secreted by specialized glands into the general blood circulation. Much of the work on the relationship between hormonal influences and aggressive behaviour has been concerned with the influence of sex steroids (e.g. testosterone and oestrogen) in animals.

Psychosurgery and critical organ surgery

There is a substantial literature identifying the effects of surgical interventions of various kinds on different parts of the brain, made in an attempt to afford relief from intractable and uncontrollable aggression. Much of the research has been hard to evaluate systematically because of faulty sampling, inadequate follow-up, and so forth. Thus it has been difficult to determine the degree to which such interventions have been clinically effective or ethically desirable. *Critical organ surgery* (e.g. castration) has been held to diminish *libido* but not to influence perverse *desires*.

Drug treatments

As we shall see in Chapter 6, some sexually aggressive offenders have been treated effectively with cyproterone acetate

(Andracur); this seems to have the effect of controlling libido, sex behaviour, and performance, *without* the widespread undesirable side-effects of some other compounds. In addition, some of the anti-psychotic drugs (such as the phenothiazines) also reduce hostility and aggression, as have some of the other drugs used to suppress epileptic seizures. Moderate doses of the benzodiazepines (e.g. Diazepam) are also effective in reducing aggressive excitability and hostility. I am not advocating 'chemical coshing'; I am simply describing instances in which such drugs have been used *appropriately and under carefully controlled and monitored conditions*.

Chromosomal abnormalities

Before leaving the subject of the biological aspects of violence, brief mention must be made of the relationship between chromosomal abnormalities and violent crime. In the early 1960s, a considerable degree of interest was aroused by the finding that there were a number of men detained in special hospitals and prisons carrying an extra Y chromosome (XYY).[1] Such men were often found to be taller than average, came from essentially *non-delinquent backgrounds*, and occasionally had records of violence. Later research has produced somewhat inconclusive evidence concerning the prevalence of such abnormalities not only in penal and similar populations but in the population at large. Although the leads offered have potential for further and interesting development, there appears to be no firm evidence to suggest that there is a strong causal link between specific genetic defects or abnormalities and violent criminality. However, if the cytological and other sophisticated techniques that are required in this field are further developed, we may find at some future date that there is a stronger genetic link than appears to be the case at present. (For reviews of this interesting area see Theilgaard 1983 and Craft 1984a.)

With these facts in mind we can proceed to examine some other organic and physical factors that may be of importance in relation to violent and dangerous behaviour.

INFECTIONS AND DISEASES

Infections of the brain

These include meningitis, encephalitis, and a number of viral conditions. It is not uncommon for marked changes in behaviour to occur following encephalitis and these may be accompanied by the development of aggressive tendencies. It is of interest to note here that a very serious outbreak of epidemic *encephalitis lethargica* occurred in the 1920s; this resulted in many children showing serious behaviour disturbance. As we shall see in Chapter 5, some forms of aggressive psychopathy *may* be caused by such infections. It is also thought that one form of *herpes* virus may be responsible for some cases of mild brain damage, which may result in behaviour disorder. The incidence in such cases is, however, hard to determine.

Huntington's chorea

This is a comparatively rare, directly transmitted hereditary and irreversible condition. The onset of the illness is more likely to occur in the middle years of life. It is characterized by a progressive deterioration of mental, physical, and emotional functioning. Occasionally, sufferers from this disorder may behave unpredictably and aggressively.

General paralysis of the insane

This disorder develops as a result of a syphilitic infection, attacking the central nervous system (CNS). Symptoms may appear many years after the original infective incident and the sufferer may sometimes indulge in uncharacteristic violent behaviour. The condition may present occasionally in very similar fashion to hypomania. There are, however, some fairly simple physical and neurological tests that can determine the conclusive presence of GPI. Fortunately, this illness is seen fairly rarely these days, largely owing to earlier diagnosis and to the use of antibiotic drugs.

ALCOHOL AND OTHER SUBSTANCES

Alcoholic poisoning

Alcohol-related problems and their relationship to serious offending are dealt with in Chapter 8 but it is worth pointing out here that brain damage as a result of alcoholic poisoning may occasionally be very important in relation to the exhibition of violent behaviour (see Brewer 1974 and Taylor 1981).

Toxic substances

Very occasionally, an individual may indulge in quite atypical and aggressive behaviour for no apparent reason. All preliminary exploratory investigations may prove negative. Later and more detailed enquiries, however, may reveal that the person concerned has been exposed to toxic substances, such as carbon monoxide fumes, lead, or industrial chemicals. Such cases will arise rarely but it is the rare and apparently inexplicable case that should merit our closest attention. Some of these issues are discussed in a useful article by Blair (1977).

ENDOCRINE, HORMONAL, AND ASSOCIATED DISORDERS

A state of hypoglycaemia may occur in certain predisposed individuals, particularly if they are diabetic and have gone without food for a prolonged period. (The legal importance of such conditions was noted in Chapter 2.) A person so suffering may show serious lack of judgement and may, on occasion, also behave impulsively and aggressively. Moreover, the underlying diabetic condition may sometimes not come to light until some oddness of behaviour has occurred. An abnormality of thyroid function may sometimes produce conduct that may be accompanied by aggressive acts. Fortunately, thyroid malfunctions, once properly diagnosed, are comparatively easy to correct.

It is a commonplace that serious swings of mood may be observed at adolescence and at the 'change of life' in women and, to a lesser extent, in men. Such mood swings may sometimes be accompanied by disturbances in behaviour and by irrational, impulsive conduct. In recent years, considerable interest has been shown in the association between seriously aggressive conduct and pre-menstrual tension. Dalton, an authority on this topic, has recently suggested that the true pre-menstrual syndrome (known for short as PMS) is a condition marked by progesterone deficiency, which starts from ovulation and reaches its climax some seven days before menstruation. PMS is held to be associated with a number of symptoms, including irritability, migraine, depression, and instability. Dalton also suggests that, in addition to these symptoms, seriously assaultive behaviour may sometimes occur. Offences of this sort tend to be unpremeditated and motiveless and may arise out of 'a sudden and momentary surge of uncontrollable emotions resulting in violence' (Dalton 1982). (See also Clare 1983 and D'Orban 1983 for reviews of recent work in this area.) Dalton has been involved in giving expert medical evidence in two fairly recent cases, in which PMS was successfully raised as a defence in order to obtain Section 2 manslaughter verdicts. It is yet another interesting example of the way in which we should be on the look-out for the *possibility* of a physical cause for inexplicable forms of violent behaviour.

MORE COMMON STATES

Extreme hunger or deprivation of sleep may induce abnormal reactions even in the most robust individuals. If these deprivations are also coupled with the ingestion of alcohol, other drugs, or prescribed medicines, they *may* lead to highly abnormal or aggressive behaviour. It is the *combination* of social, psychological, and physical factors that may prove to be important—as we saw in the case quoted by Scott (see page 99). In recent years, interest has also been shown in the possible relationship of dietary deficiencies to delinquency and aggressively anti-social behaviour (*Guardian* 22 December, 1984, and Feingold 1979).

BRAIN TRAUMA, BRAIN TUMOUR, AND BRAIN DISEASE

It is important to emphasize that, from time to time, cases of brain trauma or tumour are missed—sometimes with tragic consequences. An injury to the brain (however caused) is more than likely to produce a degree of concussion, which may sometimes be prolonged. Such injuries may give rise to mental retardation or to a form of epilepsy (see below). Such persons may also be amnesic but such amnesia will differ from the forms of amnesia described earlier. Following recovery of consciousness there may be noisy delirium—a condition *not* seen in hysterical or malingered amnesia. Organically amnesic persons may sometimes appear to be normal initially and only gradually, following careful examination, does it emerge that they have been behaving 'automatically'. In contrast, in cases of hysterical amnesia, memory may return spontaneously within twenty-four hours or so. The organically amnesic person is likely to want to do his or her best to remember events and may appear to be annoyed by their defective memory; in contrast, the hysterical amnesic may show a complete inability to recall any events before a specific time (see also Lasky 1982). In addition, the hysterically amnesic person, unlike the organically amnesic individual, may have perfect command of their speech and be well in control of their other faculties. Taylor and Kopelman (1984) have offered a useful survey of the numerous factors involved.

Lidberg (1971) studied the degree to which concussion following head injury was related to criminality. He found a statistically significant correlation between crimes of *violence* and concussion in his (admittedly small) sample. Brewer (1976) considers it essential that anyone charged with serious violence should be afforded full X-ray, EEG, and psychological investigations if there is the slightest possibility of brain disease. In a further paper, he suggested that cerebral *tumours* as such are a rare cause of criminal violence but he provides interesting case material in which he shows that cerebral *atrophy* (degeneration) may be of importance in some cases (Brewer 1978). Such atrophy may be a common sequel to many kinds of brain disease and may also be a sequel to head injury. The increased use of sophisticated radiological 'scanning' devices, which are a considerable improvement on ordinary X-ray techniques, now offers the chance of more accurate, thorough, investigation.

Occasionally, the dementing processes of advancing or old age may be associated with behaviour that is not only out of character but which may also be highly impulsive and aggressive. In summary, we may say that any behaviour occurring in mid-life that seems odd, quite out of character, is particularly aggressive, and for which there does not appear to be any immediate psychological or environmental explanation, should make us reflect very seriously upon the possibilities of an organic or similar cause.

EPILEPSY AND ASSOCIATED DISORDERS

Epilepsy, in its various forms, is not strictly speaking a psychiatric illness but a neurological disorder, manifested primarily by an excessive or abnormal discharge of electrical activity in the brain. In fact, it may be said to constitute a symptom as much as an illness. Many thousands of people will have an epileptic attack of one kind or another at some stage in their lives; even for those who have major attacks, it is usually possible to lead a perfectly normal life with the help of medication. There are many different forms and causes of epilepsy and these are well summarized by Fenton (1984). Some forms of epilepsy may be caused by head injury or brain damage, others are of unknown origin (*idiopathic*). There are several types of epileptic phenomena; *Grand Mal* (a major convulsion); *Petit Mal*; Temporal Lobe epilepsy, often characterized by sudden, unexpected alterations of mood and behaviour; Jacksonian epilepsy (a localized cerebral convulsion following traumatic brain damage); partial seizures and more generalized convulsive seizures.

As we saw in Chapter 2, epileptic automatism may sometimes be pleaded as a defence in cases of serious crime, such as homicide. Gunn has carried out a number of very important studies into the relationship between epilepsy and crime, particularly serious crime (see Gunn 1977 for a summary). He found that more epileptic males were taken into custody than would be expected by chance—a ratio of some 7–8:1,000. This is considerably higher than the proportion of epileptics found in the general population. About one-third of Gunn's cases were found to be suffering from temporal lobe epilepsy and temporal lobe cases were found to have a higher previous conviction rate. It was the group suffering from idiopathic epilepsy, however, who received disproportionately more previous convictions for violence than any other group. Gunn has suggested that undue emphasis should not be placed upon the relationship between epilepsy and serious crime. He makes three important points. First, the epilepsy itself may generate social and psychological problems, which in their turn may lead to anti-social reactions. Second, harmful social factors such as overcrowding, parental neglect, and allied problems may lead to a more than average degree of both epilepsy and anti-social behaviour. Third, environmental factors such as those just described may lead to behavioural disturbances that not only produce brushes with the law but may also produce accident and illness proneness. Gunn points out that such disturbances may, in themselves, produce an excess prevalence of epileptic phenomena. Although there is no strong proof of a general relationship between epilepsy (notably temporal lobe epilepsy) and violence, it may well be important in the individual case. For this reason, referral for expert opinion and diagnosis in cases of doubt is of great importance (see also Fenton 1984).

Episodic Dyscontrol Syndrome

This is a collection of signs and symptoms akin to epileptic phenomena. It has been suggested that there may be a very small group of people who, in the absence of demonstrable epilepsy, brain damage, or psychotic illness, may show explosively violent behaviour in the absence of any clearly discernible stimuli. Their life histories show an early onset of violent tendencies in a setting of chaotic domestic and social lives. The family may include other members who have also shown anti-social behaviour. The histories of men and women who show episodic dyscontrol syndrome have much in common with those of psychopathically disordered people (see Chapter 5). Fenton suggests that within the group of people suffering from episodic dyscontrol syndrome, there may be a small number of

'emotionally inhibited people, who habitually exercise tight control over their aggressive feeling . . . such people have led blameless lives in the past. However, if exposed to prolonged and intolerable provocation, especially from a person with whom they have a close emotional involvement, they may react with explosive aggressive behaviour, for which they have much remorse afterwards.' (Fenton 1984: 201)

Finally, it is as well to bear in mind Fenton's comment that, 'though epilepsy is more common in prison populations than might be expected, antisocial behaviour as a direct consequence of epileptic automatism is rare' (Fenton 1984: 209).

MENTAL IMPAIRMENT

Occasionally, a person adjudged to be mentally impaired will be accused of a serious crime of personal violence or of arson. It is as well to remember here that mental impairment is not correlated highly with criminal behaviour generally, although I have pointed out elsewhere that there are some instances where it may be (Prins 1980b). Such acts of violence as do occur are likely to do so when the mentally impaired person has made an inapt or inappropriate approach and then been rebuffed; for example, a clumsy and inapt sexual overture. The mentally impaired individual may not understand why he or she is repulsed and persist in making the same type of advance. The victim may then become frightened and resist, and the mentally impaired offender may then commit an assault. Some quite serious sexual offences, and even murder, may occur in such circumstances. On the other hand, it is important to remember that some mentally impaired individuals (particularly if the degree of impairment is moderately severe) may be apprehended for serious offences that they have not, in fact, committed. In recent years, there have been one or two unhappy instances in which a mentally impaired person has succumbed to pressure to make a false confession. As a result of these cases, certain safeguards have been introduced, such as the need for the presence of a parent, guardian, or other responsible person during police questioning. (For a useful discussion of this aspect and the caution that must be exercised in assessing degrees of mental impairment, see Craft 1984b.)

Two cases may illustrate some of the more general difficulties. The first concerns a man of twenty-six, who was charged with causing grievous bodily harm to a young woman by hitting her over the head with an iron bar. She was entirely unknown to him and, although he denied the offence vehemently, he was convicted by the Crown Court on the clearest possible evidence. He had suffered brain damage as a child, which had resulted in a moderate degree of mental impairment, accompanied by impulsive, unpredictable behaviour. He had come before the courts on a number of occasions, and had been eventually committed to a hospital for the mentally subnormal. He was discharged some years later to the care of his mother. Subsequent to his discharge, he committed the offence described above and was placed on probation. His response was poor. He was impulsive and erratic, and regressed to very childish forms of conduct when under stress. The family background was quite disturbed; mother and father had divorced when the offender/patient was quite small. A brother suffered from a disabling form of epilepsy and other members of the family had led decidedly eccentric lives. Shortly after the probation period expired, he committed a particularly vicious and unprovoked assault on a small girl; he was sentenced to a long term of imprisonment.

The second case illustrates the way in which the mildly mentally impaired person is particularly susceptible to the goading and provocation of those more well-endowed. This concerned a man in his forties. For many years he had worked quite happily as a farm labourer, under friendly but firm supervision. His work situation changed, with the result that his new employers felt he was being lazy and they did not have much sympathy for his disability. In addition, his new workmates teased and picked on him. On the day in question, one of them taunted him about his lack of ability with the opposite sex. Taunted beyond endurance, the defendant stabbed his tormentor in the chest with a pitchfork. When the case came before the Crown Court, evidence was heard as to his mental condition, social status, and the manner in which he had been provoked. The court made a hospital order. (For further details of this case, see McCulloch and Prins 1978: 171–72.)

A typology and a framework

TYPOLOGY

Although, as already made clear, violence and dangerousness are not coterminous, it is probably helpful to have some kind of classification of those violent individuals who may become involved in behaviour considered to be dangerous or potentially dangerous. Greenland (1980) has suggested four groupings that are helpful from this point of view.

Group I

Chronic anti-social offenders, whose personalities may be described as paranoid and whose life styles are characterized by excessive long-term use of alcohol. Such people are habitually aggressive and their assaultive and alcoholic behaviour suggests chronic maladaptation to society.

Group II

Those offenders whose violent behaviour occurs during an acute psychotic episode with either a marked delusional system and/or loss of contact with reality. Such a state may be associated with an internal experience of tension, which builds up to an unbearable level. Such persons show histories of chronic instability, poor family ties, and an incapacity for holding down a job.

Group III

Offenders who are *situationally or intermittently* violent. Greenland suggests this may occur as a result of recurrent manic-depressive illness, organic brain dysfunctions, which result in periodic loss of control, or cyclical drinking patterns resulting in rage states and disinhibition. Such persons may tend to become violent *only in specific circumstances*.

Group IV

Offenders who have committed serious violence in a state of *severe depression*. These are the offenders who often seek help (by showing warning signals) or who make suicidal attempts prior to the offence.

FRAMEWORK

It is obvious that there will always be a combination of what might best be described as *extrinsic and intrinsic factors* in the causation of violent conduct. These can best be illustrated by means of the following framework, which has been modified after Gosnold (1978) and Prins (1983d). This framework lists possible influential factors.

1. Social/psychological factors
2. Psychiatric factors (including such phenomena as hysteria, functional psychoses, hypomania, etc.)
3. Epileptic conditions/temporal lobe disease
4. Other organic states
5. Hypoglycaemia—from whatever cause
6. Toxic states (for example, uraemia or toxic compound poisoning)
7. Inflammation and infections of the brain (meningitis and encephalitis)
8. Head injuries (including cerebral irritation and concussion)
9. Alcohol ingestion, alcoholic poisoning
10. Ingestion of other drugs (including substance abuse)

Some of these factors will of course overlap. Important clues as to their presence may be looked for under the following headings:

(a) Drug Abuse (injection marks, pupil changes, general neglect)
(b) Alcohol Abuse (neglect, dietary deficiencies, smell of alcohol)
(c) Psychiatric illness (disordered speech and conversation, confusion, disorientation, hallucinations, delusions, 'hysterical' outbursts)
(d) Presence of physical illness

This typology and the framework provide us with a useful summary of some of the aetiological and situational factors already described. (See also Mednick and Volavka 1980.) From this, we can now go on to examine how dangerous or potentially dangerous situations may best be managed and how workers may become more effective and skilful in this field of work.

Management

In addition to the knowledge already outlined, we also have to ask ourselves what skills we need to acquire in order to become more effective in this area of work. To achieve this we must be prepared to examine ourselves and our attitudes—especially towards those who have committed grave offences which may frighten and sometimes horrify us. I shall begin with a discussion of the importance of acquiring a *detailed* knowledge of the violent or dangerous offence or incident.

GETTING THE FACTS RIGHT

There is no 'magic' that we can bring to the assessment and management of violent or dangerous behaviour. As Scott says,

'it is patience, thoroughness and persistence in this process, rather than any diagnostic or interviewing brilliance, that produces results. In this sense the telephone, the written request for past records, and the checking of information against other informants, are the important diagnostic devices.'   (Scott 1977: 129)

The factual or legal description of a piece of violent or dangerous behaviour on its own does not help us, either. Rape, for example, is a terrifying experience for any woman under any circumstances but there is an important qualitative difference between what might be described as 'ordinary' rape and the type of attack where the offender ties the victim up, rapes her, renders her unconscious, brings her round again and then commits further assaults, and so on. In addition, such an offender may force the victim to engage in deviant sexual practices or attempt to defile her in other ways. The legal charge of rape thus affords no clues as to the real nature of the attack and the psychology of the attacker.

Similar problems arise in homicide cases. An assault on a child may end in death, for example, not because this was the original intention of the offender but because the child struggled and screamed and death occurred as a result of attempts to keep the victim quiet. Tragically, it is all too easy to kill a small child. A hand placed over the mouth to stifle a scream may easily lead to suffocation and even a light blow to the head may, in some circumstances, cause death. Such 'accidental' deaths, if they can be so called, must be distinguished from those where the killing was part of the sexual attack and where the killer derived sexual pleasure from the pain or death of his small victim. In these cases, the nature of the wounds inflicted, their distribution, and whether they occurred before or after death, may provide most important prognostic indicators. The same applies to adult homicide. It is comparatively difficult to kill a healthy (and not elderly) adult by stabbing. The victim is likely to struggle a good deal; the offender, in his or her turn, may be scared by the struggle and the difficulty involved in quietening the victim. Thus, there may be many stab wounds and a great deal of blood or other body matter. The distribution of such wounds may help to distinguish whether this was a normal or an abnormal killing. One is reminded of Lady Macbeth's conscience-stricken statement about the killing of King Duncan: 'Yet who would have thought the old man to have had so much blood in him?' (*Macbeth* Act V, scene i).

There may, of course, be more simple indicators of pathology. A man had been sentenced to a two-year prison sentence for indecent assault on a boy of fifteen. It was only when the detailed police reports of the offence were made available that it became clear that a knife was used to induce compliance and that the youth was put in considerable fear by his assailant; a fear that had long-term damaging psychological effects.

In all such cases, the report by the pathologist and the full police account of the incident are essential for those who have the responsibility of trying to determine the true nature of the offence and whether it is likely to occur again. As we shall see later, the role of the victim and his or her relationship to the offender is often vitally important, in relation to both present and future understanding. The need to examine and assess the total situation has been usefully identified by Scott in the form of the following equation:

$$\text{Offender} + \text{victim} + \text{circumstances} = \text{offence}.$$

Scott also stressed that 'each element of the equation is equally important' (Scott 1977: 130). It is therefore vitally important not to view the offence in isolation but to try to see the extent to which it was situationally determined. Thus, it is wiser to think in terms of dangerous situations rather than dangerous persons. The importance of assessing and understanding the situational determinants of violent and dangerous events has been examined by Brody and Tarling (1980); Danto (1980); Showalter, Bonnie, and Roddy (1980); Suedfeld (1980); Steadman (1982); Hawkins (1983); Dobash and Dobash (1984); Maguire, Pinter, and Collis (1984).

THE UNASKABLE AND UNTHINKABLE QUESTION

There is no doubt that many serious and high-risk offenders have committed offences that are likely to fill those who have to deal with them with fear, horror, and revulsion (Prins 1984). There is, therefore, an initial hurdle to overcome; namely, having to examine one's *own* feelings and act with what might best be described as dispassionate compassion towards such people. There is also the added serious burden of feeling responsible for trying to see that such offences do not occur again. As we saw in Chapter 3, there are serious obligations placed upon those who are responsible for the supervision of such offenders in the community. Let us assume that the person for whom an after-care agent is responsible seems to be progressing well and that this good progress and good working relationship have continued for, perhaps, a year or two. Under these circumstances, there may be a tendency to relax one's vigilance, not necessarily because familiarity has bred contempt (though it might) but because one does not *want* to have knowledge of, or observe, signs that all is not well. Thus warning signs (changes in behaviour or mood, for example) may be ignored, as may be the warning signs being given by the offender/patient's relatives that all is not well. Sometimes, quite obvious areas of vulnerability may be overlooked, as we saw in the case of Graham Young, discussed at the beginning of this chapter.

In addition, some social workers are reluctant to exercise what they regard as a 'police rôle' and do not take kindly to the type of more intrusive supervision required in this area of work (see Floud and Young 1981). It is true, of course, that ethical issues are important; and sometimes fine judgements may have to be made between the liberty of the subject and the protection of the public. Some of these issues have been identified by Walker (1978). The problems were highlighted recently in the case of Colin Evans, referred to on page 83.

If we accept that there are no magic means of predicting future mayhem, then we are forced to acknowledge that we must use ourselves in this process and sometimes ask the unaskable and the unthinkable question. With this important fact in mind, we can begin to consider those questions that should be uppermost in our minds when dealing with potentially dangerous offenders/patients, particularly those who have already committed grave crimes, such as homicide.

SOME QUESTIONS

(1) What seem to have been the nature of past possible precipitating stress factors in the offender/patient's social environment? Have these been modified or removed?

It has to be recognized that those who have killed a close relative may need to destroy a surrogate. Take, for example, the case of the man who killed his mother and did sufficiently well in hospital to be discharged. In the course of a fairly short time it became apparent that he was forming a close relationship with a woman who in all respects was very much like the mother he had killed. Clearly, such a case would merit the most careful monitoring and perhaps a recall to hospital. It would be all too easy to be misled by appearances that he had found someone to care for him and to be cared about. That would be the lay and uninformed view; our approach must go deeper and, as already suggested, examine the unpalatable and the unthinkable. This is where advice from, and consultation with, other experienced colleagues is so important. They can offer a more detached and objective viewpoint. It is useful to bear in mind that progress within one sphere of life in an institution does not necessarily mean that other problems have been resolved. The inmate who does well on an educational or Open University course may still be harbouring murderous or fire-raising intentions. The man praised for his regular attendance at body-building and keep fit classes may well be using his time to keep himself occupied and 'in trim'; on the other hand, if he has a long history of violence towards others as a means of getting his way, he may be keeping himself fit merely for the commission of further mayhem on release. It is very easy to adopt a naïve and unquestioning view of such endeavours. It cannot be emphasized sufficiently that all such behaviour needs to be reviewed longitudinally and against the offender's general life-style, even if this results in a charge of over-suspiciousness being levelled against us. As professionals, we must be prepared to tolerate such accusations and learn to live with them.

(2)   To what extent was the original offence caused by provocation, conscious or unconscious?

Spouses may make themselves particularly vulnerable to fur-ther attack by vacillating in their attitudes towards the offender; for example, a flirtatious wife may insist on continuing this course of behaviour, knowing full well that she has a very jealous husband. The capacity to cope with provocation will vary, of course, from offender to offender. As Scott says, 'the impact of a breaking marriage may be very different in a man whose mother deserted when he was five' (Scott 1977: 130). It is only when the *history* of the behaviour is examined step by step over time that the true pattern may emerge. It is, therefore, of vital importance for all those who would counsel in this area to recognize not only the desirability of good history taking but, in addition, the need to examine *pieces* of behaviour in great depth before the be-haviour can be understood as a whole. This can be achieved only if staff keep adequate records of their work with such offenders/patients. In doing so, care should be taken to separate facts from feelings. In addition, on-going records of counselling should be consulted regularly.

We all have a rather arrogant notion that we can recall important details of our work with clients/patients. In point of fact, our recall of detail is quite poor and it is stupid and unprofessional to think otherwise. Regular re-examination of the records of our on-going work is likely to reveal gaps or inconsistencies in the offender/patient's account of his or her life, or we may well discern a pattern of repeated attempts to communicate facts or feelings to us that *we* have avoided. This kind of avoidance tactic is extremely common in the assessment and management of cases of non-accidental injury to children. Social workers and others may be very reluctant to ask searching questions as to the progress of the child at risk, especially (as I indicated earlier) if they have known the family a long time. This reluctance is excused on the spurious assumption that it 'might spoil a good relationship'. The weakness of this argument is that a 'good' relationship does not mean a cosy, collusive contact but rather one that faces realities and has a regard for the protection of the child, whilst recognizing the rights and feelings of parents. It is very difficult indeed to insist on seeing a child undressed, faced with the reply that he or she is 'asleep' or 'not very well'. Failure to persist in one's enquiry may contribute to the child being placed at further risk or actually being harmed. Tragically, in the past twenty years or so there have been too many instances of such reluctance and failures in communication. Family violence (including violence towards children) is a large topic and is not dealt with specifically in this chapter. Those who wish to pursue this important area should consult the specialist reading listed at the end of the chapter. However, much of what I have to say about general approaches to the problem of the assessment and management of dangerous behaviour is also applicable to family violence.

(3) What capacity does the offender/patient seem to have for sympathetic identification with others?

In what ways does the offender/patient's story of his or her previous history or the accounts of those near to him or her tend to confirm or refute this? Has he or she still some capacity left for learning by experience? Some indications may be obtained by the way in which the offender/patient behaved *at the time of the offence*. For example, did the behaviour seem wantonly and aggressively cruel? (See my earlier remarks concerning the need for firm factual evidence of what actually happened.) Did the offender summon help immediately after the perpetration of the deed, run off, appear quite unmoved, or even suffer a fugue or other more general amnesic state? Did the offence seem to be an isolated instance of the need to inflict pain or suffering on others? Was it directed towards a particular individual, or for a specific purpose, or was it merely a means of getting back at society in general (as, for example, in some cases of arson)? Is the offender/patient the kind of person who continually feels threatened or persecuted? (See earlier remarks about paranoid states.) All these questions need careful consideration.

(4) Are there any other indicators that we might use, if only we have the courage to ask about them?

Occasionally, the eliciting of violent and aggressive phantasies or preoccupations may provide useful clues. (The role of phantasy and its place in counselling and psychotherapy is usefully described and discussed by Segal (1985).) Too much importance should not be attached to these, however, since the extent to which such preoccupations are indulged in by those who never *behave* with serious violence is not known. Having said this, *some* clues do seem to have possible ominous prognostications, especially when phantasies are acted upon or used as a *rehearsal* for actual violence (see MacCulloch *et al.* 1983). Williams has an interesting observation to make on this phenomenon. He describes the case of a young man who assaulted pre-pubertal girls, who said, 'You see, I have already committed the assault in my mind and when this gets unbearable, I go out and find a girl and do to her what I have done in my mind. Then I feel better and often get caught' (Williams 1982: 130). Brittain, in his classic paper on the sadistic murderer, provided a very full account of the manner in which some people develop but, at the same time, attempt to conceal their sadistic and murderous phantasies (Brittain 1970). Again, the case of Graham Young, described earlier in this chapter, comes to mind.

(5) To what extent is it possible to engage offenders/patients in a discussion of how they see themselves?

What kind of self-image do they have? As we shall see in Chapter 6, these questions are particularly important in relation to serious sex offending. How vulnerable do such offenders seem to be? Do we get the impression of the 'last straw' effect, or do they see everybody as hostile towards them—as some psychopaths seems to do? Do they seem to treat others as objects on which to indulge their abnormal desires? Nilsen's attitude towards his victims (see Chapter 3) seems to have had this quality to it, as did that of Christie, the multiple killer of women.

(6) In how far is the offender/patient prepared to talk about his or her relationship with the victim?

What was the *extent* of the provocation, if any? We should remember that serious violence may be displaced from a highly provoking source to an area that may be scarcely provoking at all. Scott (1977) reminds us of this when he recalls the legendary Medea who, wanting to get back at her husband, killed her baby, saying to her husband, 'that will stab thy heart'. The notion of displaced violence is extremely important, as we saw in the case of the young man who assaulted a complete stranger, described earlier.

(7) Can employment or occupations offer us any useful cues or clues?

Occasionally, these may provide us with some useful hints. Butchering and work in abattoirs, for example, is sometimes found in the histories of those convicted of particularly sadistic offences. It is of interest to recall that Nilsen acquired such skills in the Army Catering Corps (see Chapter 2). Those with necrophilic tendencies may seek work as mortuary attendants. Scott makes the interesting observation that children given to sadistic behaviour sometimes evince an interest in veterinary work, showing an unusual interest in sick and damaged animals (Scott 1977).

(8) What can we learn from the way offenders/patients talk about their offence and past behaviour?

Have they been able to come to terms with what they did? Have they showed some capacity for self-examination? Murray Cox provides a very apt quotation from Virginia Woolf's *The Waves*, which captures the essence of the problem admirably. 'It was only for a moment, catching sight of myself as I always prepare myself for the sight of myself, that I quailed' (Cox 1982: 84). Cox goes on to make the very important point that it is the task of the counsellor to help the offender/patient face feelings and experiences that hitherto have been intolerable. It *may* be an ominous sign if an offender/patient talks about their offence in an apparently guilt-free or callous manner. As counsellors, we tend to hope for protestations of guilt and/or remorse; when these are not forthcoming we may tend to think the worst. It should be noted, however, that after the perpetration of a particularly horrendous crime a number of mechanisms may come into play—conscious and unconscious; for example, the act *may* indeed have been so horrendous that the offender/patient has had to 'blot' it out of consciousness, in which case only prolonged psychotherapy, possibly aided by chemical abreactive techniques, may bring the events and the surrounding feelings into full consciousness.

In other cases, the offender may have been under the influence of drink or drugs at the time and have no clear recollection of the events. Considerable care should be exercised in accepting such an explanation because, as we saw in Chapter 2, the ingestion of alcohol and other drugs may be proffered as an excuse or an extenuating circumstance. There may be reluctance on the part of the offender/patient to acknowledge that they have actually committed the crime, for fear of the distress such acknowledgement would cause to close family and/or friends. In these situations, work with the offender/patient and his or her family is essential. In some cases, the offender/patient may have been in an institution for so long that they have genuinely forgotten the *full* details of the offence or have become confused by being asked to talk about it on many occasions to a variety of interviewers over many years. Careful eliciting of the surrounding facts and checking back into past records should help to clarify this particular issue.

In considering all these matters, it cannot be over-emphasized that a careful review of the offender/patient's *total* life experience and the impressions gained by a *variety* of staff are of crucial importance in trying to answer the question, 'Will it happen again?' In connection with serious sexual offenders, for example, an 'unease' expressed by more than one female member of staff may be particularly revealing and suggest a need for caution in considering discharge.

WHAT OF THE WORKER'S FEELINGS?

So far I have written almost exclusively about the offender/ patient and said very little about the worker (counsellor), the fears and attributes or skills that he or she brings to this difficult task. This is partly because few of us are prepared to admit that some of the people I have been describing may frighten us. Often, we cannot put the reason for this very clearly into words. Some say, 'they have a hunch'; others will say, 'it's something in their eyes'. This may *sound* absurd—indeed, I was once taken to task by a former colleague for explaining dangerous behaviour *post hoc* and for suggesting that hunches should be relied upon (Webb 1976); but, as professionals working in this demanding field, we do, from time to time, have to rely on 'hunches'. Our task is to try to make them *informed* hunches and by learning from one case to the next to hope to improve our skills. There is certainly little doubt that the way in which some offenders/ patients present themselves to us can fill us with an intangible disquiet and even apprehension. I am reminded of the second witch in Macbeth when she says, 'By the pricking of my thumbs, something wicked this way comes' (*Macbeth* Act IV, scene i).

Can we be any more precise about what it is that we are afraid of? We are all afraid of physical violence (see later discussion). Lion (1972) drew attention to this aspect, and also to the fact that some dangerous or potentially dangerous people not only may wish to be controlled but are, in addition, afraid of their own dangerous impulses. With such offenders/patients it may be helpful to bring this out into the open. A phrase such as 'I know that you are fearful of losing control, but I'm going to try to help you' may be quite useful. Cox (1974) has suggested in this context that some offenders/patients may be frightened to talk about their feelings and phantasies because they feel that the therapist or counsellor is too frightened to listen to them (see also Cox 1983, Casement 1985). It is, therefore, essential that counsellors make some attempt to overcome these fears, though the process is a very demanding one. Are we afraid that we may *unwittingly* provoke a violent assault or are we afraid that somehow we may be overcome by the dangerous offender/patient's violent phantasy system? As already indicated, it is only after a full and intensive investigation of such individuals, their life-styles and past histories, that clues may be afforded as to the possibility of future dangerous and/or unpredictable outbursts.

Sarbin (1967) has a helpful formulation in this context. He says that there are three ways (amongst others) of meeting a crisis: the autistic, the social, and explosive violence (quoted in Scott 1977: 139). One can withdraw and do without, or one copes on a realistic basis of new adjustment, or one goes like a 'bull in a china shop' for the simple solution. Scott uses the case of a non-commissioned officer to illustrate Sarbin's formulation. This man had suffered long conflict with his wife; he went through a period of very heavy drinking (autistic) and tried to get a divorce (social). He then got himself posted to Ireland and volunteered for dangerous duty (the commencement of the violent solution, but against himself). He subsequently deserted his post, hoping to be dismissed from the service (a variety of suicide) and finally shot his wife with a high velocity rifle in their kitchen (the final violent solution). (Scott 1977: 139–40.) This case also illustrates yet again the importance of a careful analysis of *all* the facts.

Another useful illustration of the importance of understanding an apparently irrational and unpredictable outburst would be an assault or murder committed in circumstances that amounted to homosexual panic. The so-called normal individual who violently attacks another because of an alleged homosexual overture, may well need to have their own actions understood more in terms of their own possible repressed homosexuality than solely as the reactions of an outraged victim responding to an unwelcome overture. Certainly, some murders that *appear* to have a sexual setting need to be understood in this way. (For a discussion of the range of motivations in murder and murderous assaults see MacDonald 1968, Abrahamsen 1973, Pasternack (ed.) 1975 (especially the chapter by Woods), Revitch and Schlesinger 1981, and Schreiber 1984).

CLOSE ENCOUNTERS OF A DANGEROUS KIND

In bringing this chapter to a close, it seems important to say something about the management of those potentially violent situations in which the worker (counsellor) may himself or herself be subjected to threats or actual assaults. Such situations will not be all that common but it is as well to be aware that they can occur and be informed about some of the precautions that may help to avert disaster.

(1) We should try to keep the 'scream' out of our voice. This is much easier said than done, particularly if it does appear that we are in imminent danger of violent attack (see Kaplan and Wheeler 1983).

(2) We should try to be on the lookout for warning signals that danger may be looming on the horizon; examples include changes in mood, in conversation, avoidance tactics, failures to keep prearranged appointments, and 'bad news' from other family members, suggesting that all is not well.

(3) We should try wherever possible not to see those with reputations for unprovoked assaults in an empty office late at night. This is all the more important for those offenders/patients whose violence appears to be precipitated by alcohol (see classification described earlier). It is wise to ensure that another member of staff can be on hand, or that one's door is left slightly open. Some offices have alarm facilities available (in the form of a buzzer or bell that sounds in an adjacent room). If a violent outburst is expected, it is as well to warn other staff and have help discreetly on hand if needed. Of course, the fewer people who are obviously in evidence, the better.

(4) We should make an effort to be as calm and confident in our approach as possible. With the advantage of foresight, it is wise to remove breakable and potentially dangerous objects (ashtrays, for example) from easy reach. It is sensible to allow oneself an escape route, where possible; for example, not to place a chair or table between oneself and a possible exit route. By the same token, we should try not to make the offender/patient feel hemmed in or unduly threatened. Changes in posture may help to determine the latter reaction. (See Aiken 1984.)

(5) We should try not to act over-suddenly or issue a strident command. This may serve only to inflame an already volatile individual. The advice of Polonius in *Hamlet* is relevant here: 'Beware of entrance to a quarrel; but being in . . . give every man thy ear, but few thy voice; take each man's censure but reserve thy judgement' (*Hamlet* Act I, scene iii). Eyeball-to-eyeball confrontation is possibly best avoided; looking obliquely at an already hostile and inflamed individual may be more helpful, although some workers suggest that a steady calm gaze may be best. There is no 'golden rule'; one has to operate at the level and in the manner at which one feels most comfortable in a decidedly uncomfortable situation.

(6) It may be necessary to attempt to remove a weapon or dangerous implement from someone who is threatening to use it. This is always a finely poised matter. There may be little time for calm reflection and the situation has to be judged on its merits. Just occasionally, a calming phrase like 'I think you might hurt someone with that, would you like me to keep it for you?' may help, or, 'I find it very difficult to talk to you with that knife (or whatever) in your hand. Perhaps we'd get further if you gave it to me.' Such phrases are *not* offered as magic formulae, merely as *examples* of what might be tried. Above all, one has to try to keep calm, not lose one's temper or show one's level of anxiety to the extent that the offender/patient feels that *you are not in control of the situation*. As already suggested, a calm voice, an averted gaze, and *slow calm movements* augur for a more helpful response than a panic-stricken grab or strident command. To stand in a confronting position in relation to a potentially dangerous offender/patient may make him or her feel even more tense, threatened, and panic-stricken. Such a position taken at the rear of some offenders/patients may be particularly threatening, particularly those with sexual abnormalities.

(7) Sometimes, the likelihood of potentially dangerous situations arising can be defused by responding quickly to a rapidly developing crisis. Dangerous offenders/patients not infrequently feel that things are beginning to 'blow up'. The opportunity to talk through such episodes and to point out

calmly the consequences of further dangerous behaviour may not only be helpful in itself but may also enhance the offender/patient's self-esteem, their feeling of being 'rational' and 'in command'. In addition (as suggested in Chapter 3), opportunities for temporary re-admission to institutional care should not be missed, even if this is under compulsory powers in some cases. As already indicated, some dangerous offenders/patients are well aware that they are not in control of their potentially dangerous urges and very much welcome efforts to assist them in regaining control. If we had more adequate resources for the temporary admission of such persons, either compulsorily or voluntarily, some tragedies that have occurred in the past might have been averted.

(8) Finally, in the event of force being needed, try to ensure that this reduces rather than provokes further violence. Discretion in such cases may indeed be the 'better part of valour' and a hasty departure to protect oneself, summon help, and to avoid the possibility of injury to all parties concerned, may be the best course to adopt. It is well to remember that although the law allows a degree of 'reasonable force' to be used in self-protection, it is for the courts to determine what is reasonable. Naturally, physical confrontations should be avoided if at all possible. Hindsight may sometimes suggest to us ways of reducing such risks and to this extent there is much to be said for being 'wise after the event'.

Conclusions

In this chapter, I have endeavoured to define the meaning of dangerous behaviour, to examine some of its components and to offer some observations on its prediction and assessment. This has involved some discussion of violence and aggression in general, followed by an examination of some of the more important factors that might precipitate dangerous conduct. I have discussed management in some detail and concluded by offering some guidance on the handling of potentially dangerous encounters of a personal kind. In the remaining chapters, some of the disorders and offences referred to in this and preceding chapters will be examined in more detail. In addition, some further suggestions are made concerning management. It is important, once again, to stress that the material presented in this book *should be viewed as a whole*.

References

Abrahamsen, D. (1973) *The Murdering Mind*. London: Harper and Row.

Aiken, G.J. (1984) Assaults on Staff in a Locked Ward: Prediction and Consequences. *Medicine, Science and the Law* **24**: 199–207.

Armond, A.D. (1982) Violence in the Semi-Secure Ward of a Psychiatric Hospital. *Medicine, Science and the Law* **22**: 203–09.

Berger, L.S. and Dietrich, S.G. (1979) The Clinical Prediction of Dangerousness: The Logic of the Process. *International Journal of Offender Therapy and Comparative Criminology* **23**: 35–46.

Blair, D. (1977) The Medico-Legal Aspects of Automatism. *Medicine, Science and the Law* **17**: 167–82.

Bluglass, R. (1980) Indecent Exposure in the West Midlands. In D.J. West (ed.) *Sex Offenders and the Criminal Justice System*. Cambridge: Institute of Criminology.

Bottoms, A.E. (1977) Reflections on the Renaissance of Dangerousness. *Howard Journal of Penology and Crime Prevention* **16**: 70–96.

Brearley, C.P. (1982) *Risk and Social Work*. London: Routledge and Kegan Paul.

Brewer, C. (1974) Alcoholic Brain Damage: Implications For Sentencing Policy (With a Note on the Air Encephalogram). *Medicine, Science and the Law* **14**: 40–3.

—— (1976) Psychiatry and The Control of Criminal Behaviour—Two Cheers for the Medical Model. In J.F.S. King (ed.) *Control Without Custody?* Cambridge: Institute of Criminology.

—— (1978) Bad Brains and Bad Behaviour. *World Medicine* 8 August: 33–6.

Brittain, R.P. (1970) The Sadistic Murderer. *Medicine, Science and the Law* **10**: 198–208.

Brody, S.A. and Tarling, R. (1980) *Taking Offenders Out of Circulation*. HORU Research Study No. 64. London: HMSO.

Casement, P. (1985) *On Learning from the Patient*. London: Tavistock.

Clare, A.W. (1983) *Psychiatric and Social Aspects of Pre-Menstrual Complaint*. Psychological Medicine Monographs, Supplement No. 4. Cambridge: Cambridge University Press.

Conrad, J.P. (1984) Research and Development in Corrections. Terminating the Executioner: How The Empiricist Can Help. *Federal Probation* **XXXXVIII**: 59–62.

Cox, M. (1974) The Psychotherapist's Anxiety: Liability or Asset? (With Special Reference to The Offender-Patient.) *British Journal of Criminology* **14**: 1–17.

—— (1982) The Psychotherapist as Assessor of Dangerousness. In J.R. Hamilton and H. Freeman (eds) *Dangerousness: Psychiatric Assessment and Management*. London: Gaskell.

—— (1983) The Contribution of Dynamic Psychotherapy to Forensic Psychiatry and *Vice Versa*. *International Journal of Law and Psychiatry* **6**: 88–99.

Craft, M. (1984a) Genetic Endowment and the XYY Syndrome. In M. and A. Craft (eds) *Mentally Abnormal Offenders*. London: Baillière Tindall.

—— (1984b) Low Intelligence, Mental Handicap and Criminality. In M. and A. Craft (eds) *Mentally Abnormal Offenders*. London: Baillière Tindall.

Crawford, D. A. (1984) Problems with the Assessment of Dangerousness in England and Wales. *Medicine and the Law* **3**: 141–50.

Dalton, K. (1982) Legal Implications of PMS. *World Medicine* **17**: 93–4.

Danto, B.L. (1980) Managing the Man with the Gun. *International Journal of Offender Therapy and Comparative Criminology* **24**: 118–27.

Dobash, R.E. and Dobash, R.P. (1984) The Nature and Antecedents of Violent Events. *British Journal of Criminology* **24**: 268–88.

D'Orban, P.T. (1983) Medico-Legal Aspects of the Pre-Menstrual Syndrome. *British Journal of Hospital Medicine* **30**: 404–09.

Dowie, J. and Lefrere, P. (eds) (1980) *Risk and Chance: Selected Readings*. Milton Keynes: Open University Press.

Enoch, M.D. and Trethowan, W. (1979) *Uncommon Psychiatric Syndromes* (second edition). Bristol: Wright.

Faulk, M. (1976) A Psychiatric Study of Men Serving Sentences in Winchester Prison. *Medicine, Science and the Law* **16**: 244–57.

Feingold, B. (1979) Dietary Management of Juvenile Delinquency. *International Journal of Offender Therapy and Comparative Criminology* **23**: 73–84.

Fenton, G.W. (1984) Epilepsy, Mental Abnormality and Criminal Behaviour. In M. and A. Craft (eds) *Mentally Abnormal Offenders*. London: Baillière Tindall.

Floud, J. and Young, W. (1981) *Dangerousness and Criminal Justice*. London: Heinemann.

Foucault, M. (1978) About the Concept of the 'Dangerous Individual' in Nineteenth Century Legal Psychiatry. *International Journal of Law and Psychiatry* **1**: 1–18.

Fromm, E. (1977) *The Anatomy of Human Destructiveness*. Harmondsworth: Penguin.

Gathercole, C.E., Craft, M.J., McDougall, J., Barnes, H.M., and Peck,

D.F. (1968) A Review of 100 Discharges From a Special Hospital. *British Journal of Criminology* **8**: 419–24.

Gibbens, T.C.N. and Hall Williams, J.E. (1977) Medico-Legal Aspects of Amnesia. In C.W.M. Whitty and O.L. Zangwill (eds) *Amnesia: Clinical, Psychological and Medico-Legal Aspects.* London: Butterworths.

Gosnold, J.K. (1978) The Violent Patient in The Accident and Emergency Department. *Journal of The Royal Society of Health* **98**: 189–91, 198.

Greenland, C. (1978a) Comments in D. Weisstub (ed.) *Law and Psychiatry* (pp. 69–73). Oxford: Pergamon.

—— (1978b) The Prediction and Management of Dangerous Behaviour: Social Policy Issues. *International Journal of Law and Psychiatry* **I**: 205–22.

—— (1980) Psychiatry and The Prediction of Dangerousness. *Journal of Psychiatric Treatment and Evaluation* **2**: 97–103.

Gunn, J. (1977) *Epileptics in Prison.* London: Academic.

Gunn, J., Robertson, G., Dell, S., and Way, C. (1978) *Psychiatric Aspects of Imprisonment.* London: Academic.

Harding, T. and Adserballe, H. (1983) Assessments of Dangerousness: Observations in Six Countries. A Summary of Results from a WHO Co-ordinated Study. *International Journal of Law and Psychiatry* **6**: 391–98.

Hawkins, K. (1983) Assessing Evil: Decision Behaviour and Parole Board Justice. *British Journal of Criminology* **23**: 101–27.

Hays, P. (1961) Hysterical Illness and The Podola Trial. *Medico-Legal Journal* **29**: 27–32.

Hepworth, D. (1982) The Influence of the Concept of 'Danger' on the Assessment of 'Danger to Self and to Others'. *Medicine, Science and the Law* **22**: 245–54.

Holden, A. (1974) *The St Albans Poisoner: The Life and Crimes of Graham Young.* London: Hodder and Stoughton.

Home Office and DHSS (1973) *Report on the Review of Procedures for the Discharge and Supervision of Psychiatric Patients Subject to Special Restrictions (Aarvold Report).* Cmnd. 5191. London: HMSO.

—— (1975) *Report of the Committee on Mentally Abnormal Offenders (Butler Committee).* Cmnd. 6244. London: HMSO.

Howells, K. (1982) Mental Disorder and Violent Behaviour. In M.P. Feldman (ed.) *Developments in The Study of Criminal Behaviour, Volume II.* Chichester: Wiley.

Kaplan, S.G. and Wheeler, G.G. (1983) Survival Skills for Working with Potentially Violent Clients. *Social Casework* **June**: 339–46.

Klein, M. (1963) *Our Adult World and Other Essays.* London: Heinemann.

Kloek, J. (1969) Schizophrenia and Delinquency: The Inadequacy of our Conceptual Framework. In A.V.S. de Rueck and R. Porter (eds) *The Mentally Abnormal Offender*. London: J. and A. Churchill. (For CIBA Foundation.)

Kozol, H.L., Boucher, R.J., and Garofalo, R.F. (1972) The Diagnosis and Treatment of Dangerousness. *Crime and Delinquency* **18**: 371–92.

Lasky, R. (1982) *Evaluation of Criminal Responsibility in Multiple Personality and the Related Dissociative Disorders*. Especially Chapter 8. Illinois: Charles C Thomas.

Lawson, W.K. (1984) Depression and Crime: A Discursive Approach. In M. and A. Craft (eds) *Mentally Abnormal Offenders*. London: Baillière Tindall.

Lidberg, L. (1971) Frequency of Concussion and Type of Criminality. *Acta Psychiatrica Scandinavica* **47**: 452–61.

Lion, J.R. (1972) *Evaluation and Management of The Violent Patient*. Illinois: Charles C Thomas.

Lorenz, K. (1966) *On Aggression*. London: Methuen.

McCulloch, J.W. and Prins, H. (1978) *Signs of Stress: The Social Problems of Psychiatric Illness*. London: Woburn.

MacCulloch, M., Snowden, P.R., Wood, P.J.W., and Mills, H.E. (1983) Sadistic Phantasy, Sadistic Behaviour and Offending. *British Journal of Psychiatry* **143**: 20–9.

MacDonald, J.M. (1968) *Homicidal Threats*. Illinois: Charles C Thomas.

Maguire, M., Pinter, F., and Collis, C. (1984) Dangerousness and the Tariff. *British Journal of Criminology* **24**: 250–68.

Mednick, S.A. and Volavka, J. (1980) Biology and Crime. In N. Morris and M. Tonry (eds) *Crime and Justice—An Annual Review of Research, Volume II*. Chicago: Chicago University Press.

Megargee, E. (1976) The Prediction of Dangerous Behaviour. *Criminal Justice and Behaviour* **3**: 3–22.

Monahan, J. (1981) *Predicting Violent Behaviour: An Assessment of Clinical Techniques*. London: Sage Foundation.

Monahan, J. and Steadman, H.J. (1983) Crime and Mental Disorder: An Epidemiological Approach. In N. Morris and M. Tonry (eds) *Crime and Justice—An Annual Review of Research, Volume IV*. Chicago: Chicago University Press.

Montanden, C. and Harding, T. (1984) The Reliability of Dangerousness Assessments: A Decision-Making Exercise. *British Journal of Psychiatry* **144**: 145–49.

Mullen, P.E. and Maack, L.H. (1985) Jealousy, Pathological Jealousy and Aggression. In D.P. Farrington and J. Gunn (eds) *Aggression and Dangerousness*. Chichester: Wiley.

Neustatter, W.L. (1953) *Psychological Disorder and Crime.* London: Christopher Johnson.

O'Connell, B.A. (1960) Amnesia and Homicide: A Study of Fifty Murderers. *British Journal of Delinquency* **X**: 262–76.

Pasternack, S.A. (ed.) (1975) *Violence and Victims.* Especially chapters by Kozol, Rubin, and Woods. New York: Spectrum.

Payne, C., McCabe, S., and Walker, N. (1974) Predicting Offender-Patients' Reconvictions. *British Journal of Psychiatry* **125**: 60–4.

Petrunik, M. (1982) The Politics of Dangerousness. *International Journal of Law and Psychiatry* **5**: 225–53.

Pfohl, S.J. (1979) From Whom Will We Be Protected? Comparative Approaches To The Assessment of Dangerousness. *International Journal of Law and Psychiatry* **2**: 55–78.

Power, D.J. (1977) Memory, Identification and Crime. *Medicine, Science and the Law* **17**: 132–39.

Prins, H. (1975) A Danger to Themselves and to Others: Social Workers and Potentially Dangerous Clients. *British Journal of Social Work* **5**: 297–309.

—— (1980a) A Sense of Danger. *Social Work Today* **11**: 14–16.

—— (1980b) *Offenders, Deviants, or Patients? An Introduction to the Study of Socio-Forensic Problems.* London: Tavistock.

—— (1980c) Mad or Bad—Thoughts on the Equivocal Relationship between Mental Disorder and Criminality. *International Journal of Law and Psychiatry* **3**: 421–33.

—— (1981) Dangerous People or Dangerous Situations? Some Implications for Assessment and Management. *Medicine, Science and the Law* **21**: 125–33.

—— (1983a) Dangerous Behaviour: Some Implications for Mental Health Professionals. In P. Bean (ed.) *Mental Illness: Changes and Trends.* Chichester: Wiley.

—— (1983b) Counselling the Mentally Abnormal (Dangerous) Offender. *Federal Probation* **XXXXVII**: 42–51.

—— (1983c) Literature Review: Dangerous Offenders. *British Journal of Social Work* **13**: 443–48.

—— (1983d) Safe to Release. *Prison Service Journal* **50**: 8–14.

—— (1984) Vampirism—Legendary or Clinical Phenomenon? *Medicine, Science and the Law* **24**: 283–93.

Quinsey, V.L. (1979) Assessments of the Dangerousness of Mental Patients Held in Maximum Security. *International Journal of Law and Psychiatry* **2**: 389–406.

Quinsey, V.L., Pruesse, M., and Fernley, R. (1975) Oak-Ridge Patients: Pre-Release Characteristics and Post-Release Adjustment. *Journal of Psychiatry and Law* **Spring**: 63–77.

Rennie, Y. (1978) *The Search for Criminal Man.* Toronto: Lexington.

Revitch, E. and Schlesinger, L.B. (1981) *Psychopathology of Homicide*. Illinois: Charles C Thomas.

Sarbin, T.R. (1967) The Dangerous Individual: An Outcome of Social Identity Transformations. *British Journal of Criminology* **7**: 285–95.

Schipkowensky, N. (1969) Cyclophrenia and Murder. In A.V.S. de Rueck and R. Porter (eds) *The Mentally Abnormal Offender*. London: J. and A. Churchill. (For CIBA Foundation.)

Schreiber, F. R. (1984) *The Shoemaker: The Anatomy of a Psychotic*. Harmondsworth: Penguin.

Scott, P.D. (1977) Assessing Dangerousness in Criminals. *British Journal of Psychiatry* **131**: 127–42.

Segal, H. (1964) *Introduction to the Work of Melanie Klein*. London: Heinemann.

Segal, J. (1985) *Phantasy in Everyday Life*. Harmondsworth: Penguin.

Shah, S.A. (1981) Legal and Mental Health System Interactions: Major Developments and Research Needs. *International Journal of Law and Psychiatry* **4**: 219–70.

Sheppard, C. (1971) The Violent Offender: Let's Examine The Taboo. *Federal Probation* **4**: 12–19.

Showalter, C.R., Bonnie, R.J., and Roddy, V. (1980) The Spousal-Homicide Syndrome. *International Journal of Law and Psychiatry* **3**: 117–41.

Soothill, K.L., Way, C.K., and Gibbens, T.C.N. (1980) Subsequent Dangerousness Among Compulsory Hospital Patients. *British Journal of Criminology* **20**: 289–95.

Spry, W. (1984) Schizophrenia and Crime. In M. and A. Craft (eds) *Mentally Abnormal Offenders*. London: Baillière Tindall.

Steadman, H.J. (1976) Predicting Dangerousness. In D.J. Madden and J.R. Lion (eds) *Rage, Hate, Assault And Other Forms of Violence*. New York: Spectrum.

—— (1982) A Situational Approach to Violence. *International Journal of Law and Psychiatry* **5**: 171–86.

—— (1983) Predicting Dangerousness Among the Mentally Ill: Art, Magic and Science. *International Journal of Law and Psychiatry* **6**: 381–90.

Steadman, H.J. and Cocozza, J.J. (1974) *Careers of the Criminally Insane*. Toronto: Lexington.

Storr, A. (1975) *Human Aggression*. Harmondsworth: Penguin.

Suedfeld, P. (1980) Environmental Effects on Violent Behaviour in Prisons. *International Journal of Offender Therapy and Comparative Criminology* **24**: 107–16.

Taylor, D. (1981) *Alcohol*. London: Office of Health Economics.

Taylor, P. (1982) Schizophrenia and Crime. In J. Gunn and D.F.

Farrington (eds) *Abnormal Offenders, Delinquency and the Criminal Justice System*. Chichester: Wiley.

Taylor, P.J. and Kopelman, M.D. (1984) Amnesia for Criminal Offences. *Psychological Medicine* **14**: 581–88.

Tennent, T.G. (1975) The Dangerous Offender. In B. Barraclough and T. Silverstone (eds) *Contemporary Psychiatry*. Ashford: Headley Brothers.

Theilgaard, A. (1983) Aggression and the XYY Personality. *International Journal of Law and Psychiatry* **6**: 413–21.

Thornberry, T.P. and Jacoby, J.E. (1979) *The Criminally Insane*. Chicago: Chicago University Press.

Tidmarsh, D. (1982) Implications from Research Studies. In J.R. Hamilton and H. Freeman (eds) *Dangerousness: Psychiatric Assessment and Management*. London: Gaskell.

Tong, J.E. and Mackay, G.W. (1959) A Statistical Follow-Up of Mental Defectives of Dangerous and Violent Propensities. *British Journal of Delinquency* **IX**: 276–84.

Topp, D.O. (1973) Fire as a Symbol and as a Weapon of Death. *Medicine, Science and the Law* **13**: 79–86.

Walker, N. (1978) Dangerous People. *International Journal of Law and Psychiatry* **11**: 37–50.

Webb, D. (1976) Wise After the Event: Some Comments on 'A Danger to themselves and to Others'. *British Journal of Social Work* **6**: 91–6.

West, D.J. (1965) *Murder Followed by Suicide*. London: Heinemann.

Williams, A.H. (1982) Adolescents, Violence and Crime. *Journal of Adolescence* **5**: 125–34.

Woddis, G.M. (1957) Depression and Crime. *British Journal of Delinquency* **VIII**: 85–94.

—— (1964) Clinical Psychiatry and Crime. *British Journal of Criminology* **4**: 443–60.

FURTHER READING

On violence (general):

Gunn, J. (1973) *Violence in Human Society*. Newton Abbot: David and Charles.

Johnson, R.N. (1972) *Aggression in Man and Animals*. Philadelphia: W.B. Saunders.

Lefkowitz, M.M., Eron, L.D., Walder, L.O., and Huesman, L.R. (1977) *Growing Up To Be Violent: A Longitudinal Study Of The Development Of Aggression*. Oxford: Pergamon.

Lion, J.R. and Reid, W.H. (1983) *Assaults Within Psychiatric Facilities*. Especially Part III. New York: Grune and Stratton.

Macdonald, J.M. (1975) *Armed Robbery: Offenders and their Victims*. Illinois: Charles C Thomas.

Toch, H. (1972) *Violent Men*. Harmondsworth: Penguin.

On family violence:

(See also Chapter 6.)

Barkowski, M., Murch, M., and Walker, V. (1983) *Martial Violence: The Community Response*. London: Tavistock.

Carver, V. (1978) *Child Abuse: A Study Text*. Milton Keynes: Open University Press.

Dobash, R.E. and Dobash, R.P. (1980) *Violence Against Wives: A Case Against the Patriarchy*. London: Open.

Gil, D.G. (1979) *Child Abuse and Violence*. New York: AMS.

Helfer, R.E. and Kemp, C.H. (eds) (1974) *The Battered Child*. Chicago: Chicago University Press.

Jones, D.M. (ed.) (1982) *Understanding Child Abuse*. Sevenoaks: Teach Yourself.

Kempe, S. and Kempe, C.H. (1980) *Child Abuse*. London: Fontana/Open.

Lee, C.M. (1978) *Child Abuse: A Reader and Source Book*. Milton Keynes: Open University Press.

Martin, J.P. (ed.) (1978) *Violence and the Family*. Chichester: Wiley.

Pizzey, E. and Shapiro, J. (1982) *Prone to Violence*. Feltham: Hamlyn.

Renvoize, J. (1978) *Web of Violence: A Study of Family Violence*. London: Routledge and Kegan Paul.

Smith, S.M. (1975) *The Battered Child Syndrome*. London: Butterworths.

Wilson, E. (1983) *What is to be Done about Violence against Women?* Harmondsworth: Penguin.

On homicide:

Coid, J. (1983) The Epidemiology of Abnormal Homicide and Murder Followed by Suicide. *Psychological Medicine* **13**: 855–60.

Cuthbert, T.M. (1970) A Portfolio of Murders. *British Journal of Psychiatry* **116**: 1–10.

Driver, M.V., West, L.R., and Faulk, M. (1974) Clinical and EEG Studies of Prisoners Charged with Murder. *British Journal of Psychiatry* **125**: 583–87.

Gillies, H. (1976) Homicide in the West of Scotland. *British Journal of Psychiatry* **128**: 105–27.

Macdonald, J.M. (1961) *The Murderer and his Victim*. Illinois: Charles C Thomas.

Reinhardt, M. (1962) *The Psychology of Strange Killers*. Illinois: Charles C Thomas.

Williams, A.H. (1965) The Treatment of Abnormal Murderers. *Howard Journal* **XI**: 286–96.

On hostage-taking, sieges, terrorist activity, etc.:

Corrado, R.R. (1981) A Critique of the Mental Disorder Perspective of Political Terrorism. *International Journal of Law and Psychiatry* **4**: 293–309.

Danto, B. (1979) Firearms and Violence. *International Journal of Offender Therapy and Comparative Criminology* **23**: 135–46.

—— (1980) The Boomerang Bullet: Suicide Among Snipers and Assassins. *International Journal of Offender Therapy and Comparative Criminology* **24**: 41–57.

Davies, W. (1982) Violence in Prisons. In M.P. Feldman (ed.) *Developments in the Study of Criminal Behaviour, Volume II*. Chichester: Wiley.

Scott, P.D. (1978) The Psychiatry of Kidnapping and Hostage Taking. In R.N. Gaind and B.L. Hudson (eds) *Current Themes in Psychiatry, Volume I*. London: Macmillan.

Wright, F., Bahn, C., and Rieber, R.W. (eds) (1980) *Forensic Psychology and Psychiatry, Part III*. Notably papers by Schlossberg, Knutson, Symonds, and Strentz. New York: New York Academy of Sciences.

On biological and organic factors:

Jeffery, C.R. (ed.) (1979) *Biology and Crime*. London: Sage.

Mark, V.H. and Ervin, F.R. (1970) *Violence and the Brain*. London: Harper and Row.

Mednick, S.A. and Christiansen, K.O. (1977) *Biosocial Bases of Criminal Behaviour*. New York: Gardner.

Monroe, R.R. (1978) *Brain Dysfunction in Aggressive Criminals*. Lexington: D.C. Heath.

Noback, C.R. and Demarest, R.J. (1977) *The Nervous System: Introduction and Review* (second edition). New York: McGraw-Hill.

Penfield, W. (1978) *The Mystery of the Mind: A Critical Study of Consciousness and the Human Brain*. Princeton: Princeton University Press.

Prentky, R. (1985) The Neurochemistry and Neuroendocrinology of Sexual Aggression. In D.P. Farrington and J. Gunn (eds) *Aggression and Dangerousness*. Chichester: Wiley.

Scott, D.F. (1978) *About Epilepsy* (third edition). London: Duckworth.

Weller, M.P.I. (1985) Head Injury—Organic and Psychogenic Issues in Compensation Claims. (A useful overview of the forensic aspects of injury and damage to the brain.) *Medicine, Science and the Law* **25**: 11–25.

On general management:

The books marked with an asterisk provide excellent accounts of therapy with dangerous offenders/patients.

Bridges, P.K. (1971) *Psychiatric Emergencies: Diagnosis and Management.* Illinois: Charles C Thomas.

British Journal of Criminology (1982) *Special Issues on Dangerousness.* **July**. (Vol. 23(3).)

Conrad, J.P. and Dinitz, S. (1977) *In Fear of Each Other.* Lexington: D.C. Heath.

*Cox, M. (1978) *Structuring the Therapeutic Process: Compromise with Chaos.* Oxford: Pergamon.

*—— (1978) *Coding the Therapeutic Process: Emblems of Encounter. A Manual for Counsellors and Therapists.* Oxford: Pergamon.

Hinton, J.W. (ed.) (1983) *Dangerousness: Problems of Assessment and Prediction.* London: Allen and Unwin.

Home Office (1982) *Workshop on the Supervision of Offenders at Risk of Committing Dangerous Offences.* London: Home Office.

Moore, M.H., Estrich, S.R., McGillis, D. and Spelman, W. (1984) *Dangerous Offenders: The Elusive Target of Justice.* London: Harvard University Press.

Norris, M. (1984) *Integration of Special Hospital Patients into the Community.* Research report on the community resettlement of ex-Broadmoor patients. Aldershot: Gower.

Rappeport, J.R. (ed.) (1967) *The Clinical Evaluation of the Dangerousness of the Mentally Ill.* Illinois: Charles C Thomas.

Stuart, R.B. (ed.) (1981) *Violent Behaviour: Social Learning Approaches to Prediction, Management and Treatment.* New York: Brunner Mazel.

Note

1 A brief word of explanation concerning normal chromosome disposition may be helpful. Normal human cells contain 46 chromosomes; these are arranged in 23 pairs of different shapes and sizes. They may be seen and classified under a high power microscope, once they have been suitably prepared for examination. Different chromosomes contain different genes. One pair of chromosomes called X and Y determine sex. In the female, these consist of a matched pair XX and in the male, a pair XY. This normal patterning may sometimes become altered in a variety of ways, resulting in an extra X or extra Y chromosome or other variants.

CHAPTER FIVE

Psychopathic personality disorder

'Thou cam'st on earth to make the earth my hell.
A grievous burden was thy birth to me;
Tetchy and wayward was thy infancy;
Thy school-days frightful, desp'rate, wild, and furious;
Thy prime of manhood daring, bold, and venturous;
Thy age confirm'd, proud, subtle, sly, and bloody,
More mild but yet more harmful, kind in hatred:
What comfortable hour canst thou name
That ever grac'd me in thy company?'
                SHAKESPEARE
                Duchess of York in *Richard III* Act IV, scene iv

In the above quotation, King Richard's mother, the aged
Duchess of York, attributes to him many of the attitudes and
experiences we have come to associate with that most elusive
concept—*psychopathic personality disorder*. Elusive though the concept may be (see Lewis 1974), Shakespeare has depicted, with
his usual penetrating insight into the human condition, some
of the essential clinical features. Thus, the ageing Duchess
describes an apparently eventful birth, long-standing anti-
sociality becoming more marked in adulthood and accompanied by a veneer of charm and sophistication that serves to
mask the underlying themes of chaos and frequent violence. In
Chapters 2 and 3, I made reference to psychopathic personality
disorder. In this chapter, I shall trace briefly the historical
development of the concept against the background of some
more general observations on personality. I shall then describe
possible causal factors, some of the key characteristics of
psychopathic disorder and management problems, paying

special attention to those adjudged to be manifesting aggressive psychopathy.

Personality

Within the constraints of this chapter, it would be impossible to write at length about personality in general terms; however, a few words are necessary in order to provide a context for what follows. Not only are there difficulties in defining 'personality' with any degree of accuracy but the issue is further confused by the word's use in common parlance to cover a variety of attributes. Trethowan and Sims suggest that 'personality may be either considered subjectively, i.e. in terms of what the . . . (person) . . . believes and describes about himself as an individual, or objectively in terms of what an observer notices about his more consistent patterns of behaviour' (Trethowan and Sims 1983: 225). Personality will include such things as mood state, attitudes, and opinions and all these must be measured against how people comport themselves in their social environments. If we describe a person as having a 'normal' personality, we use the word in a statistical sense 'indicating that various personality traits are present to a broadly normal extent, neither to gross excess nor extreme deficiency. Abnormal personality is, therefore, a variation upon an accepted, yet broadly conceived, range of personality' (Trethowan and Sims 1983: 225).

There are a very large number of personality variations that may constitute 'disorders' if they stray far enough from this spectrum of normality. Some examples of personality variations are the paranoid, schizoid, explosive, hysterical, obsessive, depressive, and affectionless. The great German psychiatrist Schneider (1958) regarded personality disorder not as an illness in the conventional medical sense but as a variation of personality, which could only be defined in relation to the average man or woman—the 'man (or woman) on the Clapham omnibus' so beloved of lawyers. The modern concept of personality disorder seems to represent two interlocking notions. The first suggests that the disorder is present when *any* abnormality of personality causes problems *either* to the person himself or herself *or* to others. The second, and the one with which we are more specifically concerned in this chapter, carries a more pejorative connotation; it implies unacceptable, anti-social behaviour coupled with a notion of dislike for the person showing such behaviour and a rejection of them. As we shall see, the word 'psychopath' is sometimes used for this purpose. Such usage has led to many difficulties for lawyers, sentencers, psychiatrists, and other caring professionals.

One way of regarding psychopathic disorder is to view it as lying at the far end of a spectrum of behaviour disorders (see *Figure 5(2)*). The *danger in doing so* will be that we may make precipitate moral judgments about such behaviour, without giving enough consideration to its possible aetiology. In summary, we may say that the personality disorders (of which psychopathy is but one) consist of a group of disorders in which the basic personality appears to be noticeably abnormal, either in the balance of its components and their quality and expression, or in its total aspect. The condition is well described in the *Glossary of Mental Disorders*:

> 'This category refers to a group of more or less well defined anomalies or deviations of personality which are not the result of psychosis or any other illness. The differentiation of these personalities is to some extent arbitrary and the reference to a given group will depend initially on the relative predominance of one or other group of character traits.'
>
> (General Register Office 1968: 14)

Defining psychopathic personality disorder

'a rose
By any other name. . . .'
(*Romeo and Juliet* Act II, scene ii)

The dilemma involved in trying to describe the psychopath was aptly indicated many years ago by Curran and Mallinson with the statement 'I can't define an elephant, but I know one when I see one' (East 1949: 130). The history of the development of the concept of psychopathic personality disorder has been very well documented; see, for example, Maughs 1941, Gurvitz 1951, Walker and McCabe 1973, Pichot 1978, and McCord 1982. The eminent French psychiatrist Pinel is usually credited with providing the first description of what we would now regard as psychopathic personality disorder; the term he used was '*manie sans délire*'. However, Pinel probably included in his descriptions cases that we should not regard today as psychopathic. In the 1830s, the English psychiatrist and anthropologist Prichard formulated the concept of *moral insanity*. He described it as a 'madness, consisting of a morbid perversion of the natural feelings, affections, inclinations, temper, habits, moral disposi- tions and natural impulses, without any remarkable disorder or defect of the interest or knowing and reasoning faculties' (Prichard 1835). We should note that 'moral' in the sense in which Prichard used it meant emotional and psychological and not the opposite of immoral, as in today's parlance. This view of 'moral insanity' rested upon the, then, fairly widely held but controversial belief that there could be a separate moral sense, which could be deranged.

To understand such beliefs fully, we need to see them against the very rudimentary state of psychological and psychiatric knowledge at that time. (See also Chapter 2.) In the 1880s, Koch formulated the concept of *constitutional psychopathy*, im- plying that there was a considerable constitutional (innate) predisposition towards the development of the disorder. This approach was, no doubt, influenced by the contemporary in- terest in hereditary factors in the causation of delinquency and deviation. In 1917, Mercier laid claim to being the originator of the terms *moral defective* and *moral imbecile*—these eventually found their way into the Mental Deficiency Act of 1913, thus enshrining a pejorative and condemnatory element in an English statute. This served to make it even more difficult to regard such individuals as deserving of understanding and further study.

In the 1930s, findings from the fields of neurology and physiology were of importance. They helped to further the understanding of such disorders as encephalitis, epilepsy, chorea and their relevance to the kind of seriously aggressive behaviour often associated with psychopathic states. (See also Chapter 4.) For some time, psychoanalysts had taken an interest in this field; Alexander described the 'neurotic character' as a form of personality deviation, attempting to fit it into a Freudian perspective (Gurvitz 1951). Of even greater significance was the work of Partridge; he suggested that *socio-pathy* was a more appropriate description of the condition, since it emphasized the importance of the psychopath's lack of ability in social relations and the harm he caused others (Gurvitz 1951). The term *sociopath* is the preferred term in the United States. Henderson (1939) considered that psychopathy constituted a true illness and was not to be seen as mere wilfulness or evil, which could be beaten out of a person. He suggested that there were three main categories of psychopath: the predominantly aggressive, the predominantly inadequate, and the predominantly creative. The inclusion of the latter group has always attracted controversy, since the notion of creativity appears to be diametrically opposed to the failure and chaos that are the hallmarks of the lives of most psychopaths. The notion of the psychopath as suffering from a true illness is one that has characterized the work of Cleckley (1976) and we shall return to his views later. Further work on the intra-psychic life of the psychopath was carried out by the psychoanalysts, Lindner (1944) and Karpman (1948).

In more recent years, the works of Craft (1968, 1984), Whiteley (1968), and Jones (1963) in this country—particularly in the area of institutional treatment—have been of considerable significance. When considering the development of the concept of psychopathy, it is as well to remember, as Treves-Brown (1977) has pointed out, that it is a concept much influenced by prevailing cultural notions of responsibility and what is regarded as 'decent' behaviour. During the last decade, increasing debate has taken place as to the desirability of retaining the term for legal and penal purposes. The Butler Committee (Home Office and DHSS 1975) considered that the term 'psychopath' might be deleted from the definition of mental disorder in the Mental Health Act of 1959 with the substitution of the much broader term 'personality disorder'. In addition, the Committee also considered that dangerous anti-social psychopaths who had shown no previous mental, organic, or identifiable psychological or physical defect should be dealt with through the prison rather than the hospital system. Such a recommendation presupposes that the prison system would be able to provide adequate training and rehabilitation; a presupposition unlikely to be realized for some time in the present parlous state of our prison system. Further dissatis-faction with the use of the term was expressed in the Depart-ment of Health and Social Security report, *A Review of the Mental Health Act, 1959* (DHSS *et al.* 1976). The report suggested the substitution of the term 'severe personality disorder'. They defined this as such a persistent abnormality of mind as would seriously affect an individual's life and adjustment to society and which was so severe as to render them a serious risk to themselves or to others. The Mental Health Act of 1959 defined psychopathic disorder as a 'persistent disorder or disability of mind (whether or not including subnormality of intelligence) which results in abnormally aggressive or seriously irrespon-sible conduct on the part of the patient and requires or is susceptible to medical treatment' (Section 4(2)). It should be noted that the 1959 Act retained the association with defect of intelligence (see my remarks on the Mental Deficiency Act of 1913, above) and the definition included as a criterion suscepti-bility to medical treatment. (Medical treatment in this context included other forms of treatment under medical supervision.)

The new Mental Health Act of 1983 retains the classification of psychopathic disorder in the following form: 'psychopathic disorder means a persistent disorder or disability of mind (whether or not including significant impairment of intelli-gence) which results in abnormally aggressive or seriously irresponsible conduct on the part of the person concerned' (Section 1(4)). Because strong feelings had been expressed that the compulsory detention of those suffering from psychopathic disorder should be dependent upon a reasonable prospect of response to treatment, the diagnostic criteria in the definition have been separated from the 'susceptibility to treatment' clauses. These are contained in sections 3, 37, and 47 of the Act. These make compulsory admission for treatment available only *if it can be stated that medical treatment is likely to alleviate or prevent a deterioration in the individual's condition.* This is an important proviso because it recognizes the difficulties involved in treating psychopaths but it also keeps the door open for therapeutic optimism. It also serves to emphasize the fact that the term 'psychopathic disorder' should be used sparingly and not as a 'dustbin' label for those clients or patients who are merely difficult, unco-operative, or unlikeable (see discussion on pages

Figure 5(1)   Development of terminology

manie sans délire → moral insanity → moral imbecility (defectiveness) →
(constitutional) psychopathic inferiority → neurotic character → psychopathy
and sociopathy → severe (anti-social) personality disorder (reaction)

157–60. Nearly forty years ago, an eminent psychiatrist, Eliot Slater, suggested that 'if we were to drop the term altogether, we should be obliged to invent an equivalent or to overlook a whole series of clinically very important phenomena' (Slater 1948: 277). In my view, this statement is as true today as it was then. The historical development of the term 'psychopathic disorder' is summarized in *Figure 5(1)*.

It is important to stress that these descriptive terms and the theorizing that has accompanied them are derived, in the main, from studies of incarcerated and criminal psychopaths. As Widom and Newman (1985) have pointed out, we also need detailed studies of the prevalence of psychopathic disorder in non-institutionalized populations.

Possible causal factors

I have inserted the word *possible* before 'causal factors' for good reason. The aetiology of psychopathic disorder is obscure and based more upon emotively held beliefs than upon proven aetiological facts. The literature is vast and readers who wish to pursue the subject in more depth are advised to consult the references cited in this chapter. I shall concentrate on one or two aspects that seem to merit further consideration and then formulate a simple classification, which attempts to locate the features of the condition upon a spectrum of personality (behaviour) disorder (see *Figures 5(2)* and *5(3)*).

As is the case with many other disorders and deviations, the 'nature' versus 'nurture' debate has raged for many years in relation to psychopathy. Evidence has been adduced from twin, neurological, chromosomal, and other studies to suggest the importance of innate factors. Equally convincing evidence has been provided by the environmentalists, who suggest that family background and social milieu are all important, particularly in relation to the psychopath's singular incapacity for 'rôle taking' (Gough 1956). This theory of rôle taking deficiency finds some support from the work of Blackburn, a clinical psychologist who has undertaken seminal work in attempting to refine the concept of psychopathy. Blackburn suggests that seriously psychopathically disordered individuals (such as those seen in Special Hospitals and prisons) tend to view others as being malevolently disposed towards them (Blackburn 1984). Other psychologists, such as Hare and Schalling (Hare 1970, Hare and Schalling 1978), have made substantial contributions to the study of psychopathic disorder. Hare has undertaken the major task in summarizing and bringing together research findings from the fields of abnormal psychology, neuro- and psychophysiology, learning theory, and theories of socialization. Much of the evidence obtained under experimental (laboratory) conditions seems to be in accord with the day-to-day experience of clinicians and others in this field. The following appraisal attempts to summarize some of the most important findings reported by Hare and his colleagues and due acknowledgement is made to these authors in quoting from their pioneering work.

STUDIES OF THE CEREBRAL CORTEX

In Chapter 4, I referred to the importance of certain 'organic' and physical factors in the aetiology of violent or dangerous behaviour. These factors are very relevant in attempting to understand the behaviour of the psychopath, particularly the seriously aggressive psychopath. Studies using the EEG (electroencephalogram) have tended to show that the slow wave activity found in the brain rhythms of some aggressive psychopaths bears some degree of resemblance to the EEG tracings found in children. These findings (which I have oversimplified here) have led to a hypothesis of *cortical immaturity*. The theory may also explain why the behaviour of some aggressive psychopaths seems to become less violent with advancing years. Two further conclusions derived from work in this field are also relevant here. First, psychopathy may be associated with a defect or malfunction of certain brain mechanisms concerned with emotional activity and the regulation of behaviour. Second, it has been suggested that psychopathy may be related to a lowered state of cortical excitability and to the attenuation of sensory input, particularly input that would, in ordinary circumstances, have disturbing consequences. This may partially explain the apparent callous and cold indifference to the pain and suffering of others that is demonstrated by some seriously psychopathically disordered individuals. Woodman (1980), reporting on work with a group of Broadmoor patients, lends further support to the view that organic factors may be more important than has been appreciated in the past. His research also lends support to the view that some seriously psychopathically disordered individuals lack conditioned anticipatory fear. (See also Craft 1984: 358.)

THE IMPORTANCE OF THE AUTONOMIC NERVOUS SYSTEM

Clinical and other experience has always tended to show the psychopath's general apparent lack of anxiety, guilt, and emotional tension. In recent years, experiments carried out under laboratory conditions have tended to give confirmation to these clinical impressions. It has been shown, for example, that during periods of relative quiescence, psychopathic subjects tend to be *hypoactive* on several indices of autonomic activity, including resting level of skin conductance and cardiac activity. This activity can be measured comparatively easily by galvanometric and similar devices. It is worth noting, however, that some of these findings have been criticized. Feldman (1977) suggests that too many conclusions have been based solely upon laboratory tests and that too few comparative studies have been undertaken of 'control' populations derived from non-penal or non-specialist hospital sources. Also, it should be pointed out that lack of anxiety, guilt, and emotional tension are not characteristics peculiar to the psychopathically disordered. Rather is it the case that they seem to show this lack in *a more extreme form* than the general population.

PSYCHOPATHIC DISORDER AND THE CONCEPT OF AROUSAL

There is some laboratory evidence to suggest that psychopathy is related to cortical *under-arousal*. Because of this, the psychopath (particularly the seriously aggressive) may seek stimulation with arousing or exciting qualities. It is certainly true that even so-called 'normal' offenders, when asked about their motivation for offences, often report that they derived a 'high' from the act committed or that they did it 'for kicks'. McCord states that 'most psychopaths do not seek security as a goal in itself; rather they crave constant change, whirlwind variety, and new stimuli' (1982: 28). McCord suggests that Ian Brady and Myra Hindley illustrate the 'psychopath's craving for excitement'. He says that they 'explained their actions as simply ways to attain new levels of excitement, a new "consciousness" and a temporary escape from boredom' (1982: 28).

In an entirely different field, that of wife abuse, Pizzey and Shapiro (1982) have recently suggested that certain women may obtain a 'high' from the pain they suffer as a result of being abused. They point out, very tentatively, that some women may become 'addicted' to this kind of arousal and that the addiction is likely to be associated with hormonal functions. Although such a theory is largely speculative, it would seem to have elements in common with the phenomena described above and to be worthy of serious further consideration. The craving for excitement commented upon by McCord and others may render the psychopath unaware of or inattentive to many of the more subtle cues required for the maintenance of socially acceptable behaviour and for adequate socialization.

Mawson and Mawson (1977) suggest that psychopaths show a greater degree of variability in autonomic functioning than non-psychopaths. They theorize that a biochemical disturbance may manifest itself in abnormal oscillations in neuro-transmitter functioning. They also make the further very interesting suggestion that future research might elucidate possible links in disturbances in neuro-transmitter functioning in such diverse conditions as the schizophrenias, Parkinson's Disease, and hyperactivity in children.

PSYCHOPATHY AND LEARNING

It is also possible to conclude, albeit tentatively, that psychopaths do not develop conditioned fear responses readily. Because of this, they find it difficult to learn responses that are motivated by fear and reinforced by fear reduction. There is also experimental evidence (again confirmed in clinical practice) to suggest that psychopaths are less influenced than are normal persons by their capacity to make connections between past events and the consequences of their present behaviour. The significance or otherwise of the influence of close family and social environment will be commented upon later in this chapter, when I consider some of the key characteristics of the psychopath and the need to try to make a differential diagnosis.

Classification

In *Figures 5(2)* and *5(3)* I attempt to provide a classification of psychopathic personality disorder and to summarize possible causal factors.

The terms *pseudo-psychopathy* and *essential psychopathy* referred to in *Figure 5(2)* require some expansion. In the first place, they are very closely linked. The term 'pseudo-psychopathy' is meant to denote an 'as if' situation; that is, the disorder has the appearance of 'essential psychopathy' but is one in which it seems possible to ascribe some reasonably clear cause. As already indicated in Chapter 4, there is much evidence to suggest a fairly clear link between the development of seriously anti-social behaviour (particularly that associated with serious

Figure 5(2)   Classification of psychopathic personality disorder

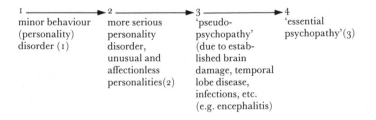

Notes to Figure 5(2)
(1) In this figure I have used the terms 'personality' and 'behaviour' disorder synonymously. Some authorities reserve the term 'behaviour disorder' for use in childhood conditions only.
(2) See McCulloch and Prins 1978.
(3) Sometimes described as 'true' or 'nuclear' psychopathy.

Figure 5(3) Aetiological factors

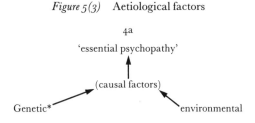

* Operating singly or in combination but of unknown origin.

aggression) and exposure to infections of various kinds. Work by Cleobury *et al.* (1971), for example, suggests that a particular strain of *herpes* virus infection *may* have an important rôle to play in producing psychopathic disorder. As we have already seen, illnesses such as encephalitis or meningitis may be particularly important. The same considerations apply to brain damage. Supporting evidence for such links can be found, for example, in cases where psychosurgery has been used inappropriately in the treatment of certain cases of neurosis. Such treatment may produce side-effects that can consist of bouts of aggression and highly anti-social conduct.

The classification I have suggested in column 2 of *Figure 5(2)* would have assigned to it the swindlers, cheats, and suchlike (the affectionless personalities) who act without remorse. It might also include those ruthless businessmen and women and politicians who trample on others to fight their way to the top. The category would also include those that Henderson (1939) described as 'predominantly creative psychopaths'. According to Henderson, these would embrace such personalities as Lawrence of Arabia. As indicated earlier, this seems to be stretching the concept of psychopathic disorder somewhat too far, thus rendering it meaningless. Gunn and Robertson have indicated that those individuals whom I would consign to column 2 could best be given a diagnostic category of 'neurosis (anti-social) behaviour' (1976: 634). It should be noted here that psychiatrists seem to differ quite widely in the extent to which they agree upon the particular diagnostic signs that go to make up the diagnosis of psychopath. Davies and Feldman (1981), in a study of 34 psychiatric specialists, found that although only 2 did not regard psychopathy as a clinical entity, there was considerable disagreement about the precise importance of each diagnostic sign (see discussion of differential diagnosis, below). It is also of interest to observe at this point that those labelled as psychopaths are almost invariably male. It is possible to speculate that a number of females who may well be psychopathic are labelled by psychiatric professionals as hysterics or as hysterical personalities. In a carefully executed piece of research, Guze (1976) found an unexpected association between psychopathy and hysteria. He suggested that, were this finding to be confirmed by further research, it would help to account for the apparent striking sex differences in the two disorders. Such research would have interesting parameters; for example, what are the respective parts played by biological and cultural factors that contribute to the sex differences, and to what extent will the continually changing status of women affect these so-called sex differences?

A number of workers have tried to discriminate between primary and secondary psychopaths (see, for example, Karpman 1948). More recently, Blackburn has carried such work further; he, too, suggests primary and secondary types. In addition, he has suggested that it is possible to identify four profile types for the psychopath. The first of these seems to be essentially similar to Karpman's primary type, to Cleckley's 'true' psychopath, and to my classification of 'essential psychopathy'. (See Blackburn 1974, 1975, 1982, 1983.)

THE NEED FOR DIFFERENTIAL DIAGNOSIS

Having made some attempt to delineate two major types of psychopathic disorder (the 'pseudo' and the 'essential'), it now seems important to examine the extent to which such disorder may be differentiated from ordinary criminal recidivism. In the first place, Blair suggests that psychopathic disorder must be distinguished from:

'1. Personality Disorders
2. Severe Psychoneurosis
3. Ordinary Adolescents
4. Hardened Criminals'

(Blair 1975: 56)

He also emphasizes that in order to make an adequate assessment of the condition, it is vital to obtain a detailed life history,
since in almost all cases the true or essential psychopath has
exhibited severe disturbance in all areas of behaviour *from a very
early age*. Indeed, it is important to remember that the presence
of long-standing disturbance is implicit in the criteria for the
diagnosis of psychopathic disorder within the meaning of the
Mental Health Act of 1983. What, then, are some of the
characteristics that distinguish true psychopaths from ordinary
recidivists (Blair's 'hardened criminals')? Cleckley (1976) suggests that the following may be some of the distinguishing
features:

(1) Ordinary recidivist criminals often seem to work to their
    own advantage through their offending; by this it is meant
    that they seem to be more purposive. Psychopaths, on the
    other hand, appear so much more likely to be detected that
    their criminality has an almost irrational or 'insane' quality
    to it.
(2) As already suggested, the criminal career of the psychopath
    seems to begin earlier than that of the ordinary criminal
    and, in addition, it spreads into many areas of his or her
    social and personal behaviour. Psychopaths appear to be
    more unmoved than ordinary recidivist offenders by over-
    tures of help or by punishment and their criminal careers
    seem more rapidly continuous. Their words appear to bear no
    relationship to their feelings or activities. (This important
    aspect will be commented upon later.)
(3) The psychopath's anti-social acts are often quite incompre-
    hensible and he or she seems to indulge in them for quite
    obscure reasons. Psychopaths also seem to be injuring
    themselves; in fact, the greatest degree of harm they may do
    to others is often brought about largely through others'
    concern for the psychopath and the psychopath's sub-
    sequent rejection of them. Reid suggests that this quality
    represents the essential 'sadness' of their lives (Reid (ed.)
    1978: 7). Thus, they often leave a *characteristic chain of chaos in
    their wake*. I would regard this feature as being one of the
    most important points in trying to distinguish the true
    psychopath from the ordinary recidivist.

(4) The male psychopath's sexual behaviour is not infrequently abnormal and seems to be indulged in at whim.

(5) The ordinary recidivist criminal seems, generally speaking, to have a certain degree of loyalty to family and to fellow criminals. The psychopath almost always appears to have none and is essentially a 'loner'. Indeed, McCord describes the psychopath as 'The Lonely Stranger' (McCord 1982: 9). (See also Smith 1978.)

(6) Hare and Jutai (1983) have observed that psychopaths commit a disproportionate number of crimes, compared to other male criminals. Hare and McPherson have provided recent evidence that 'the crimes and behaviour of psychopaths are also more violent and aggressive than are those of other criminals' (Hare and McPherson 1984: 35). The results of their three separate retrospective studies (which involved about 500 male criminals) showed that psychopaths were much more likely to use violent and aggressive behaviour than were criminals in general. Hare and McPherson used very careful and explicit criteria for the diagnosis of psychopathy and the assessment procedures used in the studies were rated as highly reliable and valid. It is also of interest to note that Hare and Jutai suggest that the aggressive psychopath may in fact engage in his or her aggressive activities for a longer period than has been supposed hitherto.

The criteria suggested above go some way towards indicating the possibilities of framing a differential diagnosis. There will, of course, be areas of overlap and ambiguity. Scott, however, a highly respected authority in this field, once questioned the need to distinguish between psychopaths and recidivists and suggested that there was not a great deal to be gained by it (Scott 1960: 1642).

SOME KEY CHARACTERISTICS

I shall now attempt to delineate some further characteristics of the psychopath, in order to expand upon the more general picture painted above. Cleckley makes the very telling observation that 'a race of men congenitally without pain sense would not find it easy to estimate the effects of physical torture on others. A man who has never understood visual experience would lack appreciation of what is sustained when the ordinary person loses his eye.'   (Cleckley 1976: 322)

He also states that the psychopath 'is invincibly ignorant of what life means to others' (1976: 386). In order to emphasize some of the key characteristics, Cleckley's list of sixteen cardinal features, in an earlier work, is very useful:

'1. Superficial charm and good intelligence
2. Absence of delusions and other signs of irrational thinking
3. Absence of 'nervousness' or psychoneurotic manifestations
4. Unreliability
5. Untruthfulness and insincerity
6. Lack of remorse or shame
7. Inadequately motivated anti-social behaviour
8. Poor judgement and failure to learn by experience
9. Pathological egocentricity and incapacity to love
10. General poverty in major affective reactions
11. Specific loss of insight
12. Unresponsiveness in general interpersonal relations
13. Fantastic and uninviting behaviour with drink and sometimes without
14. Suicide rarely carried out
15. Sex life impersonal, trivial and poorly integrated
16. Failure to follow any life plan.'   (Cleckley 1964: 363)

Taken overall, these features provide a very thorough framework for trying to distinguish the main characteristics of the true or essential psychopath. Obviously not *all* sixteen characteristics will necessarily be present in every case but for the diagnosis to be made the majority should be.

In this list of cardinal characteristics and in the points and two quotations from Cleckley cited earlier, we may readily grasp the core features; namely, *lack of real affect, an inability to relate feelings to the words with which they are expressed*, and *the chaos and destruction that the essential psychopath leaves behind*. The lack of

affect and chaos have been well described by numerous authorities but less attention has been given to the singular disparity
between speech and feelings. In this connection, it has been well
stated that the psychopath 'knows the words but not the music'
(Johns and Quay 1962: 217). I can think of one clear example,
from my own experience, of this singular disparity. I once
interviewed an offender/patient (who admittedly had already
been labelled as a psychopath). He told me a highly complicated tale, which was so obviously untrue from start to finish
that his story had a quality of complete irrationality and a
feeling akin to madness about it. This offender knew that the
facts could have been checked with the minimum of difficulty
and that they were so glaringly untrue that any normal individual would have known that they could not possibly deceive.
In addition, the statements he was presenting as truth were
clearly lies of such a grandiose nature that, again, this curious
quality of madness came across even more forcefully. He was
not, however, regarded as clinically deluded, in the sense that he
might have been suffering from delusions of grandeur due to
psychotic illness. His lying was, in my view, the clearest possible
example of that demonstrated by Cleckley's true or essential
psychopath. It was no doubt this disparity between speech and
feelings that led Cleckley to formulate his interesting concept of
semantic disorder or dementia.

In developing this idea, Cleckley drew upon work that had
been done by the neurologist Henry Head, in relation to a
condition known as semantic aphasia. This concept of
Cleckley's has received relatively little attention, perhaps because of its complexity; it is admittedly difficult to prove, though
clearly it deserves further exploration. Crudely put, and at the
risk of some distortion through compression, Cleckley suggests
that just as damage to certain higher nerve centres in the brain
may produce a physical inability to comprehend or produce
language so, with the psychopath, some form of neural damage
(unspecified but likely to be within that part of the brain dealing
with the higher functions of speech and meaning) might produce this strange inability to gear in to the needs and wants of
others. Cleckley indicates that the psychopath is able to present
to the outside world a façade of normality, which in fact conceals
a seriously disabled and often irresponsible individual.

This connection (or rather lack of it) between words and emotion is also of interest from another angle. In his book *The Murdering Mind* Abrahamsen (1973) illustrates how an unusually large proportion of murderers and others charged with acts of serious personal violence seemed to share two common characteristics—serious errors in verbal usage and curious, but strangely consistent, spelling mistakes. Such mis-spellings he describes as *onomatopoësis*—the making of a word or a name from a sound. Abrahamsen suggests that such people are not really anxious to communicate; their verbal communication is merely a way of exhibiting themselves. He goes on to suggest that such phenomena may offer diagnostic and predictive clues. Clearly, one cannot make too much use of such findings; they would require careful experimental validation and they are no more than peripherally linked with Cleckley's formulation. Nevertheless, they do provide food for further serious thought. Cleckley's concept of semantic aphasia is perhaps exemplified to some extent by what the psychopath Patrick Mackay had to say about the senseless and horrific crimes he committed. 'I feel terrible about what happened all the more because I do not know why or what made me do it. I find it all a confusing matter' (Clark and Penycate 1976: 2).

One final, important characteristic of the psychopath which is worth commenting on is a lack of time sense. Harrington, an American lay author, collected information on the characteristics of psychopaths from a variety of expert sources. One of his expert witnesses pointed out that psychopaths

> 'never see their behaviour in the context of tomorrow . . . if I'm a psychopath and I have an appointment to meet you but—all at once, unexpectedly—I run into an old friend on the street I might spend my afternoon with him and simply not show up for our meeting.'   (Harrington 1972: 215)

Such behaviour obviously has important implications for those who have the task of managing psychopaths and trying to help them—a topic to which we must now address ourselves.

Problems of management

There is little doubt, both from research findings and from clinical practice, that personality disorders in general and psychopathy in particular are very difficult conditions to treat or to ameliorate. In child psychiatric practice, for example, it is a well-established fact that it is easier to treat anxiety states and phobic conditions in children than it is to treat behaviour disorders; though some such disorders, particularly those involving hyperactivity, seem to be amenable to behaviour modification techniques. As for the more serious cases, we have to admit that, in the present state of our knowledge and skills, these are most intractable. This is the more distressing, since we know from careful research studies such as those carried out by Robins (1969) that the behaviour disordered children of today not infrequently become the psychopaths of tomorrow. Such failure, in the light of my earlier remarks about our lack of accurate knowledge concerning explanations of psychopathy, is hardly surprising. It is, therefore, very tempting to write off all such offenders as untreatable. One of the arguments often advanced for finding a new term for psychopathy is that it has become a word of abuse and a 'dustbin' category, to which we have assigned all those patients, residents, inmates, and offenders who seem unwilling to be helped, are unpredictable, unresponsive, and who, in addition, may show aggressive behaviour to a severe degree. There is, of course, much truth in this, but it is only a partial explanation.

It seems that whatever label we are going to use—be it psychopath, sociopath, psychopathic personality, or severe personality disorder—we are *still* going to have to face problems of engagement, acceptance, and communication. Many people have drawn attention to the reluctance of professionals in the penal and mental health care services to deal with psychopaths (particularly the more aggressive types). Admittedly, the label we use *can* be used pejoratively and as a defence against involvement. The basic difficulty lies in developing a special awareness not only of the rejecting feelings that such clients arouse in us but also of the way in which we can rationalize our negative responses by the use of the label. Somehow, we have to rise above the rejecting behaviour of these clients, to 'hang on' to them, sometimes over many years, and hope that gradually there may be some modification of their attitudes; this is a theme to which I shall return shortly. There is little doubt that 'some workers intuitively obtain good results with certain psychopaths' (Scott 1960: 1645); also, as Scott went on to point out, 'it should be possible to find out how they do it' (1960: 1645).

By adopting the type of classification I have suggested in *Figure 5(2)* it should be possible to make our attempts at management more discriminating and realistic. Those individuals I have assigned to categories 1 and 2, for example, may well respond to comparatively simple methods of management, though some should be left to go their own way, provided always that they do not come into serious conflict with the law and are not a danger to themselves or to others. Psychopaths in my category 3 may well respond to certain forms of medication or other methods aimed at improving, modifying, or even curing the underlying 'physical' condition that has given rise to what I have described as 'pseudo-psychopathy'. Such individuals may also need the application of additional measures; for example, containment for a time or exposure to one of the varieties of behaviour modification or retraining (see, for example, the chapter by Suedfeld and London in Hare and Schalling 1978).

Those psychopaths I have assigned to category 4—the 'essential', 'true', or 'nuclear' psychopaths—present the most difficult problems in management. We must acknowledge that as yet we have no 'cure' available. For some, containment under conditions of strict security within penal or other establishments for very long periods of time *may be* the only solution. The emphasis, however, should be on the *may be*, for there is some clinical evidence to suggest that even the essential psychopath may be enabled to modify attitudes over time (see, for example, Schmideberg 1965, McCord 1982, and Craft 1984). Schmideberg, who gave up using traditional psychoanalytic approaches in therapy with offenders (many of whom were psychopaths), found that a much more reality-based confronting approach was necessary. Psychopaths need, time and time again, to be brought up against the consequences of their behaviour. This seems to be brought about best when done by peers in a group situation (see, for example, Whiteley 1968 and Craft 1984). Benefit can also accrue, however, from one-to-one encounters. In order to achieve success with this type of confrontational technique, the worker needs to bear in mind the realities of the behaviour exhibited by the essential psychopath and not allow himself or herself to be *personally* affronted at being misled, lied to, evaded, or made to feel helpless and surrounded by chaos. (See my earlier observations about the key character-istics of the psychopath.) We are really talking about something as deceptively simple as the possession of *patience* in dealing with such people. The late George Lyward, who was a gifted worker with highly disturbed adolescents (some of whom showed early signs of psychopathic disorder), is said to have once remarked that 'patience is love that can wait'. Readers may think this a very apt observation within the context of the present discussion.

The possession of patience was also one of the keynotes of George Stürup's management regime at Denmark's famous institution for chronic criminals (psychopaths) at Hersted-vester (Stürup 1968). He also stressed the importance of con-tinuity of staff contact with such offenders; many of his own institution staff were responsible also for the long-term follow-up and after-care of such psychopaths when they had left the institution. This would be difficult to achieve in this country, since most of our prisons and Special Hospitals have national catchment areas. Stürup also stresses the point that manage-ment goals should not be set too high and that an eclectic approach is better than one marked by dogmatic adherence to a particular theoretical framework or mode of treatment. In discussing management, he also emphasized the need for work-ers to be aware of their own deeply held prejudices, which could prevent the possibility of a productive therapeutic alliance. In this connection Scott suggested that:

> 'wherever possible . . . psychopaths should be kept out of custody, for detention carries risks of its own. As soon as offenders or the anti-socially inclined are segregated there is the tendency for staff and inmates to consolidate at opposite poles; a hierarchy tends to develop among the offenders; a threat is thus offered to the staff which calls out a repressive authorative regime and the possibility of a vicious circle of resentment and counter-resentment.'   (Scott 1960: 1644)

The dangers of such an atmosphere are brought out very clearly in Boyle's (1984) account of the attempts to develop the special unit at Barlinnie Prison and the manner in which these attempts appear to have been subverted because of the anxieties engendered by this new approach to managing 'dangerous' (psychopathic) men.

Over the years, a number of other institutions have attempted to use more open group-work techniques with psychopaths. Craft's pioneering work at various units in Devon, Nottinghamshire, and Wales is worth careful study (Craft 1984). (See also Miles 1969.) McCord (1982) summarizes work carried out in the USA using 'milieu therapy'. For the less seriously psychopathically disordered (i.e. the aggressive but the non-dangerous), Watts and Bennett (1978) and Woodside *et al.* (1976) have shown that quite seriously deviant patients can be coped with satisfactorily in a psychiatric day hospital or small ward setting. In summary, there are three keynote words that spring to mind in managing the psychopathically disordered—particularly those at the more serious end of the spectrum—*consistency*, *persistence*, and *insistence*. These would seem to encapsulate the essentials of all work in this area.

Conclusions

By way of conclusion, we may return to the charges laid at Richard III's door by his elderly mother. They graphically demonstrate some of the key characteristics of the essential psychopath that we have been discussing in this chapter: ambivalent parental feelings, provoking in turn a cold, wayward response, resultant long-standing behaviour difficulties, lovelessness, cunning, evasion, and deceit, coupled with a superficial charm. All the 'hallmarks' appear to be there.[1] Taken together, they represent a tremendous challenge to those charged with the task of management. In addition, such a challenge presupposes the capacity to step outside narrow boundaries of learning and experience and to take on board findings from a wide range of disciplines. Some words by Professor Rawnsley in his Presidential Address to the Royal College of Psychiatrists on the subject of the future of psychiatry are also highly relevant to the problem of understanding and managing the psychopath. He suggested that there should be

'a willingness to embrace a truly eclectic approach, which rejoices in the complexity of the human mind and is aware of the equally valid contributions from genetics, biochemistry, pharmacology and psychology (both in its dynamic and behavioural mode) and from the social sciences.'

(Rawnsley 1984: 575)

If we can rid ourselves of our preconceptions and prejudices and broaden our horizons, we may be able to improve our skills in managing the most problematic and enigmatic group of individuals known to the caring and containing professions.

References

Abrahamsen, D. (1973) *The Murdering Mind*. London: Harper and Row.

Blackburn, R. (1974) *Personality and the Classification of Psychopathic Disorders*. Special Hospitals Research Report No. 10. London: DHSS.

—— (1975) An Empirical Classification of Psychopathic Personality. *British Journal of Psychiatry* **127**: 456–60.

—— (1982) On the Relevance of the Concept of the Psychopath. In D. Black (ed.) *Symposium: Broadmoor Psychology Department's 21st Birthday*. Issues in Criminological and Legal Psychology No. 2. Leicester: British Psychological Society.

—— (1983) Are Personality Disorders Treatable? In J. Shapland and T. Williams (eds) *Mental Disorder and the Law: Effects of the New Legislation*. Issues in Criminological and Legal Psychology No. 4. Leicester: British Psychological Society.

—— (1984) Unpublished lecture given as part of the commemoration of the opening of the Park Lane Hospital, Liverpool, 4 October, 1984.

Blair, D. (1975) The Medico-Legal Implications of the Terms 'Psychopath', 'Psychopathic Personality' and 'Psychopathic Disorder'. *Medicine, Science and the Law* **15**: 51–61, 110–23.

Boyle, J. (1984) *The Pain of Confinement: Prison Diaries*. Edinburgh: Canongate.

Clark, T. and Penycate, J. (1976) *Psychopath: The Case of Patrick Mackay*. London: Routledge and Kegan Paul.

Cleckley, H. (1964) *The Mask of Sanity* (fourth edition). St Louis: C.V. Mosby.

—— (1976) *The Mask of Sanity* (fifth edition). St Louis: C.V. Mosby.

Cleobury, J.R., Skinner, G.R.B., Thouless, M.E., and Wildy, P. (1971) Association between Psychopathic Disorder and Serum Antibody to Herpes Simplex Virus (Type I). *British Medical Journal* **I**: 438–39.

Craft, M. (1968) Psychopathic Disorder: A Second Trial of Treatment. *British Journal of Psychiatry* **114**: 813–20.

—— (1984) Should One Treat or Gaol Psychopaths? In M. and A. Craft (eds) *Mentally Abnormal Offenders*. London: Baillière Tindall.

Davies, W. and Feldman, P. (1981) The Diagnosis of Psychopathy by Forensic Specialists. *British Journal of Psychiatry* **138**: 329–31.

Department of Health and Social Security, Home Office, Welsh Office, Lord Chancellor's Department (1976) *A Review of the Mental Health Act, 1959*. London: HMSO.

East, N. (1949) *Society and the Criminal*. London: HMSO.

Feldman, M. (1977) *Criminal Behaviour. A Psychological Analysis*. London: Wiley.

General Register Office (1968) *A Glossary of Mental Disorders*. Studies on Medical and Population Subjects, No. 22. London: HMSO.

Gough, H.G. (1956) A Sociological Study of Psychopathy. In A.M. Rose (ed.) *Mental Health and Mental Disorder*. London: Routledge and Kegan Paul.

Gunn, J. and Robertson, G. (1976) Psychopathic Personality: A Conceptual Problem. *Psychological Medicine* **6**: 631–34.

Gurvitz, M. (1951) Developments in the Concept of Psychopathic Personality. *British Journal of Delinquency* **II**: 88–102.

Guze, S.B. (1976) *Criminality and Psychiatric Disorders*. Oxford: Oxford University Press.

Hare, R.D. (1970) *Psychopathy: Theory and Research*. London: Wiley.

Hare, R.D. and Jutai, J.W. (1983) Criminal History of the Male Psychopath: Some Preliminary Data. In K.T. van Dusen and S.A. Mednick (eds) *Prospective Studies of Crime and Delinquency*. Boston: Kluwer Nijhoff.

Hare, R.D. and McPherson, L.M. (1984) Violent and Criminal Behaviour by Criminal Psychopaths. *International Journal of Law and Psychiatry* **7**: 33–50.

Hare, R.D. and Schalling, D. (eds) (1978) *Psychopathic Behaviour: Approaches to Research*. London: Wiley.

Harrington, A. (1972) *Psychopaths*. London: If.

Henderson, D. (1939) *Psychopathic States*. New York: W.W. Norton.

Home Office and DHSS (1975) *Report of the Committee on Mentally Abnormal Offenders (Butler Committee)*. Cmnd. 6244. London: HMSO.

Johns, J.H. and Quay, H.C. (1962) The Effect of Social Reward on Verbal Conditioning in Psychopathic and Neurotic Military Offenders. *Journal of Consulting Psychology* **26**: 217–20.

Jones, M. (1963) The Treatment of Character Disorders. *British Journal of Criminology* **3**: 276–82.

Karpman, B. (1948) Conscience in the Psychopath. *American Journal of Orthopsychiatry* **18**: 455–91.

Lewis, A. (1974) Psychopathic Personality: A Most Elusive Category. *Psychological Medicine* **4**: 133–40.

Lindner, R.M. (1944) *Rebel Without a Cause*. New York: Grune and Stratton.

McCord, W. (1982) *The Psychopath and Milieu Therapy: A Longitudinal Study*. New York: Academic.

McCulloch, J.W. and Prins, H. (1978) *Signs of Stress: The Social Problems of Psychiatric Illness*. London: Woburn.

Maughs, S.B. (1941) Concept of Psychopathic Personality: Its Evolution and Historical Development. *Journal of Criminal Psychopathology* **2**: 329–56, 365–99.

Mawson, A.R. and Mawson, C.D. (1977) Psychopathy and Arousal: A New Interpretation of the Psychophysiological Literature. *Biological Psychiatry* **12**: 49–74.

Miles, A.E. (1969) The Effects of a Therapeutic Community on the Interpersonal Relationships of a Group of Psychopaths. *British Journal of Criminology* **9**: 22–38.

Pichot, P. (1978) Psychopathic Behaviour: A Historical Overview. In R.D. Hare and D. Schalling (eds) *Psychopathic Behaviour: Approaches to Research*. London: Wiley.

Pizzey, E. and Shapiro, J. (1982) *Prone to Violence*. Feltham: Hamlyn.

Prichard, J.C. (1835) *A Treatise on Insanity and Other Disorders Affecting the Mind*. Philadelphia: Haswell, Barrington and Haswell.

Rawnsley, K. (1984) Psychiatry in Jeopardy (Presidential Address at the Annual General Meeting of the Royal College of Psychiatrists, July, 1984). *British Journal of Psychiatry* **145**: 573–78.

Reid, W.H. (ed.) (1978) *The Psychopath: A Comprehensive Study of Antisocial Disorders and Behaviour*. New York: Brunner Mazel.

Robins, L.N. (1969) *Deviant Children Grown Up: A Sociological and Psychiatric Study of Sociopathic Personality*. Baltimore: Williams and Wilkins.

Schmideberg, M. (1965) Reality Therapy with Offenders. *British Journal of Criminology* **5**: 168–82.

Schneider, K. (1958) *Psychopathic Personalities*. (Tr. M. Hamilton.) London: Cassell.

Scott, P.D. (1960) The Treatment of Psychopaths. *British Medical Journal* **2**: 1641–646.

Slater, E.T.O. (1948) Psychopathic Personality as a Genetical Concept. *Journal of Mental Science* **94**: 277–80.

Smith, R.J. (1978) *The Psychopath in Society*. New York: Academic Press.

Stürup, G. (1968) *Treating the Untreatable: Chronic Criminals at Herstedvester*. Baltimore: Johns Hopkins Press.

Trethowan, W. and Sims, A.C.P. (1983) *Psychiatry* (fifth edition). London: Baillière Tindall.

Treves-Brown, C. (1977) Who is the Psychopath? *Medicine, Science and the Law* **17**: 56–63.

Walker, N. and McCabe, S. (1973) *Crime and Insanity in England and Wales, Volume II*. (Chapters 9 and 10.) Edinburgh: Edinburgh University Press.

Watts, F.N. and Bennett, D.H. (1978) Social Deviance in a Day Hospital. *British Journal of Psychiatry* **132**: 455–62.

Whiteley, S. (1968) Factors in the Treatment and Management of Psychopaths. In D.J. West (ed.) *Psychopathic Offenders*. Cambridge: Institute of Criminology.

Widom, C.S. and Newman, J.P. (1985) Characteristics of Non-Institutionalized Psychopaths. In D.P. Farrington and J. Gunn (eds) *Aggression and Dangerousness*. Chichester: Wiley.

Woodman, D.D. (1980) What Makes a Psychopath? *New Society*, 4 September: 447–49.

Woodside, M., Harrow, A., Basson, J.V., and Affleck, J.W. (1976) Experiment in Managing Sociopathic Behaviour Disorders. *British Medical Journal* **2**: 1056–059.

FURTHER READING

Bleechmore, J.F. (1975) Towards a Rational Theory of Criminal Responsibility: The Psychopathic Offender. *Melbourne University Law Review* Parts I and II, **May, September**: 19–46, 207–24.

Craft, M. (1965) *Ten Studies into Psychopathic Personality*. Bristol: John Wright.

Jensen, O.N. (1978) The Mask of Psychopathy. *International Journal of Law and Psychiatry* **I**: 153–66.

Lion, J.R. (1974) *Personality Disorders: Diagnosis and Management*. Baltimore: Williams and Wilkins.

Reicher, J.W. (1979) Psychoanalytically Orientated Treatment of Offenders Diagnosed as Developmental Psychopaths: The Mesdag-kliniek Experience. *International Journal of Law and Psychiatry* **2**: 87–98.

Note
1 It is of considerable interest to note that in his account of his preparation for portraying the part of Richard, Anthony Sher placed great stress on Richard's relationship with his mother. See Sher, A., (1985) *The Year of the King: An Actor's Diary and Sketchbook*. London: Chatto and Windus.

CHAPTER SIX

Serious sexual attack

'Few love to hear the sins they love to act'
SHAKESPEARE
Pericles Act I, scene i

In this chapter, I propose to deal with a fairly limited range of sexual offences; in so doing, I am aware that my selection has been arbitrary and is thus open to criticism. It can be argued that any sexual offence is serious and that although in some cases only minor physical harm may result, the psychological trauma may be considerable. The extent to which the criminal law should be used to control sexual behaviour is open to controversy but, as West points out, 'the right of citizens to be protected by the criminal law from un-wanted or forcible sexual intrusion is everywhere acknowledged' (West 1983a: 184). It is also important to locate any discussion of deviant sexual behaviour within a socio-cultural context, for this will affect the type of legislation introduced to control it; it will also reflect apparent inconsistencies and idiosyncratic modes of enforcement (see Honoré 1978).

It is necessary to make several further important points by way of introduction. Those who have to deal with sexually deviant behaviour (particularly serious sexual deviancy) have to learn to become aware of their own 'blind-spots' and prejudices and to recognize the wide variations that exist in sexual practices between human beings. In recent years, many workers (for example, Kinsey, Pomeroy, and Martin 1948; Kinsey *et al.* 1953; Ford and Beach 1965; Masters and Johnson 1966) have shed considerable light on the infinite variety of human behaviour and response. As a result, people *may* be less guilty about acknowledging their own sexuality and that of others. One possible side-effect of the recent emphasis on improving knowledge and developing skill in sexual techniques, however, is to place too much importance upon 'performance'; this may tend to establish a dichotomy between the physical expression of sexuality and human relationships in their wider context.

This development is paralleled by the manner in which the media, and more particularly advertising, place considerable emphasis upon sexual attractiveness. Overall, there is nowadays much more open presentation—literary, verbal, and visual—of sex. It is debatable whether this has led to people being any more substantially informed or less anxious about sexuality but we have at least rid ourselves of some quainter euphemisms. No longer do newspapers describe buggery as a 'serious offence' or as an 'unnatural act', though it is probably true to say that few people realize the real implications of calling someone a 'bugger'!

This information explosion, combined with the fact that we *appear* to be taking a more liberal view of some forms of sexual activity (for example, homosexual acts between adult consenting males in private), has made it increasingly difficult to draw sharp distinctions between so-called 'normal' and deviant sexual behaviour. In addition, we all tend to use the word *sexuality* in a fairly imprecise fashion, forgetting that it encompasses contributions from chromosome sex, gonadal sex, internal and external (morphological) characteristics, and gender. (For reviews of some of these aspects, see Zuger 1980, MacCulloch and Waddington 1981, Goodman 1983, and West 1983b.) The notion of gender is especially important. Gender *identity* is what an individual feels about his or her maleness or femaleness; gender *rôle* is concerned with an individual's manifest behaviour of masculinity or femininity. These concepts are of particular interest to those charged with the responsibility of counselling so-called sexually deviant individuals, for it is a mistake to think that maleness and femaleness are distinct and separate attributes. There is enough evidence from work carried out in the field of bi- or ambi-sexuality to validate the assertion that all of us have components of the opposite sex within us. The balance of these components will vary within individuals (see, for example, Wolff 1977). For many people, this is an uncomfortable notion; but it is one that has to be faced by those wishing to work helpfully with people requiring or thought to need help with sexual problems. (For more specific discussion of these aspects, see Bender 1977 and Cohen 1977).

In view of all these factors, can we make any useful distinctions between so-called 'normality' and 'deviation'? I think the answer is 'yes', but I must emphasize again that the distinctions will be culture-bound, that they may change over time, and that they can be seen only as broad generalizations. They will also be dependent upon differences in individual aesthetic beliefs. We can assert that normal sexual behaviour encompasses those forms of sexual activity between two adults (as currently defined by law) which are acceptable to both parties, *do not involve coercion, exploitation, or degradation*, and, if performed in public, do not cause offence to the average man or woman in the street. The material that follows is almost exclusively concerned with those aspects of sexual behaviour that involve the words italicized. I shall be concerned with those sexual offences normally defined as serious. For this purpose, Walmsley and White's classification is useful: it includes rape and attempted rape, buggery and attempted buggery, incest and attempted incest, and unlawful sexual intercourse with girls under 13 (Walmsley and White 1979). To this classification I shall add sexual assaults against children and young persons more generally, and sexual murders. Some reference will also be made to certain other offences.

The incidence of sexual offences

Contrary to common belief, sexual offences constitute a minute proportion of all crimes. In 1980, they constituted less than 1 per cent of all *recorded* offences and about 1.5 per cent of all persons *found guilty* of indictable (more serious) offences (Walmsley 1984). There is also a wide discrepancy between the numbers of sexual offences recorded as known to the police and the numbers actually *dealt with* or *prosecuted*. The reasons for this are not hard to find. Victims (and witnesses) may be reluctant to come forward and corroboration may thus prove difficult. In addition, consenting parties may be reluctant to admit to having engaged in unlawful sexual activity, so that it may be difficult to prove that an offence has occurred. Many more sexual offences are committed *than are ever reported to the police*. There may be a reluctance to admit involvement, or a degree of blackmail may be involved, so that the victim may prefer to remain silent. In some cases (rape, for example), the victim may not wish to suffer the embarrassment and trauma of medical and police enquiries, followed by a public court appearance, which may involve rigorous cross-examination of both fact and reputation. Parents of sexually assaulted children may wish to spare them a similar ordeal. There is evidence to suggest that many young adult males who have been subjected to serious sexual assault (for example, buggery) are very reluctant to report the offence because of the sense of humiliation they feel. If such assaults have been carried out in an institutional setting, victims may be reluctant to report them for fear of reprisals. There is a paucity of literature on this subject in the UK but Sccaco has written extensively about the topic in the USA (Sccaco 1975, 1982).

In considering the volume of sexual crime, it is also as well to remember that certain other, apparently non-sexual, crimes may be sexually motivated. The offence of aggravated burglary is a good example of this. If such offences appear in the antecedent history of a person who has gone on to commit a serious sexual assault, the outlook concerning the commission of further serious sexual offences is not good. The significance of sexually motivated burglaries is described by Revitch (1983) and more general aspects by Morneau and Rockwell (1980). My remarks in Chapter 4 concerning the need to obtain exact and full details of an offender's past criminal record and offence behaviour are highly relevant in this context. In 1983, about 9,300 offenders were found guilty of, or cautioned for, indictable sexual offences. This figure is the lowest for ten years—the average for the years 1973–83 being round about the 10,000 mark. *Table 6(1)* provides a breakdown of these figures into major offence categories. (Source for all statistics: Home Office 1984: 73, 95.) These figures do not include other offences that may have been sexually motivated (for example, aggravated burglary or sexual murder). It is apparent that the number of serious sexual offences actually dealt with is comparatively small. Many of these offences, however, cause grave physical and emotional trauma to their victims and in some cases the perpetrators pose a serious threat to the safety of the general public. As Gunn has said, 'Paedophilia . . . (for example) . . . can . . . occasionally, go on to physical assault and murder. Indeed all sexual behaviour both normal and abnormal, can lead to violence' (Gunn 1976: 63).

Most serious sexual offences are dealt with by custodial penalties. Rape almost always attracts a sentence of imprisonment and on the rare occasions where a judge decides otherwise, the media are quick to comment—sometimes without adequate knowledge of the detailed facts of the individual case. Incest is dealt with by a custodial sentence in about 70 per cent of cases. As Walmsley (1984) points out, however, this total percentage ignores considerable variations within sentencing as between

Table 6(1) (1) *Offenders found guilty or cautioned for indictable sexual offences, 1983*

buggery (2)		254
indecent assault on a male (3)		789
indecency between males		1,338
rape		330
indecent assault on a female		3,235
unlawful sexual intercourse with a girl under 13		149
unlawful sexual intercourse with a girl under 16		1,673
incest		152
procuration, abduction, bigamy		400
soliciting by a man		739
gross indecency with a child		255
	Total	9,314

(Source: Home Office 1984: 73, 95)

Notes to Table 6(1)
(1) This table includes only the more serious, 'indictable' offences. Certain summary (less serious) offences, such as indecent exposure, are not included.
(2) In this chapter, we are predominantly concerned with the offences of buggery, rape, incest, unlawful sexual intercourse with females, indecent assaults on males, and certain cases of indecency with children.
(3) In some categories, comparisons with figures for previous years are not possible because of changes in counting and recording procedures introduced in 1979 (see Home Office 1984: 191–92).

father/daughter incest (which almost always attracts a custodial penalty) and brother/sister incest (which does not). Buggery with victims under the age of 14 will almost always attract a prison sentence but the likelihood of a custodial penalty will decrease with the increasing age of the victim. Similar variations appear to occur concerning the offence of unlawful sexual intercourse with a female. Indecent assaults on males and females appear to be dealt with by a custodial penalty in about 20 to 30 per cent of cases. Overall, 'the proportion of persons found guilty who receive a custodial sentence has remained fairly stable since 1946 in respect of the most serious sexual offences' (Walmsley 1984: 49). It is also of interest to note that the use of Hospital Orders for sex offenders seems to have declined considerably in the past ten years (Walmsley 1984). The reasons for this may be similar to those suggested in Chapter 2 for the decline in the use of Hospital Orders in cases of diminished responsibility.

With these outline statistics in mind, we can now examine a selection of serious sexual offences in a little more detail. There are dangers in singling out offence categories in this way; an offender may commit more than one type of sexual offence and some of the offence categories will, in any case, overlap. Rape, for example, may end in murder, either because the killing was a planned part of the rape, because the victim died as a result of the attack, or because the assailant was over-zealous in silencing his victim. It is important, therefore, to remember that *every case is different* and great care should be taken in reaching any generalized conclusions. Despite these caveats, it seems helpful to try to separate the categories in a fairly crude way. I shall begin with a consideration of serious sexual assault on children and young persons, and incest. The reason for linking the two categories is that incestuous behaviour (particularly with young victims) may be regarded as a highly specific form of serious indecent assault.

Serious sexual offences against children, young persons (paedophilia), and incest

It is often difficult to obtain adequate data concerning the prevalence of serious sexual assaults on the young but it has recently been estimated that more than one million children can expect to be sexually assaulted by the age of 15 (*Guardian* 5 March, 1985). Some of the reasons for the absence of hard data have already been suggested. In addition, the criminal statistics are not always very helpful; for example, the figures for buggery do not differentiate between those offences committed against adults and those against children and young persons. Of one thing we can be certain: those who commit serious sexual assaults on the young (sometimes described somewhat emotively as child molesters) span the age spectrum and come from very diverse social backgrounds. Such offenders have included those in high office, from the notorious fifteenth-century Marshal of France, Gilles de Rais, to the most lowly and illiterate itinerant. Love of children is as old as civilization itself; at various times it has been both praised and vilified (see Kraemer (ed.) 1976, Abel, Becker, and Cunningham-Rathner 1984, Brongersma 1984). Despite the asseverations of those who would wish to sanction a greater degree of licence for children to engage more freely in sexual relations with adults, most thinking and concerned people are conscious of the possible dangers that can exist in such relationships. Such so-called loving relationships may become warped and selfish (as described, for example, in Nabokov's *Lolita* and Mann's *Death in Venice*). The child or young person may never grow to independent adulthood; because of this, the sexual 'games' of childhood may persist into adult life. In addition, the love of such adults may go far beyond the limits of normal care and protection and become physically and emotionally traumatic for the child.

It comes as no surprise to find that this darker side of adult love is reflected in the opportunities and occupations afforded to those who sexually abuse the young. Many are in positions of trust and tutelage. Parents certainly number among their ranks as recent evidence so sadly attests (see Finkelhor 1979, Mrazek and Kempe (eds) 1981, and Porter (ed.) 1984). Others include members of the wider family circle, friends, youth workers, teachers, and the clergy; a sad but telling commentary on the vulnerability of those who would seek to serve those they offend against. Tragically, many of these offenders have themselves been the victims of assault in their own childhood or adolescence. As we saw in Chapter 4, the rôle of the victim is particularly important. Some victims crave affection and it is all too easy for them to behave seductively towards vulnerable adults (Abel, Becker, and Cunningham-Rathner 1984). Sometimes such behaviour is barely conscious; at others, it may be quite deliberate and engaged in for financial or other rewards. Both Virkunnen (1975) and Ingram (1979) have stressed the importance of seductive and provocative behaviour.

It is difficult to be precise as to the harm that sexual assaults may cause. There is little doubt that the *physical* effects have often been underestimated. Abel *et al.* (1981) suggest that serious physical violence is more common in both homosexual and heterosexual paedophilia than is sometimes supposed. Serious tears in the rectum or vagina are not uncommon and the risk of infections of various kinds is high. Although a good deal has been written about the *emotional* trauma (see, for example, Groth 1979), the evidence is often conflicting (Tsai and Wagner 1978). The most significant determinants of trauma will be:

(a) the victims's previous and current social and psychological environment;
(b) the anxiety caused by being forced to keep a 'guilty' secret;
(c) the opportunities (or lack of them) for the victim to off-load this guilt (Elliot 1985);
(d) the nature of the pre-existing or current relationship with the assailant and avenues of 'escape' from it, if any;
(e) the reactions of those having care of the victim.

The latter are probably more important than any other factor and do much to foster or limit later guilt and trauma. It is perhaps worth pointing out that some young people *appear* to be markedly resilient in the face of even quite serious sexual assaults. If the assault has been *violent and unexpected* (either in respect of the location or in respect of the person carrying it out), however, the experience is likely to be highly traumatic. Such trauma will increase with the degree of terror that the offender may seek to induce in the victim. It is very important that this element is explored carefully. Crawford (1982) has pointed out that it is essential to distinguish between those who use force as a means of gaining co-operation in the act and those offenders for whom the infliction of pain or terror is an end in itself. He suggests that elicitation of this information will help to distinguish those whose problem is an overpowering *love* of children from those whose problem is one of *hatred*.

It will be obvious that some form of differential diagnosis (assessment) is vital in *all* cases. For this reason, I have produced the following rudimentary classification of such offenders. It is important however, to bear in mind my earlier comments about the arbitrary and overlapping nature of such classifications. It is generally recognized that there are significant differences between *homosexual* and *heterosexual* paedophiles, although very occasionally individuals may assault victims of both sexes. (This is likely in the case of some mentally retarded paedophiles—see Shepherd 1982.) Bluglass (1982) suggests that *homosexual* paedophiles are more likely to have had past involvement with children, to prefer them as sexual partners, and to show deviant patterns of sexual arousal. *Heterosexual* paedophiles are more likely to be situationally motivated and to prefer adult women but may seek a child because of social and personal stresses of various kinds (see later discussion).

CLASSIFICATION

(a) Young offenders

(1) Ambi-sexual (as distinct from homosexual) inadequate adolescents, who bribe younger children to engage in deviant sexual practices. Such offenders may have been placed by adults in positions of trust towards their victims. Some of these victims stand in danger of becoming sexually deviant themselves. (See, for example, Longo 1982).

(2) A rather more dangerous adolescent offender, who indulges in quite serious sexually assaultive behaviour. He, too, often has a history of being sexually abused in childhood. These offenders often show a history of sexually inappropriate behaviour from an early age; they may go on to become seriously sexually deviant adults (Longo and Groth 1983). When compared with non-sex offence delinquents, these offenders are more likely to come from a middle-class background, to be less intellectually able, but to show a

less-marked history of truancy or alcohol abuse (Awad, Saunders, and Levene 1984).

(b) Adult offenders

(1) The middle-aged heterosexual paedophile. He is almost always a lonely and isolated individual, seeking the company of small girls for affection and companionship. Such offenders seem quite unable to fulfil an adult sex role and are often socially incompetent in other areas of their lives.

(2) Senile or pre-senile homosexual paedophiles whose sexual predilections do not seem to be dulled by age, even though their sexual ability may be. It is foolhardy to think that such offenders are necessarily likely to be less potentially dangerous merely because of their advancing years. They may in fact become more easily frustrated, feel less 'in command' (powerful), and, because of this, may resort to violence —including homicide—during the pursuit of their desires. Any act imputed to the victim as humiliating may also end in violently assaultive behaviour. 'Hell' may have 'no fury' like an ageing paedophile scorned.

(3) Paedophiles of low or subnormal intelligence. Such individuals may commit serious sexual offences for a number of reasons. First, they may not be fully aware of the likely consequences of their behaviour or know that it is wrong. Second, since many of them lack social skills, they may make inapt sexual overtures; when these are rebuffed, violence may ensue. Third, there are those who may not appreciate their own strength; because of this, they may cause injury. (See also Chapter 4 and Shepherd 1982.)

(4) Those whose sexual offences against the young seem to be part of a more generalized inability to achieve social conformity. Such offenders frequently have histories of alcohol-related problems and convictions for non-sexual offences.

(5) The exclusively homosexual paedophile (sometimes referred to as the *pederast*). This offender often sees himself as the 'protector' of disadvantaged youths, does not see that his activities are wrong or unusual, exerts a powerful and coercive influence over his victims, and seems quite impervious to treatment.

MANAGEMENT

For management to achieve any degree of success, careful assessment is essential (see my remarks on the need for full assessment in Chapter 4). One of our main concerns must be with the prediction (and possible prevention) of repetition. During the last two decades, a great deal of experimental work has demonstrated that the measurement of penile responses to a variety of sexually arousing stimuli offers a surer basis of prediction than social and psychological measures alone.[1] A very useful description of this technique (known as penile plethysmography) may be found in Earls 1983. Earls also makes the point that good interviewing skills are required *in addition* to physiological measurements, to enable the worker (counsellor) to make adequate investigation and verification of the offender's self-reports of sexual preferences.

Work in this area clearly demonstrates the need for a multi-disciplinary approach. Clinical and allied experience suggests that seriously deviant sexual preference is a very difficult condition to alter and that permanent 'cure' is highly unlikely. (Useful summaries of major treatment modalities may be found in Brodsky 1980, Crawford 1981, Perkins 1983, and West 1983.) As already suggested, management is made difficult by the fact that, in many cases, sexual preference has been fixed at a very early age. Techniques based on traditional insight giving therapy (such as classical psychoanalysis) are not likely to be successful, though group-work techniques may be. The less seriously deviant adolescent may respond quite well to supportive counselling; in such cases, group approaches have also met with some success (Margolin 1984). Many of these offenders are singularly deficient in social skills, so training in this area can be very helpful. Some success has been reported even with serious sex offenders detained in a Special Hospital (Crawford and Allen 1979). In cases where the behaviour appears to be situational and to this extent transient, attempts to locate and manage these difficulties may expect to be met with a degree of success, particularly if a friendly follow-up service is available. Many of those who commit serious sex offences against the young, however, are highly reluctant to change their life-styles and they lack capacity for insight. For such offenders, particularly the exclusively homosexual paedophile, the most realistic course may be to attempt to 'damp down' sexual desire. The use of anti- (feminizing) hormones, such as cyproterone acetate (Andracur), has met with some success, though unpleasant side-effects have been recorded (for example, nausea, depression, and breast enlargement). Chemotherapy of this kind is more likely to be successful if it is accompanied by counselling and mutual support group activities (see Shaw 1978a and 1978b, Weaver and Fox 1984).

Procedures derived from learning theory, such as a wide variety of behaviour modification techniques, have been successful in less serious cases. Techniques have included aversion therapy (though this is less popular now); such procedures make use of a controlled aversive reaction (such as a mild electric shock) to the deviant sexual stimulus. 'Shaming' has also been used. This involves the offender being subjected to public exhibition of his deviancy, which is then criticized by the audience. Other techniques include positive conditioning (more popular these days), in which attempts are made to establish a relationship between well-regarded sexual thoughts and orgasm, and 'shaping'. Shaping involves the substitution of a less deviant sexual activity (as presented on a slide) as orgasm approaches during masturbation. In some countries, castration (critical organ surgery) has been used and some success has been claimed. The ethical problems associated with the use of such an irreversible procedure, however, are considerable and it has rightly never been popular as a form of treatment (see Ortmann 1980). There are also serious ethical implications in the use of even reversible procedures, such as hormone implant therapy. The serious sexual assaulter of young people undergoing a long period of hospitalization or imprisonment may find it very tempting to facilitate his release by agreeing to subject himself to one or other of the varieties of hormonal treatment (such as an implant), even though, as we have already seen, his real motivation for change may be slight.

Since the passing of the Mental Health Act of 1983, there are now more stringent safeguards concerning such procedures; a recent case reported in the *Guardian* (4 and 5 December, 1984) highlighted some of these dilemmas. In this case a judge had made a requirement in a probation order that the accused be treated by hormone therapy and the offender had agreed. The civil liberties lobby were quick to point out some of the pitfalls in making such an order (although they also appeared to have ignored the fact that the offender would otherwise have gone to prison for a very long time; he had numerous prior convictions for sex assaults on small girls). *If* an offender has given his informed consent, *if* he has been made aware of the full social and medical consequences of treatment, and *if* he is prepared to involve himself in rigorous follow-up on release, not only may he be less likely to be a menace to children but he may also be able to make some useful contribution to society. Research indicates that in such cases long-term follow-up is crucial. Gibbens, Soothill, and Way (1981) conducted a long-term study of men who had committed sexual offences against girls under thirteen (unlawful sexual intercourse, or USI). When followed up for a *twenty-year period*, it appeared there was a low but *persistent* tendency to reconviction and *that this was greater than that found in property offenders.*

I shall now turn to another aspect of serious sexual offending against the young—incest.

INCEST

The history of incest, the nature of the taboos against it, and the genetic complications arising from close consanguinous mating have been well documented and do not need recapitulating here. (See, for example, Adams and Neal 1967, Roberts 1967, Nakashima and Zakus 1977, Bluglass 1979, and Goodwin 1982 (Chapter 15 and Appendix I).) Incest did not become a criminal offence in England and Wales until 1908, having been an ecclesiastical crime up to that time. In Scotland, it had been a crime since very early times and was punishable by death until the late 1880s. The present law derives from the Sexual Offences Act of 1956. The crime of incest is committed if a man has sexual intercourse with a woman whom he knows to be his granddaughter, daughter, sister, or mother. A woman commits the same crime if, being of or above the age of sixteen, with consent, she permits her grandfather, father, brother, or son to have sexual intercourse with her. The terms brother and sister extend to half-blood relationships and they need not be legitimate offspring. In other countries, there are variations concerning the proscribed degree of consanguinity; in this country, there have been disagreements as to whether the term 'incest' should be used and whether it should continue to be a specific offence. The Criminal Law Revision Committee recommended that it should, though they also recommended that prosecutions should only be brought by or with the consent of the Director of Public Prosecutions, and that incest committed by brothers and sisters over the age of 21 should not be an offence (Criminal Law Revision Committee 1984). The offence is currently punishable by a maximum sentence of seven years' imprisonment; in the case of its commission against a girl under the age of thirteen, it is punishable by a life sentence. As can be seen from *Table 6(1)*, comparatively few cases are prosecuted. It has been conservatively estimated that there may be some 1,500 cases of incest a year; of these, only about 300 come to the attention of the police. The number of prosecutions is, therefore, very small and appears to be but a fraction of the estimated incidence. This is hardly surprising when one considers the secrecy and guilt that surrounds this behaviour and the consequent problems of obtaining confessions and corroboration.

Offender populations

In a survey of 68 imprisoned incest offenders, Hall Williams (1974) found that most had been sentenced to imprisonment for three years or more and that 25 per cent of his sample *had previous convictions for sexual offences*. In addition, 22 per cent had been concurrently charged with buggery, 27 per cent with unlawful sexual intercourse (USI), and 4 per cent with rape. The number and range of other sexual offences in his sample is of interest; they lend support to the findings of Abel *et al.* (1981) that some incest offenders may also have paedophilic characteristics. Gibbens, Way, and Soothill (1978) conducted a long-term comparative follow-up of sibling and parent-child incest offenders. Of the *fathers*, 61 per cent were first offenders, 12 per cent had subsequent convictions, and 13 per cent had prior convictions for sexual offences (a smaller number than that found by Hall Williams but his sample was an imprisoned group, whereas those studied by Gibbens, Way, and Soothill consisted of *all* cases dealt with by the higher courts for the period in question); 90 per cent of the *fathers* went to prison, whereas 74 per cent of the *brothers'* cases were dealt with by non-custodial penalties. Of the brothers, 54 per cent had previous convictions but few were for sexual crimes. During a twelve-year follow-up period, 49 per cent of the brothers were convicted for property offences and 14 per cent for violence. These results tend to support the view that brother-sister incest relationships are likely to occur in socially disorganized families, in which other anti-social behaviour is likely to be manifested.

Family characteristics and incest-promoting situations

Nearly all the studies into incestuous behaviour indicate disturbances of some kind or another in family relationships (see, for example, Lukianowicz 1972, Maisch 1973, Meiselman 1978, Canepa and Bandini 1980, Goodwin 1982, and Porter 1984). As most of these studies tend, inevitably, to report generalized conclusions, it is none the less as well to remember the need to examine each case individually. We should also remember the need to be on the alert for the collusion and denial I referred to in Chapter 4; in addition, it is not as uncommon as is sometimes supposed for children to make false accusations of incest. *The following may be a helpful classification of incest-promoting situations*:

(1) Incest taking place in large, overcrowded families. Participants may almost 'slip into' incestuous behaviour. In some cases, this tendency may be exacerbated by alcohol abuse and by the threat of, or use of, violence by the father or by an older brother (Virkunnen 1974). Such cases are more likely to occur where the family is geographically or socially isolated (Bluglass 1979).

(2) Incestuous relationships developing because of intellectual impairment or psychotic illness in either or both of the parties (the latter phenomenon would appear to be rare).

(3) The absence of the wife, through death or separation, which may lead the daughter(s) to take over the wife's sexual rôle as part of a wider attempt to provide comfort for the father. In other cases, the wife is present but has clearly abdicated her sexual rôle; in these instances, she appears to be quite

cognizant of what is occurring and colludes in the practice (Meiselman 1978, Dietz and Craft 1980).

(4) Families in which the father is a dominating, aggressive individual; he seduces the children in the full knowledge that such behaviour is wrong. There is no feeling of guilt on his part and each daughter may be seduced in turn as she becomes old enough to satisfy the father's desires. In these families, one also sometimes finds that the boys have been subjected to incestuous assault. The picture that emerges in these cases is one of gross family pathology.

(5) Families in which 'object fixation incest' occurs (Bagley 1969). In these cases, incest may occur where the dominant partner has been sexually fixated on an earlier object of sexual gratification, a child or an adolescent, with whom he had his first sexual experience. Such phenomena emphasize the harmful effects of the 'sexual games' referred to earlier in the context of paedophilia.

Management

Workers have to learn to overcome understandable feelings of repugnance (Hart 1979). The continued use of the word 'incest' is not helpful in this respect. It is, therefore, better to regard incest as part of a broader spectrum of sexual abuse of the young and as an offence emanating, in the main, from highly disturbed family relationships. Although imprisonment may be necessary in some cases (for example, those in my categories 1 and 4, above), the severe disruption caused to the family and the additional guilt engendered in the victim ('What have I done to dad?') must be set against what some people consider to be the need for condign punishment. In any event, there is a strong possibility that the father will wish to return to the family at some point and a period of prolonged incarceration only makes family rehabilitation that much more difficult. It might be more productive to effect the temporary removal of the father by means of a probation order with a requirement of residence, so that a phased plan of return to the family may be worked out by the appropriate authorities. Local authority social service departments and health authorities already have adequate provisions available under the child care legislation to safeguard (by speedy removal, if necessary) any child or young person who may be at risk. The aim should be to try to restore family functioning by means of individual, family, or group treatment, rather than to disrupt it further by the invocation of punitive and inflexible disposals.

There is evidence to suggest that family treatment approaches seem to offer the best hope of success (see, for example, Mrazek and Kempe 1981 and Porter (ed.) 1984), although the difficulties of such approaches should not be underestimated. It takes a great degree of skill and patience to enable families to talk about forbidden and guilt-laden behaviour. Those working in this field occasionally have the additional problem of having to report certain information —albeit received in confidence—to legal authorities. The result of this may be court action or the removal of the child or children from home. In California, interesting pioneering work indicates that in a number of cases prompt intervention by caring agencies may prevent the need for a court appearance, provided that the offender and his or her family are prepared to enter into a formal contract for treatment. This does not appear to be a 'soft option' but consists of a rigorous and demanding programme of social intervention. It also takes account of both *individual and family* needs and would seem to be suitable for all but the most grossly pathological situations I have outlined above (Giarretto 1981).

Rape

Appreciation of the real impact of rape on a woman has been much enhanced in recent years by the activities and advocacy of the Women's Movement, particularly by those women who have been active in establishing rape crisis and counselling centres. Convictions for rape and indecent assaults on females seem to remain fairly constant over the years. (It is recognized that a serious indecent assault may be as traumatic for the victim, in some cases, as rape or attempted rape.) Although recent changes in legislation have made it somewhat easier for women to report the offence to the police, often they remain reluctant to do so. As already indicated, rape almost always attracts a custodial penalty. As with those who commit serious sexual assaults on girls under thirteen, a considerable number of rapists tend to be reconvicted *a long time after their first convictions* (Soothill, Jack, and Gibbens 1976, Soothill and Gibbens 1978). It is also of interest to note that when serious sexual offenders and non-sexual offenders are compared psychometrically, the sex offenders are found to have greater problems in the area of self-control than non-sex offenders (Howells and Wright 1978). Numerous studies have examined the epidemiology of rape (see, for example, Amir 1971). Such studies tend to show that assailant and victim have often had prior contact, that the assault is often planned carefully (though exacerbated by alcohol), and that multiple rape is not uncommon. Amir concludes not only that the rôle of the victim has been neglected in the past but that the degree of brutality involved in some cases was found to be less serious than had been anticipated. Later research has tended to refute this latter finding. Wright (1980) found that in about 80 per cent of the cases he studied, some form of physical violence had been involved. This violence had less to do with *the sex act itself* than with the degree of threat or assault used in carrying out the rape. As Wright suggests, 'the attack might justifiably be seen as a life-threatening situation' (Wright 1980: 112).

THE LAW AND THE VICTIM

The historical background to the present law has been well documented (see Brownmiller 1975, Toner 1977, Honoré 1978). Under the provisions of the Sexual Offences (Amendment) Act of 1976, a man commits rape if:

(a) he has unlawful sexual intercourse with a woman who, at the time of intercourse, does not consent to it; and

(b) at that time knows that she does not consent to the intercourse or is reckless as to whether she consents to it.

The *Criminal Law Revision Committee* (1984) recommended that the offence of rape should remain substantially in its present form but that the common law presumption that a boy under fourteen be incapable of the offence should be abolished. They also recommended that it should be possible for a man to be prosecuted for raping his wife in situations where the two were not cohabiting with each other. The Committee was divided over whether the offence of rape should be extended to cases of non-consensual sexual intercourse within marriage. The Committee also recommended a continuation of the present procedure by which the anonymity of the *victim* is preserved but recommended that the present anonymity afforded to the defendant should be removed.

Reference has already been made to the under-reporting of rape incidents. When we consider that the victim has to go through the ordeal of a searching (and not always sympathetic) medical examination and police interrogation, such under-reporting is not surprising. This ordeal may be followed by an equally harrowing appearance in the witness box. In addition, some women are understandably very reluctant to report a serious sexual attack to their partners, other family members, or close friends. Despite changes in public attitudes and in the law, women are still likely to feel that others (particularly men) may say that 'there's no smoke without fire', or that 'she asked for it by walking alone or sleeping with her window open'. Women may suffer enormous anguish as a result of being raped. The physical sequelae, apart from vaginal and other injury that may have been caused, are very important. The attack may result in pregnancy, venereal disease, or genital herpes and this reality just compounds the feeling of having been defiled. These latter feelings may be so strong that some women compulsively scrub their genitalia with strong disinfectants long after the event. Skilled and sympathetic handling during the investigation *and after the attack* is vital. Fortunately, medical and police investigators are becoming more sensitive to the problem. Despite this, referral for rape crisis counselling can do much to lessen the more traumatic effects of the experience and is helpful not only to the victim but also to family and other close associates. There is now a substantial literature on this subject (for some examples, see Nadelson and Notman 1979, Holmes 1981, and Osborne 1982).

TYPOLOGIES OF RAPISTS

A number of difficulties arise in trying to classify rapists and their offences. This is because we are sometimes describing the offence by the nature of the behaviour displayed (for example, aggressive or over-inhibited), sometimes by the choice of victim (child or old person), and sometimes by the presence of other features, such as mental disorder. Two studies illustrate these problems. Gibbens, Way, and Soothill (1977) suggested three groupings:

(1) Paedophilic rapists—involving girls aged fourteen or under.
(2) Aggressive rapists; such offenders will often have committed other aggressive offences.
(3) Isolated rape offences. These would include incidents as diverse as those arising from mistaken consent to the highly pathological rape-murder.

Hall Williams (1977), studying a sample of imprisoned rapists, discerned four types:

(1) The extensively aggressive.
(2) A mixed aggressive group.
(3) Those who commit rape as a reaction to serious personal problems and/or stressful life situations.
(4) Essentially paedophilic types.

If we disregard, for a moment, those rapes that arise out of allegedly mistaken consent, we find that a key characteristic underlying or associated with most other rapes is anger or aggression. In most cases, rape is best regarded as a crime of extreme personal *violence* rather than as an offence aimed at achieving sexual satisfaction *per se*. For this reason, a classification proposed by Groth and Hobson (1983) is probably the most helpful. Their typology suggests three clear-cut but overlapping classes of rape:[2]

(1) *Anger Rape*—motivated by feeling 'put down' or by retribution for perceived wrongs.
(2) *Power Rape*—engaged in as a means of denying deep feelings of inadequacy and insecurity.
(3) *Sadistic Rape*—victims are usually complete strangers; they may be subjected to torture, bondage, and highly deviant sexual practices.

In the typology that follows I have attempted to deal with as wide a range of rape behaviours and motivations as possible; I acknowledge its rudimentary nature.

(1) (a) The normal, sexually virile young man 'out for what he can get'; his desire for sexual gratification is not counterbalanced by finer scruples or caution.

   (b) A sub-group consisting of mainly shy, younger men, trying to overcome their feelings of sexual inadequacy and clumsiness. They may well mistake their victim's responses for a 'come on'. Some of these offenders appear to be trying to compensate for a degree of latent homosexuality.

(2) A predominantly young group, who rape in group or packs ('gang-bangs'). They are likely to have previous convictions for violence and sex offences. They may engage in deviant sexual practices with their victims and subject them to other forms of defilement (such as urinating on them). Some of them may belong to gangs such as 'Hell's Angels'. A number of these rape activities tend to originate in the dynamics of youthful gang behaviour; unlike some of the following typologies, they are not characterized, in the main, by marked personal pathology (Wright and West 1981).

(3) The sexually violent and aggressive. These rapists have records of other forms of violence and abuse of alcohol. (See Chapter 7.) Alcohol may be ingested in the mistaken belief that it will heighten sexual capacity.

(4) Those rapists who are found to be suffering from a definable form of mental disorder, such as psychosis, brain disease, or mental impairment. Such cases are comparatively rare. The grossly psychotic rapist is likely to be detained in a Special Hospital.

(5) The severely sexually maladjusted rapist. These include those who need to gain reassurance for their masculinity through a show of force. They would include Groth and Hobson's categories 1 and 3. Such rapists have also been described by West, Roy, and Nichols (1978). These offenders are likely to force their victims to engage in deviant sexual activities (for example, buggery and oral sex), or to

subject them to repeated acts of intercourse. This group will also contain a proportion who are Groth and Hobson's sadistic rapists. These offenders obtain sexual pleasure from their sadistic activities (true sadists) and they may need the resistance of their victims to arouse their potency. Some of these may commit sexual murder (see next section).

MANAGEMENT

Much of what was said earlier about the management of paedophilia applies to rape. The formulation of some kind of typology based upon in-depth assessment will afford clues as to the most appropriate form of management. Some type of brief counselling or training in sexual and social skills may be of help with groups 1a and 1b. Those in group 2 may outgrow their unpleasant proclivities but they may also need to be removed from circulation for a time, both for the protection of society and for the development of their consciences. Those in group 3 may respond to measures that are aimed at improving their life-styles and at helping them with their drinking problems. Those in group 4 may well respond to efforts aimed at treating their underlying mental disorder. Cox (1980) has described some of the valuable work being done in a Special Hospital setting. Those in group 5 are much harder to manage; however, intensive group psychotherapy during long-term incarceration has been shown to have some degree of success (West, Roy, and Nichols 1978). Some success with programmes designed to develop social competence and to modify deviant sexual preferences (by means of behaviour modification) has been reported, though long-term follow-up results are not yet available (Marshall and Barbaree 1984). The use of hormonal and allied treatments has already been referred to in the discussion of paedophilia.

No *one* form of management is likely to be effective. In this field, it is highly dangerous to espouse with Messianic enthusiasm any one theory or treatment model. A multi-disciplinary approach, based upon a full assessment of the personal and situational factors in the rapist's life is essential.

Sexual murder and some associated matters

Sexual murder is, fortunately, a rare event.[3] As I have pointed
out elsewhere in this book, however, it is sometimes very
difficult to determine whether such a killing has occurred as a
result of the pursuit of sadistic pleasure, as a means of keeping
the victim quiet (or unable to give evidence), or as a result of an
unintentional act of violence that has become lethal during some
form of sexual activity (for example, it is possible for manual
strangulation to occur during some forms of anal intercourse).
West (1983a) suggests that certain groups of individuals may be
especially vulnerable to sexual murders: children because of
their physical vulnerability, prostitutes, and promiscuous male
homosexuals. (See also Rupp 1970.) Gibson and Klein (1969)
estimated that there were 10–12 sex-related murders in any one
year, out of a total of something like 500 or more murders known
to the police. In a leading article in the *British Medical Journal*
(1966), it was suggested that there were about 4 sexual murders
of *children* per year in a UK population of over 50 million.
Despite the apparent rarity of these events, it is important to
stress that some of the more disturbed and highly deviant sexual
offenders whom I have already described may go on to commit a
sexual murder, particularly the sadistic rapist.

The motivation for sexual murder may be very complex.
Hyatt Williams (1964) stresses the manner in which different
facets of the sexual murderer's personality may seem to be out of
touch with each other. He indicates that kindness and compassion can co-exist with a high degree of cruelty and savage
destructiveness; rather akin to the 'hysterical' splitting-off that I
described in Chapter 4. Such pathological phenomena are
well illustrated by Cox (1979) in his reference to the sadistic
sexual murder of the King in Marlowe's play, *Edward II*. The
illustration concerns the use of the red-hot spit that was used to
penetrate the King anally and eventually to kill him. The spit is
used in combination with a table to stamp on him, 'But not too
hard, lest that you bruise his body' (Cox 1979: 310). This
quotation is redolent of the jarring incompatabilities suggested
by Hyatt Williams.

In an important paper, Brittain (1970) provides a graphic
composite picture of the sadistic sexual murderer. It is impor-

tant to emphasize that Brittain suggests a *composite* picture and that one would not expect to find all the many features he describes in any one case. I have selected a few of them. One finds that such killers are often withdrawn, introverted, over-controlled, and even timid individuals. Some are even prudish and take offence at the telling of 'dirty jokes'. The killer is likely to be thirty years old or older and may come from any occupational status; a surprising number have worked in the butchery trade or been employed in abattoirs (on links between murder and occupation, see Chapter 4). Sexual murderers often seem to be remarkably ambivalent towards their mothers—the devoted son on the one hand and the mother-hater on the other. In other words, their personalities show a mass of contradictions, with many unresolved earlier psychological conflicts. The mothers of such killers tend to be gentle and over-indulgent, whilst the fathers are often rigidly strict or absent. Such murderers often have an active and bizarre phantasy life but, as we saw in Chapter 4, its prognostic significance is often very hard to evaluate. Such phantasies may be enhanced by a preoccupation with violent and sadistic pornography. Such persons are likely to show a marked interest in torture and atrocities, Nazi activities, black magic, and horror films. They also tend to be unreasonably preoccupied with the size of their genitalia and their sex lives are often poor or non-existent. The murder may be planned over several weeks or even months and these offenders appear quite lacking in remorse for the appalling injuries and suffering they inflict. Indeed, as suggested earlier, the sight of their helpless victims may well serve to add to their sexual frenzy. Asphyxia is a common method of sadistic sexual killing since by this means the victim's suffering may be prolonged. (He or she may be rendered unconscious by strangulation, brought round, rendered unconscious again, and so on). Sexual intercourse, or for that matter any sexual activity, may not necessarily accompany the murder. Schlesinger and Revitch suggest that 'the brutal and murderous assaults actually are a substitute for the sexual act in many cases of sexual brutality and murder' (Schlesinger and Revitch 1983: 214). These offenders may also insert objects (such as a torch, milk bottle, or poker) with great force into the victim's rectum or vagina. The prognosis for such offenders is not good. Those in charge of them and who share the responsibility for making recommendations about future dangerousness have to guard against being misled by *appearances* of good behaviour and apparently sincere protestations of reform. Revitch has said that 'many of these cases have a tendency to repeat aggression . . . even after years of imprisonment' (Revitch 1980: 10). On the other hand, a proportion of these offenders do show a desire to be controlled because they are frightened of their sadistic impulses and activities and are grateful for the containment provided by prison or Special Hospital.

NECROPHILIA AND AUTO-EROTIC FATALITY

Although the sexual molestation of corpses is not common, it is appropriate to say a word or two about it in trying to give a reasonably comprehensive review of the varieties of sexual assault. Molestation of corpses (necrophilia) is defined in a variety of ways. Some take it to cover *any* interference with a corpse, others limit it to *sexual* molestation, and others subsume it under the general heading of vampirism (Prins 1984). In a recently reported case, a man received four years' imprisonment for mutilating corpses. When his house was searched, police found a photograph of a man's severed genitals. He admitted mutilating three bodies and told the police that he had nursed a phantasy for a long time about cutting off male genitalia (*Guardian* 27 March, 1985). It is not surprising that necrophilia appears to be an uncommon phenomenon, by its very nature: its perpetration is likely to be highly secret and there is no victim to complain. Those who commit such offences are likely to be grossly disordered personalities, though there may be no formal mental illness or mental disorder such as to satisfy the mental health legislation. It has been suggested that some occupations, such as those of mortuary attendant or undertaker, may lend themselves to those motivated to necrophilic activities. The possible aetiology of such behaviour and the characteristics of those who indulge in it are discussed briefly by Bartholomew, Milte, and Galbally (1978), Lancaster (1978), and more fully by Smith and Dimock (1983).

Finally, I make brief reference to some circumstances in which deviant sexual activity may result in the death of the deviant himself. Death may occur as a result of deviant auto-erotic practices, if these are combined with the inhalation of substances such as solvents; death has also occurred from accidental electrocution (Knight 1979, Sivaloganathan 1981). Coroners' inquests occasionally indicate that death may have occurred during bondage or hanging activities. In the latter case, it is sometimes difficult to determine to what extent the fatality has occurred as a result of an auto-erotic practice that has gone badly wrong, or has been a suicide or para-suicide. There seems to be good reason to conclude that such activities may be more common than we realize (see Resnik 1983).

Conclusions

I would emphasize the need for us to recognize our prejudices and aim to respond as dispassionately as possible to what is certainly sometimes bizarre and sickening behaviour. The capacity to listen and respond non-judgementally in such cases is crucial for any success, irrespective of the treatment modality employed. Despite some appearances to the contrary, a number of serious sexual offenders are distressed and disturbed by their behaviour and its effects upon others. Only when they find a dispassionate and compassionate recipient for their feelings can they begin to unburden themselves and ease some of the tensions and conflicts that may have contributed to their offending. Workers in this field have a professional obligation not only to make themselves as well informed as possible but also to recognize that it is only by sharing the task with professionals in other disciplines that any real success will be achieved.

References

Abel, G.G., Becker, J.V., and Cunningham-Rathner, J. (1984) Perspectives on Paedophilia (2): Complications, Consent, and Cognitions in Sex Between Children and Adults. *International Journal of Law and Psychiatry* **7**: 89–103.

Abel, G.G., Becker, J.V., Murphy, W.D., and Flanagan, B. (1981) Identifying Dangerous Child Molesters. In R.B. Stuart (ed.) *Violent Behaviour: Social Learning Approaches to Prediction, Management and Treatment*. New York: Brunner Mazel.

Adams, M.S. and Neal, J.V. (1967) Children of Incest. *Paediatrics* **40**: 55–62.

Amir, M. (1971) *Patterns in Forcible Rape*. Chicago: Chicago University Press.

Awad, G.A., Saunders, E., and Levene, J. (1984) A Clinical Study of Male Adolescent Sexual Offenders. *International Journal of Offender Therapy and Comparative Criminology* **28**: 105–15.

Bagley, C. (1969) The Varieties of Incest. *New Society* 21 August: 280–82.

Bartholomew, A.A., Milte, K.L., and Galbally, F. (1978) Homosexual Necrophilia. *Medicine, Science and the Law* **18**: 29–35.

Bender, R. (1977) Problem Child or Problem Family? *Social Work Today* **8**: 7–9.

Bluglass, R. (1979) Incest. *British Journal of Hospital Medicine* **August**: 152–57.

—— (1982) Assessing Dangerous Sex Offenders. In J.R. Hamilton and H. Freeman (eds) *Dangerousness: Psychiatric Assessment and Management*. London: Gaskell. (For Royal College of Psychiatrists.)

British Medical Journal (1966) Leader. **i**: 626.

Brittain, R.P. (1970) The Sadistic Murderer. *Medicine, Science and the Law* **10**: 198–208.

Brodsky, S.L. (1980) Understanding and Treating Sexual Offenders. *Howard Journal* **XIX**: 102–15.

Brongersma, E. (1984) Perspectives on Pedophilia. 1: Aggression Against Pedophiles. *International Journal of Law and Psychiatry* **7**: 79–88.

Brownmiller, S. (1975) *Against Our Will: Men, Women and Rape*. London: Secker and Warburg.

Canepa, G. and Bandini, T. (1980) Incest and Family Dynamics: A Clinical Study. *International Journal of Law and Psychiatry* **3**: 453–60.

Cohen, M. (1977) Uncovering Sexual Problems. *Canadian Family Physician* **23**: 69–72.

Cox, M. (1979) Dynamic Psychotherapy with Sex Offenders. In I. Rosen (ed.) *Sexual Deviation* (second edition). Oxford: Oxford University Press.

—— (1980) Personal Reflections upon 3,000 Hours in Therapeutic Groups with Sex Offenders. In D.J. West (ed.) *Sex Offenders in the Criminal Justice System*. Cambridge: Institute of Criminology.

Crawford, D.A. (1981) Treatment Approaches With Pedophiles. In M. Cook and K. Howells (eds) *Adult Sexual Interest in Children*. London: Academic.

—— (1982) Problems for the Assessment and Treatment of Sexual Offenders in Closed Institutions. In D.A. Black (ed.) *Symposium: Broadmoor Psychology Department's 21st Birthday*. Issues in Criminological and Legal Psychology No. 2. Leicester: British Psychological Society.

Crawford, D.A. and Allen, J.V. (1979) A Social Skills Programme With Sex Offenders. In M. Cook and G. Wilson (eds) *Love and Attraction*. Oxford: Pergamon.

Criminal Law Revision Committee (1984) *Fifteenth Report: Sexual Offences*. Cmnd. 9213. London: HMSO.

Dietz, C.A. and Craft, J.L. (1980) Family Dynamics of Incest: A New Perspective. *Social Casework* **61 (December)**: 602–09.

Earls, C.M. (1983) Some Issues in the Assessment of Sexual Deviance. *International Journal of Law and Psychiatry* **6**: 431–41.

Elliott, M. (1985) *Preventing Child Sexual Assault*. London: Bedford Square Press.

Finkelhor, D. (1979) *Sexually Victimized Children*. New York: Free Press.

Ford, C.S. and Beach, F.A. (1965) *Patterns of Sexual Behaviour*. London: Methuen.

Giarretto, H. (1981) A Comprehensive Child Sex Abuse Programme. In P.B. Mrazek and C.H. Kempe (eds) *Sexually Abused Children and their Families*. Oxford: Pergamon.

Gibbens, T.C.N., Soothill, K.L., and Way, C. (1981) Sex Offences Against Young Girls: A Long-Term Record Study. *Psychological Medicine* **11**: 351–57.

Gibbens, T.C.N., Way, C., and Soothill, K.L. (1977) Behavioural Types of Rape. *British Journal of Psychiatry* **130**: 32–42.

—— (1978) Sibling and Parent-Child Incest Offenders. *British Journal of Criminology* **18**: 40–52.

Gibson, E. and Klein, S. (1969) *Murder, 1957–1968*. Home Office Research Studies No. 3. London: HMSO.

Goodman, R.E. (1983) Biology and Sexuality: Inborn Determinants of Human Sexual Response. *British Journal of Psychiatry* **143**: 216–20.

Goodwin, J. (1982) *Sexual Abuse: Incest Victims and their Families*. Boston: John Wright.

Groth, A.N. (1979) Sexual Trauma in the Life of Rapists and Child Molesters. *Victimology* **4**: 10–16.

Groth, A.N. and Hobson, W.F. (1983) The Dynamics of Sexual Assault. In L.B. Schlesinger and E. Revitch (eds) *Sexual Dynamics of Anti-Social Behaviour*. Illinois: Charles C Thomas.

Gunn, J. (1976) Sexual Offenders. *British Journal of Hospital Medicine* **January**: 57–65.

Hall Williams, J.E. (1974) The Neglect of Incest: A Criminologist's View. *Medicine, Science and the Law* **14**: 64–7.

—— (1977) Serious Heterosexual Attack. *Medicine, Science and the Law* **17**: 140–46.

Hart, J. (1979) *Social Work and Sexual Conduct*. London: Routledge and Kegan Paul.

Holmes, K.A. (1981) Services for Victims of Rape: A Dualistic Practice Model. *Social Casework* **62 (January)**: 30–9.

Home Office (1984) *Criminal Statistics, England and Wales, 1983: Statistics Relating to Crime and Criminal Proceedings for the Year 1983*. Cmnd. 9349. London: HMSO.

Honoré, T. (1978) *Sex Law*. London: Duckworth.

Howells, K. and Wright, R. (1978) The Sexual Attitudes of Aggressive Sexual Offenders. *British Journal of Criminology* **18**: 170–74.

Hyatt Williams, A. (1964) The Psychopathology and Treatment of Sexual Murderers. In I. Rosen (ed.) *The Pathology and Treatment of Sexual Deviation*. London: Oxford University Press.

Ingram, M. (1979) The Participating Victim: A Study of Sexual Offences Against Pre-Pubertal Boys. In M. Cook and G. Wilson (eds) *Love and Attraction*. Oxford: Pergamon.

Kinsey, A.C., Pomeroy, W.B., and Martin, C.E. (1948) *Sexual Behaviour in the Human Male*. London: W.B. Saunders.

Kinsey, A.C., Pomeroy, W.B., Martin, C.E., and Gebhard, P.M. (1953) *Sexual Behaviour in the Human Female*. London: W.B. Saunders.

Knight, B. (1979) Fatal Masochism: Accident or Suicide? *Medicine, Science and the Law* **19**: 118–20.

Kraemer, W. (ed.) (1976) *The Forbidden Love: The Normal and Abnormal Love of Children*. London: Sheldon.

Lancaster, N.P. (1978) Necrophilia, Murder and High Intelligence. *British Journal of Psychiatry* **132**: 605–08.

Longo, R.E. (1982) Sexual Learning and Experience Among Adolescent Sexual Offenders. *International Journal of Offender Therapy and Comparative Criminology* **26**: 235–41.

Longo, R.E. and Groth, A.N. (1983) Juvenile Sexual Offences in the Histories of Adult Rapists and Child Molesters. *International Journal of Offender Therapy and Comparative Criminology* **27**: 150–55.

Lukianowicz, N. (1972) Incest: (i) Paternal Incest (ii) Other Types of Incest. *British Journal of Psychiatry* **120**: 301–13.

MacCulloch, M. and Waddington, J.L. (1981) Neuroendocrine Mechanisms and the Aetiology of Male and Female Homosexuality. *British Journal of Psychiatry* **139**: 341–45.

Maisch, H. (1973) *Incest*. London: André Deutsch.

Margolin, K. (1984) Group Therapy as a Means of Learning About the Sexually Assaultive Adolescent. *International Journal of Offender Therapy and Comparative Criminology* **28**: 65–72.

Marshall, W. and Barbaree, H.E. (1984) A Behavioural View of Rape. *International Journal of Law and Psychiatry* **7**: 51–77.

Masters, W.H. and Johnson, V. (1966) *Human Sexual Response*. New York: Little Brown.

88

Meiselman, K. (1978) *Incest: A Psychological Study of Causes and Effects with Treatment Recommendations*. San Francisco: Jossey Bass.

Morneau, R.H. and Rockwell, R.R. (1980) *Sex, Motivation, and the Criminal Offender*. Illinois: Charles C Thomas.

Mrazek, P.B. and Kempe, C.H. (eds) (1981) *Sexually Abused Children and their Families*. Oxford: Pergamon.

Nadelson, C.C. and Notman, M.T. (1979) Psychoanalytic Considerations of the Response to Rape. *International Review of Psychoanalysis* **6**: 97–103.

Nakashima, I.I. and Zakus, G.E. (1977) Incest: Review and Clinical Experience. *Paediatrics for the Clinician* **60**: 676–701.

Ortmann, J. (1980) The Treatment of Sexual Offenders: Castration and Anti-Hormone Therapy. *International Journal of Law and Psychiatry* **3**: 443–52.

Osborne, K. (1982) Sexual Violence. In P. Feldman (ed.) *Developments in the Study of Criminal Behaviour, Volume II: Violence*. Chichester: Wiley.

Perkins, D. (1983) Assessment and Treatment of Dangerous Sexual Offenders. In J.W. Hinton (ed.) *Dangerousness: Problems of Assessment and Prediction*. London: Allen and Unwin.

Porter, R. (ed.) (1984) *Sexual Abuse Within the Family*. CIBA Foundation. London: Tavistock.

Prins, H. (1984) Vampirism—Legendary or Clinical Phenomenon? *Medicine, Science and the Law* **24**: 283–93.

Resnik, H.L.P. (1983) Erotized Repetitive Hangings. In L.B. Schlesinger and E. Revitch (eds) *Sexual Dynamics of Anti-Social Behaviour*. Illinois: Charles C Thomas.

Revitch, E. (1980) Gynocide and Unprovoked Attacks on Women. *Corrective and Social Psychiatry and Journal of Behaviour Technology, Methods and Therapy* **26**: 6–11.

—— (1983) Burglaries With Sexual Dynamics. In L.B. Schlesinger and E. Revitch (eds) *Sexual Dynamics of Anti-Social Behaviour*. Illinois: Charles C Thomas.

Roberts, D.F. (1967) Incest: Inbreeding and Mental Abilities. *British Medical Journal* **4**: 336.

Rupp, J.C. (1970) Sudden Death in the Gay World. *Medicine, Science and the Law* **10**: 189–91.

Sccaco, A.M. (1975) *Rape in Prison*. Illinois: Charles C Thomas.

—— (ed.) (1982) *Male Rape: A Casebook of Sexual Aggressions*. New York: AMS.

Schlesinger, L.B. and Revitch, E. (1983) Sexual Dynamics in Homicide and Assault. In L.B. Schlesinger and E. Revitch (eds) *Sexual Dynamics of Anti-Social Behaviour*. Illinois: Charles C Thomas.

Shaw, R. (1978a) The Persistent Sexual Offender—Control and Rehabilitation. *Probation Journal* **25**: 9–13.

—— (1978b) The Persistent Sexual Offender—Control and Rehabilitation: A Follow-Up. *Probation Journal* **25**: 61–3.

Shepherd, E. (1982) Assessing Dangerousness in Mentally Subnormal Patients. In J.R. Hamilton and H. Freeman (eds) *Dangerousness: Psychiatric Assessment and Management*. London: Gaskell. (For Royal College of Psychiatrists.)

Sivaloganathan, S. (1981) Curiosum Eroticum—A Case of Fatal Electrocution During Auto-Erotic Practice. *Medicine, Science and the Law* **21**: 47–50.

Smith, S. and Dimock, J. (1983) Necrophilia and Anti-Social Acts. In L.B. Schlesinger and E. Revitch (eds) *Sexual Dynamics of Anti-Social Behaviour*. Illinois: Charles C Thomas.

Soothill, K. L., and Gibbens, T.C.N. (1978) Recidivism of Sexual Offenders: A Reappraisal. *British Journal of Criminology* **18**: 267–76.

Soothill, K.L., Jack, A., and Gibbens, T.C.N. (1976) Rape: A 22-Year Cohort Study. *Medicine, Science and the Law* **16**: 62–9.

Toner, B. (1977) *The Facts of Rape*. London: Arrow.

Tsai, M. and Wagner, N.N. (1978) Therapy Groups of Women Sexually Molested as Children. *Archives of Sexual Behaviour* **7**: 417–27.

Virkunnen, M. (1974) Incest Offences and Alcoholism. *Medicine, Science and the Law* **14**: 124–28.

—— (1975) Victim Precipitated Pedophilia Offences. *British Journal of Criminology* **15**: 175–80.

Walmsley, R. (1984) Recorded Incidence and Sentencing Practice For Sexual Offences. In M. and A. Craft (eds) *Mentally Abnormal Offenders*. London: Baillière Tindall.

Walmsley, R. and White, K. (1979) *Sexual Offences, Consent and Sentencing*. Home Office Research Study No. 54. London: HMSO.

Weaver, C. and Fox, C. (1984) The Berkeley Sex Offenders Group: A Seven-Year Evaluation. *Probation Journal* **31**: 143–46.

West, D.J. (1983a) Sex Offences and Offending. In M. Tonry and N. Morris (eds) *Crime and Justice: An Annual Review of Research, Volume V*. Chicago: Chicago University Press.

—— (1983b) Homosexuality and Lesbianism. *British Journal of Psychiatry* **143**: 221–26.

West, D.J., Roy, C., and Nichols, F.L. (1978) *Understanding Sexual Attacks*. London: Heinemann.

Wolff, C. (1977) *Bisexuality: A Study*. London: Quartet.

Wright, R. (1980) Rape and Physical Violence. In D.J. West (ed.) *Sex Offenders in the Criminal Justice System*. Cambridge: Institute of Criminology.

Wright, R. and West, D.J. (1981) Rape—A Comparison of Group Offences and Lone Assaults. *Medicine, Science and the Law* **22**: 25–30.
Zuger, B. (1980) Homosexuality and Parental Guilt. *British Journal of Psychiatry* **137**: 55–7.

FURTHER READING

General works:

Gunn, J. (ed.) (1976) *Sex Offenders—A Symposium*. Special Hospitals Research Report No. 14. London: DHSS.
Howard League for Penal Reform (1985) *Unlawful Sex: Report of a Working Party*. A useful and concise summary of current thinking and practice concerning the problems presented by sexual offenders. London: Waterlow.
Krafft-Ebing, R. von (1978) *Psychopathia Sexualis*. Although now rather 'dated', this book is a useful illustration of the way in which thinking about sexual deviation has developed and changed. New York: Scarborough.
Morneau, R.H. (1983) *Sex Crimes Investigation: A Major Case Approach*. Although primarily written for police officers, this work contains interesting and useful material concerning the need to ascertain the facts about, and motivation for, offences as thoroughly as possible. Illinois: Charles C Thomas.
Parker, T. (1970) *The Twisting Lane: Some Sex Offenders*. A useful biographical account of some imprisoned sex offenders. London: Panther.
Priestley, R. (1980) *Community of Scapegoats: The Segregation of Sex Offenders*. A small-scale, in-depth study of the impact of imprisonment on sex offenders and on their custodians. Oxford: Pergamon.

On sexual variation:

Ettorre, E.M. (1980) *Lesbianism, Women and Society*. London: Routledge and Kegan Paul.
Gosselin, C. and Wilson, G. (1980) *Sexual Variations: Fetishism, Transvestism and Sado-Masochism*. London: Faber and Faber.
Marmoor, J. (ed.) (1980) *Homosexual Behaviour: A Modern Reappraisal*. Especially Part III. New York: Basic Books.
Masters, W.H. and Johnson, V.E. (1982) *Homosexuality in Perspective*. Toronto: Bantam.

On sexual abuse of the young and incest:

Forward, S. and Buck, C. (1981) *Betrayal of Innocence: Incest and Its Devastation.* Harmondsworth: Penguin.

Morris, M. (1983) *If I Should Die Before I Wake.* A novel about incest. London: Souvenir.

Schultz, L.G. (ed.) (1980) *The Sexual Victimology of Youth.* A useful over-view of the subject. Illinois: Charles C Thomas.

Taylor, B. (ed.) (1981) *Perspectives on Paedophilia.* London: Batsford.

On rape

McCahill, T.W., Meyer, L.C., and Fischmen, A.M. (1981) *The Aftermath of Rape.* Toronto: Lexington.

Macdonald, J.M. (1975) *Rape: Offenders and Their Victims.* Illinois: Charles C Thomas.

Schultz, L.G. (ed.) (1975) *Rape Victimology.* Illinois: Charles C Thomas.

Notes

1 The usual technique is to present tapes and/or slides of various sexual activities whilst measuring the degree to which the person is sexually aroused.

2 The authors also list ten key areas under each of the three headings. They are useful in making a differential diagnosis and readers should consult them, and the authors' discussion, for further details.

3 I am not including here the *crime passionnel*, or murder committed as a result of pathological (sexual) jealousy. Certain aspects of these offences were discussed in Chapter 4.

CHAPTER SEVEN

Alcohol, drugs, other substances, and dangerous behaviour

'*Macduff* What three things does drink especially provoke?
Porter Marry, sir . . . it provokes and it un-
provokes; it provokes the desire, but it
takes away the performance: therefore, much drink may be said to be an
equivocator with lechery.'

SHAKESPEARE
Macbeth Act II, scene iii

At various points in this book, particularly in Chapters 2 and 4, reference has been made to the relationship between alcohol, other drugs, and serious offending. This included some discussion of the effects of such compounds upon criminal responsibility and the way in which they might affect an individual's recollection of events. We must now consider these relationships in a little more detail. In doing so, it is useful to consider alcohol and other drugs separately; such separation is to some extent arbitrary, since, apart from other overlaps, an offender may well have ingested both substances. I shall also make a few comments upon the growing social problem of the abuse of solvents and similar substances.

Alcohol

Those readers wishing to update their knowledge of attitudes to alcohol abuse and of the various treatment approaches now in vogue should consult the texts listed at the end of this chapter. A few general observations are in order here, however, before I proceed to more specific aspects. Alcohol and the problems it may cause must be studied from a variety of perspectives. These will include those of psychiatry, psychology, pharmacology, social policy, economics, and social ethics. Two major viewpoints tend to dominate much of our thinking in this area. On the one hand, there is the view that alcohol abuse is a form of weakness and a sign of moral turpitude (the moral stance); on the other, there is the view that the problem is solely one of illness and is thus susceptible to treatment (the medical stance). Both views have elements of truth in them, but both are over-simplifications of a complex problem. These two stances also reflect a fundamental underlying ambivalence. It is said that alcohol indulgence is bad yet we cheerfully and indiscriminately advertise its benefits as a boost to self-esteem and personal attractiveness. Society's ambivalence is further demonstrated by the government's promotion of warnings as to its hazards, on the one hand, and receipt of vast tax revenues each year through sales of alcohol, on the other. As one example of the problem, it is interesting to note the situation in Scotland. It has been suggested that during the past thirty years, the doubling of alcohol consumption has resulted in a dramatic increase in the number of car crashes, murders, fire deaths, and attempted suicides. Though this may be a somewhat sweeping statement and difficult to prove in terms of exact causal connections, it does give some idea of the possible harmful effects of alcohol on various facets of social life (*Guardian* 27 March, 1985).

As is the case with mental disorder, the relationship between alcohol and crime in general is somewhat equivocal. (For a general overview see Roslund and Larson 1979, Prins 1982, and Murphy 1983; for a detailed analysis of the evidence from research studies, see Collins 1982, Chapter 8.) Five groupings of alcohol related offences may be discerned:

(1) Serious offences against persons or property due directly or extremely closely to the effects of alcohol.
(2) Other, less serious, offences against persons or property.
(3) Offences against the Road Safety and Road Traffic Acts.
(4) Offences committed in order to obtain supplies of alcohol (for example, theft or deception).
(5) Offences of habitual drunkenness ('public order' offences).

In this chapter I am concerned only with those offences in category 1.

The controversy concerning the effects of alcohol on behaviour, particularly violent and potentially dangerous behaviour, is well illustrated in the remarks of Shakespeare's Porter quoted at the beginning of this chapter; he makes an important point concerning the relationship between ingestion of alcohol and sexual activity, when he says that 'it provokes the desire, but it takes away the performance'. Shakespeare knew as well as does any good psycho-physiologist something of the effects of alcohol indulgence upon the central nervous system. Contrary to general assumption, alcohol—though often described as a stimulant (its short-term psychological effect)—does not, in fact, stimulate the higher centres of the brain but actually *depresses* them. In particular, it has a depressant effect upon those brain centres concerned with the regulation of insight, conduct, and fine judgement. By a progressive process, basic emotional control deteriorates and this is likely to be accompanied by an alteration in conduct (Paul 1975). In cases of serious crime, there is certainly abundant anecdotal evidence to show an apparently clear causal relationship. In homicide cases, alcohol appears to play a significant part in a very high proportion of cases and it is of interest to note that this applies to victims as well as to aggressors (see, for example, Gillies 1965).

As Pernanen (1982) has recently pointed out, the relationship between alcohol and violence may be quite complex. In the first place, although the disinhibiting effects of alcohol are well known, they have to be seen within the context of culture and social milieu, since these have a marked effect upon how people behave when 'in drink'. Second, indulgence in alcohol and offending may be viewed as behaviours arising from the same underlying cause, such as insecurity as a result of social and emotional deprivation. Third, there is the view that alcohol is just one of a number of factors that might increase the probability of serious crime; for example, the admixture of such factors as alcohol, youthful company, provocative music, and a degree of overcrowding might all mutually reinforce each other to increase the risk of violence. The effect of drink on the victim as a possible precipitator of the outburst would also have to be assessed (Murphy 1983). Fourth, there is the view that the relationship between alcohol and violent offending is only true in a statistical sense. Thus, as Murphy suggests, this would 'explain fights in public houses, for example, by reference only to the gathering of young male adults, the alcohol being consumed being incidental to the violence' (Murphy 1983: 8). It is, therefore, apparent that we must be cautious about suggesting definite causal links, when in fact apparent links may be highly dubious. There are, however, *some* cases or situations where there do appear to be reasonably clear-cut correlations:

(1) Spencer (1984: 88) describes a condition he calls 'chronic sozzling'. Such a state can produce brain damage, which may render an offender particularly liable to erupt into violent behaviour. It is important to emphasize again that 'the disinhibiting effects of alcohol may release suppressed feelings of aggression and hostility. Numerous investigations have associated intoxication with violence' (Royal College of Psychiatrists 1979: 34).

(2) Some offenders suffer from psychotic disorders, such as schizophrenia. In such cases, the offender may be deeply troubled by delusions and hallucinations; chronic drinking may be used to 'drown the voices'. Such illnesses, exacerbated by alcohol and/or a mixture of alcohol and medication taken to treat the illness, may lead to an outburst of unprovoked and unpredictable violence. It is obvious that a very careful history of the antecedent events in the individual's life is vitally important.

(3) There are rare instances where alcohol (even if taken in very small amounts) may exacerbate a pre-existing medical and/or physical condition. Cowen and Muller (1979) cite the case of a man with an XYY chromosomal endowment (see Chapter 4), who also suffered from cardiac problems. These difficulties were much exacerbated by alcohol. In the course of some of his aggressive outbursts, he committed serious arson offences and received a long sentence of imprisonment.

(4) In other cases, clinical experience suggests that the ingestion of even quite small amounts of alcohol may be sufficient to provoke a very violent outburst in an individual who suffers from some underlying neurological disorder. This is

highly likely to be the case if the individual has suffered from brain damage, head injury, or some form of epilepsy (see Lishman 1978 and Öjesö 1983). As with psychotic illness, the condition may be made worse if the individual mixes alcohol with the medication prescribed for the neurological disorder.

(5) There is a small group of individuals who habitually consume near-lethal 'cocktails of alcohol' and other drugs, sometimes with disastrous consequences. Some of these situations were referred to in Chapter 2.

We may conclude this brief discussion with a newspaper account of a tragic case of homicide, in which drink clearly played a very important part. This concerns the case of a previously convicted and sentenced murderer who, at the age of fifty-six, strangled a young chambermaid. He had recently been released from his previous life sentence; this had been imposed for murdering an elderly widow. He had been described as a 'model prisoner' (though presumably with no access to drink). His defending counsel stated that the defendant was 'a different man when he had been drinking'. His second victim, aged twenty-three, is alleged to have taunted him following sexual intercourse, telling him he was an 'old man'. The accused is alleged to have said: 'This upset me. I lost control and grabbed her by the throat.' The victim's body had been found the day after the accused had been taken to hospital suffering from alcoholic poisoning and exposure. Defence counsel stated that 'the tragedy is that he is two people—one when he has taken drink and one when he has not' (*Guardian* 19 March, 1980).

Drugs and other compounds

'How use doth breed a habit in a man!'
SHAKESPEARE
Two Gentlemen of Verona Act V, scene iv

It is as well to remember that the abuse of and addiction to drugs have been present in society for generations. Preoccupation with what appears to be a current increase in the problem must be seen against the same kind of ambivalence that we saw in the case of alcohol. We live in a society in which we rely far too heavily on 'pills' for almost every conceivable complaint. Advances in modern medicine and medical technology make reliance on drugs commonplace and it is all too easy to become 'hooked' on many of them. I refer, of course, to therapeutic drugs, as distinct from mainly non-therapeutic compounds. The situation is not eased by the pressure on our health services, which leads medical practitioners into the temptation of over-prescribing for ills that they cannot, or feel they have no time to, cure—namely, the large number of emotional and psychological complaints that find their way so often to the general practitioner and rather less frequently to the hospital doctor. How easy to 'push' the prescription pad and what a facilitating prelude to another kind of 'pushing', with which we have sadly become all too familiar. There are two important elements to be borne in mind in any discussion of drug-related problems. First, the *compulsive* need to continue to take drugs and to obtain supplies by any means, however unlawful. Second, the grave social and psychological repercussions for the individual and for society. Almost any compound may be abused and many are. When discussing drug-related problems, however, it is usual to refer only to those drugs that are commonly described as drugs of abuse. Readers may wish to be reminded that these are as follows:

(1) *Opiates* (for example, heroin and morphine).
(2) *Stimulants* (amphetamines and cocaine).
(3) *Major tranquillizers* (for example, the benzodiazepenes).
(4) *Sedatives and hypnotics* (for example, the barbiturates).
(5) *Hallucinogens* (LSD—lysergic acid diethylamide—and cannabis). (Home Office 1985)

It is not my intention to review the addictive properties and short- and long-term effects of these drugs (for a brief review, see Prins 1980 and the recommended further reading at the end of this chapter). Suffice it to say that in the last five years there has been a considerable increase in the importation, distribution, and consumption of 'hard' drugs, such as heroin. This increase seems to have followed a period of comparative stability in the mid-1970s. This, in turn, followed a marked increase in the 1960s and early 1970s. It would be interesting to know precisely why these peaks and troughs appeared, for they have occurred at other times in recent history and have never been explained adequately. The number of *addicts* notified in the UK in 1983 (just under 6,000) was 42 per cent up on 1982; the figure for 1984 is expected to show about a 25 per cent increase on the 1983 total (Home Office 1985). It should be emphasized that the number of addicts who are formally notified to the Home Office is 'probably only a small proportion of the number of chronic misusers' (Home Office 1985: 5). Similar increases have been noted in the number of drugs offences and drugs seizures, particularly of heroin and cocaine. In 1983, about 23,300 individuals were found guilty of, or cautioned for, offences concerning controlled drugs; 3,000 more than in 1982 and 11,500 more than in 1975 (Home Office 1985).

DRUG-RELATED OFFENCES

The following, somewhat rough and ready, classification should be read in conjunction with that already given for alcohol offences.

(1) Offences against the numerous enactments that are concerned with the importation, possession, distribution, and consumption of drugs.
(2) Offences committed in order to obtain drugs (for example, breaking and entering and stealing from pharmacies, surgeries, hospitals, and warehouses).
(3) Offences thought to be due to the ingestion of drugs. (See categories 1 and 2 under 'Alcohol', above.)

There is a substantial body of literature concerning the possible relationships between drug misuse, addiction, and criminal behaviour. As with alcohol, there is much debate as to whether these are separate phenomena or whether those who take drugs and offend do so for similar reasons. (For brief reviews of the literature see Prins 1980 and 1982.) The main conclusion to be drawn from all the studies is that the web of interaction between abuse, addiction, and criminality is highly complex and that, apart from some exceptional instances, there are no clear-cut causal connections. There are a few instances, however, in which abuse or addiction may result in dangerous

behaviour/offending against persons or property and these are
now mentioned below.

Mott says that 'it is now generally accepted that no drug has
inherent criminogenic properties' (Mott 1981: 235). In addition, it is true to say that the opiate drugs, cannabis and LSD, do
not *in general* facilitate dangerous, aggressive behaviour. Such
behaviour is more likely to be facilitated by the amphetamines,
which act as cerebral stimulants and can produce feelings of
euphoria, omnipotence, and irritability. If amphetamines are
combined with alcohol, there is a marked acceleration in loss of
control and judgement. In such circumstances, serious and
unprovoked aggression may occur. In similar fashion, barbiturates—regarded by most people as sedative drugs—may have a
highly adverse effect upon an already basically volatile individual, such as the aggressive psychopath (see Chapter 5). It is
interesting to note that a recent, large-scale research study
carried out in Sweden found a high proportion of violent crime
arrests amongst intravenous drug abusers. This study examined a birth cohort of some 15,000 persons born in 1953. It is
also interesting to note that the *intravenous drug abusers* accounted
for some 45 per cent of all male arrests and 58 per cent of all
female arrests during the time of the study (Fry 1985).

There are also occasional individual case reports of tragedies
occurring as a result of the ingestion of powerful hallucinogenic
drugs such as LSD. Readers will recall the case of Lipman in
Chapter 2. A recently reported case is a useful reminder of the
impact of such tragedies. At a coroner's inquest, evidence was
received that a 'punk rocker', aged seventeen, had killed his
mother and his grandmother and then himself, almost certainly
as a result of taking a dose of LSD. The coroner stated that 'the
state of the house, with blood spattered everywhere, showed
that someone had gone beserk'. He was in no doubt that the
young man had inflicted the wounds on his mother, grandmother, and then himself. In commenting upon the case, the
coroner made the important (and sometimes overlooked) point
that there is 'growing evidence which indicates that hallucinations and delusions can recur after the drug has actually been

dissipated or excreted from the body . . . recurring hallucinations could even occur when the drug had not been taken for some time' (*Guardian* 26 March, 1985). It is not widely realized that the abuse of common medical compounds, such as aspirin or sleeping pills, if combined with alcohol, can produce devastating results. Certain of these drugs may be taken for medicinal purposes and then be accompanied by the ingestion of alcohol. Paul (1975) cites several cases in which unprovoked violence had occurred in similar circumstances. As we have already seen, even quite small amounts of alcohol can potentiate the possible hallucinogenic effects of such drugs. Any apparently unprovoked and unpredictable eruption of gross violence should lead us to make very careful enquiries about the possible use or abuse of medication accompanied by the ingestion of alcohol.

Other substances

In the last decade or so, there has been growing concern about the problem of substance abuse, particularly among young people. As in the case of alcohol and other drugs, this is by no means a new problem. From ancient times, a wide variety of substances has been inhaled, not only as adjuncts to religious ritual and observance but to bring about relief of tension, to produce euphoria, and to achieve altered states of consciousness. The last few years, however, have witnessed an escalating epidemic of the abuse of various compounds, mainly hydrocarbons and other volatile substances (Prins 1985). Such abuse can have a wide range of harmful effects, not the least of these being permanent brain and liver damage. Fatalities are not unknown. Deaths may be due not only to the toxic effects of the substances themselves but also to the confusion and disorientation caused by them and an accompanying progressive lack of discrimination. These side-effects may lead to suicide or death by misadventure. More importantly, from our point of view, such abuse may lead to quite atypical violent behaviour against persons or property. O'Connor (1983), who has made one of the few comprehensive studies of this problem, quotes a number of illustrations where this had occurred. They included amongst others:

(1) An unprovoked and violent attack on a youth leader who remonstrated with a group of solvent-abusing youngsters.

(2) Another group, 'high' on glue, with a seeming 'grudge' against their former teachers, who set fire to a school, causing over £35,000 worth of damage.

(3) Others who set fire to a shed next door to a café; this caused extensive damage and the near-death of a mother and her child, who were in the café at the time.

(4) A series of assaults on younger children, in which the latter were forced to inhale glue by their assailants.

An even more horrific incident concerned an attack on a four-year-old boy. A group of youngsters was seen to be tossing him about like a doll. An eye-witness stated that 'they were tossing it from one to the other, then they poured paint on it and started stripping away some of the clothes' (O'Connor 1983: 97). Their tiny victim developed the most severe post-incident symptoms as a result of his traumatic experiences; these included severe breathing problems and horrific nightmares.

Conclusions

Fortunately, these and similar events are comparatively rare, though O'Connor suggests that they may be more common than we care to think. Such offences highlight the dangerous changes in behaviour that may occur when any substance is abused, be it alcohol, other drugs, or a solvent-type compound. It is worth emphasizing that in some predisposed individuals only a very small quantity may be needed to set off an explosive and potentially lethal outburst. These facts highlight yet again the need for a careful appraisal of all the evidence in the background and circumstances of each case. This plea could be said to be one of the most important messages in this book.

References

Collins, J.J. (ed.) (1982) *Drinking and Crime: Perspectives on the Relationships Between Alcohol Consumption and Criminal Behaviour.* London: Tavistock.

Cowen, P. and Muller, P.E. (1979) An XYY Man. *British Journal of Psychiatry* **135**: 79–81.

Fry, L.J. (1985) Drug Abuse and Crime in a Swedish Birth Cohort. *British Journal of Criminology* **25**: 46–59.

Gillies, H. (1965) Murder in the West of Scotland. *British Journal of Psychiatry* **111**: 1087–094.

Home Office (1985) *Tackling Drug Misuse: A Summary of Government Strategy.* London: Home Office.

Lishman, W.A. (1978) *Organic Psychiatry: The Psychological Consequences of Cerebral Disorder.* Oxford: Blackwell Scientific.

Mott, J. (1981) Criminal Involvement and Penal Response. In G. Edwards and C. Busch (eds) *Drug Problems in Great Britain: A Review of Ten Years.* London: Academic Press.

Murphy, D. (1983) Alcohol and Crime. In Home Office Research and Planning Unit *Home Office Research Bulletin No. 15.* London: Home Office.

O'Connor, D. (1983) *Glue Sniffing and Volatile Substance Abuse: Case Studies of Children and Young Adults.* Aldershot: Gower.

Öjesö, L. (1983) Alcohol, Drugs and Forensic Psychiatry. *Psychiatric Clinics of North America* **6**: 733–49.

Paul, D.M. (1975) Drugs and Aggression. *Medicine, Science and the Law* **15**: 16–21.

Pernanen, K. (1982) Theoretical Aspects of the Relationships Between Alcohol Use and Crime. In J.J. Collins (ed.) *Drinking and Crime: Perspectives on the Relationships Between Alcohol Consumption and Criminal Behaviour.* London: Tavistock.

Prins, H. (1980) *Offenders, Deviants, or Patients? An Introduction to the Study of Socio-Forensic Problems.* London: Tavistock.

—— (1982) *Criminal Behaviour: An Introduction to Criminology and the Penal System* (second edition). London: Tavistock.

—— (1985) Literature Review: An Abuse of Some Substance? *British Journal of Social Work* **15**: 403–08.

Roslund, B. and Larson, C.A. (1979) Crimes of Violence and Alcohol Abuse in Sweden. *International Journal of the Addictions* **4**: 1103–115.

Royal College of Psychiatrists (1979) *Alcohol and Alcoholism—Report of a Special Committee.* London: Tavistock.

Spencer, S. (1984) Homicide, Mental Abnormality and Offence. In M. and A. Craft (eds) *Mentally Abnormal Offenders.* London: Baillière Tindall.

FURTHER READING

Alcohol-related problems: general

These three books provide useful accounts of current thinking about alcohol-related problems. The books by Edwards and Hunt are also useful on management.

Edwards, G. (1982) *The Treatment of Drinking Problems: A Guide for the Helping Professions.* London: Grant McIntyre.

Grant, M. and Gwinner, P. (eds) (1979) *Alcoholism in Perspective.* London: Croom Helm.

Hunt, L. (1982) *Alcohol Related Problems.* London: Heinemann Educational.

Alcohol-related problems: policy issues

This book challenges many common assumptions about alcohol and the relationship between availability and abuse.

Tuck, M. (1980) *Alcoholism and Social Policy: Are We On the Right Lines?* Home Office Research Study No. 65. Home Office Research Unit. London: HMSO.

Other drugs

Stimson, G.V. and Oppenheimer, E. (1982) *Heroin Addiction: Treatment and Control in Britain.* London: Tavistock.

West, D.J. (ed.) (1978) *Problems of Drug Abuse in Britain.* Cambridge: Institute of Criminology.

CHAPTER EIGHT
Arson and arsonists

'Is not this a brand plucked out of the fire?'
BOOK OF ZECHARIAH 3. ii

'I am malicious because I am miserable.'
MARY SHELLEY
The Monster in *Frankenstein*

The universal phenomenon of fire and its symbolism is well documented in the annals of history, religious ritual, legend, and witchcraft; its powers, both of destruction and of cleansing, have been clearly described in the anthropological and associated literature (see Topp 1973, Scott 1974). Topp has summarized the phenomenon of fire very succinctly.

'There seems little doubt that fire has a deeply ingrained mystical and religious significance to man which exercises its effects both at conscious and subconscious levels of thought. It offers an Almighty-like power within the reach of the individual, though the majority carefully respect this violent potential.'   (Topp 1973: 85)

This chapter is concerned with those who, for one reason or another, do not respect 'this violent potential', and, by their fire-raising activities, cause grave harm to persons and/or property. The chapter is divided into the following sections. First, definition of terms and a consideration of the legal aspects; second, the size of the problem; third, a classification of the characteristics and motivations of arsonists; fourth, management.

Definition of terms and legal aspects

Various terms have been used to describe those who engage in deliberate fire-raising activities. *Arson* is the term commonly used in the United Kingdom but some countries prefer the terms *malicious fire-raising, incendiarism,* or *fire-setting* (the latter being popular in the USA; see, for example, Inciardi 1970 and Heath, Gayton, and Hardesty 1976). Some authorities equate 'fire-setting' with 'pyromania' (see, for example, Fras 1983) but this latter term is not much in vogue today. It was in popular use by medical men towards the latter part of the nineteenth century. When first introduced, it was used to describe motive-less, irrational fire-raising behaviour and was considered to represent a form of insanity. Today, the term tends to be reserved for compulsive acts of fire-raising in which rising sexual tension is said to be discharged by fire-setting activities. As we shall see shortly, the evidence suggests that this phenom-enon is comparatively rare.

ARSON AND THE LAW

Fire officers do not normally use the legal terms 'arson' or 'criminal damage endangering life'; they prefer to talk of fires of doubtful or malicious origin. Until the implementation of the Criminal Damage Act of 1971, arson was a common law offence. The current statutory definition is wider than that under the old common law, which confined the offence largely to its occurrence in dwelling houses. Smith and Hogan (1983) state that under *Section 1(1)* of the Criminal Damage Act, 1971:

> 'A person who without lawful excuse destroys or damages any property belonging to another intending to destroy or damage any such property or being reckless as to whether any such property would be destroyed or damaged shall be guilty of an offence . . . punishable with imprisonment for ten years.'   (Smith and Hogan 1983:628)

Section 1(3) of the Act provides that 'an offence committed under this section by destroying or damaging property by fire shall be charged as arson'; the offence is punishable with a maximum of life imprisonment. Furthermore, *Section 1(2)* of the Act provides that if a person endangers the life of another through such activity, this shall also be punishable with a maximum penalty of life imprisonment. (For a more detailed description of the law and the legal interpretations of such matters as intention, recklessness, and so forth, see Smith and Hogan 1983, Chapter 17.) As can be seen from the tables that follow, the offence of criminal damage endangering life is now separately recorded in the criminal statistics.

The size of the problem

Table 8(1) gives an indication of the number of offenders found guilty at all courts, or cautioned for arson and causing criminal damage endangering life, for the period 1979–83.

The number of cases in which individuals are actually prosecuted or cautioned for arson are comparatively few in relation

Table 8(1)   *Arson and criminal damage endangering life 1979–83*

	1979	1980	1981	1982	1983
arson	2,604	3,265	3,404	3,270	3,324
criminal damage endangering life	45	46	56	45	66

(Source: Home Office 1984: 97)

Notes to Table 8(1)

(a)   The numbers of those found guilty of, or cautioned for, arson in 1983 are the highest for the last ten years (apart from the year 1981), the figures for the years 1974, 1975, 1976, 1977, and 1978 being 2,509, 2,631, 2,625, 2,382, and 2,807, respectively. It will be observed that, apart from 1977, there was also a steady increase in this earlier five-year period. (Home Office 1984: 97.)

(b)   It should be emphasized that, although arson and criminal damage endangering life are very serious crimes they constitute only about 1 per cent of all offences against property as disclosed in the annual criminal statistics.

(c)   In 1982, some 757 persons were cautioned for arson and 11 for criminal damage endangering life. It should be noted that the majority of these were children and young persons. (Home Office 1982: 64.)

(d)   Serious cases of arson and criminal damage with intent to endanger life will normally be dealt with by custodial penalties. Less serious cases will usually be dealt with by fines or probation orders. In 1982, 90 men and 24 women were made the subject of Hospital or Guardianship Orders for offences of criminal damage—mainly arson. (Home Office 1982: 56.)

Table 8(2)   *Deliberate and possibly deliberate fires in dwellings 1978–82*

1978	1979	1980	1981	1982
2,600	3,400	3,900	4,500	5,000

to the number of fires in dwellings or other occupied buildings that are regarded by the police and fire services as being of 'doubtful' or 'malicious' ignition (Fry and le Couteur 1966). There has been a steady increase in the number of such fires in recent years; this can be seen from the statistics provided in *Tables 8(2)* and *8(3)*.

In 1982, it is estimated that there were about 60 fatal and 670 non-fatal casualties in dwellings that were ignited deliberately. Between 1978 and 1982, the number of the non-fatal casualties more than doubled and accounted for about a third of the total incidence in fire casualties by both deliberate and accidental ignition. Arson caused the most rapid increase in the number of casualties from these deliberate fires, from about 80 in 1978 to about 250 in 1981 and 160 in 1982 (the figure for 1982 is lower because the system of statistical recording was altered, so that terrorist fires were counted separately). A more detailed breakdown of the numbers of non-fatal and fatal casualties in dwellings fired deliberately or possibly deliberately is provided in *Table 8(4)*.

Comparable increases in the size of the problem have been reported in the USA. In 1964, there were about 40,000 fires of

Table 8(3)   *Deliberate and possibly deliberate fires in other occupied buildings 1978–82*

1978	1979	1980	1981	1982
6,100	6,500	7,600	8,300	8,900

(Source for Tables 8(2) and 8(3): Home Office 1983: 4)
Notes to Tables 8(2) and 8(3)
(a) All figures rounded to the nearest hundred.
(b) Figures for 1978 and 1980 include estimates covering periods of industrial action by fire services.
(c) Figures for 1982 include fires arising from terrorist activities.

Table 8(4) *Non-fatal and fatal casualties in dwellings fired deliberately or possibly deliberately 1978–82*

	1978	1979	1980	1981	1982
non-fatal	329*	507	546*	704	667
fatal	41	66	82	65	61

(Source: Home Office 1983: 11)
Note to Table 8(4)
* Figures include estimates covering periods of industrial action by fire services.

confirmed or suspected deliberate origin; in 1975, this figure had grown to 144,000 (Vreeland and Levin 1980). The estimated *cost* of fires in Great Britain, according to the British Insurance Association, was £553.6 million during 1984. Figures on the cost of 'malicious fires' are hard to obtain but it is estimated that it is in excess of £100 million per year (British Insurance Association, April, 1985: personal communication).

The reasons for the discrepancies between the criminal and fire statistics are not hard to find. Experienced fire and police officers emphasize that there is a serious problem in distinguishing between accidental and deliberate fire incidents. Even if there is good forensic evidence that arson has been committed, it is often very difficult to apprehend and charge the culprits. As we shall see later, arson is above all else an offence that can be committed at 'one remove' from the victim or victims. Because of this, it is comparatively easy to escape detection. It is also true to say that there are many more fires started deliberately than are shown in the fire statistics. It is fairly easy to find likely reasons for the increase in the number of fires of all kinds.

(1) It has been suggested that many buildings are not adequately protected against the ravages of fire; one is reminded of the tragedies that have occurred in certain homes for the elderly and infirm.
(2) Some modern building and furnishing materials are known to be liable to insidious conflagration, with the result that disaster point may be reached before the fire service can be alerted (see, for example, Marchant 1980).
(3) There has been an increase in the amount of flammable

materials available for use in incendiary devices (see Mac-donald 1977).

(4) It has been suggested that we are all less fire-conscious than people were in the past. Increasing use of indirect means of warmth (for example, central heating) prevents the exposure of children to the old open fire and the consequential parental injunctions concerning its dangers (see Clisby 1980). The less frequent use of the open fire also means that there are fewer opportunities for children to explore its properties in a legitimate and supervised fashion.

(5) It seems likely that people are being more careless in their handling of electrical and other equipment. One wonders how many people remember to unplug the television set before retiring to bed or ensure that electric blankets are installed safely. There are also still too many tragic instances of the use of defective paraffin heaters.

(6) The increase in fires of both doubtful and malicious origin must be seen against the background of violence that appears to surround us more generally and in particular the prevalence of terrorist activities of one kind or another.

Classification—the motivation and characteristics of arsonists

Various attempts have been made to classify the motives and characteristics of arsonists (for some examples, see Scott 1974, Foust 1979, Prins 1980, Vreeland and Levin 1980, Faulk 1982, and Harris and Rice 1984). Faulk suggests two interesting groupings: *Group I* contains those cases in which the fire is a means to an end (such as revenge, fraud, or a plea for help); *Group II* contains those cases where the fire itself is the phenomenon of interest (this group would contain cases of fire-raising said to be a result of irresistible impulse or as a means of attaining sexual excitement—true pyromania). All the classifications show that many different types of people commit arson for many varied reasons. It also has to be acknowledged that, despite a fairly substantial literature on the subject, much of the available information is unfortunately anecdotal and we know very little about the motivations of a good many arsonists. The classification that follows attempts to combine both motivation and characteristics. It derives in part from some research on imprisoned arsonists carried out by two psychiatrist colleagues and myself (Prins, Tennent, and Trick 1985). In formulating this classification, I have had two aims: first, to provide a composite frame of reference for *understanding* arsonists; second, to provide a basis for effective *management*, which we must hope will diminish the risk of repetition. It will be obvious that many of the categories overlap, so they should not be viewed as discrete entities.

(1) The 'professional' arsonist

Such an individual may set fires for financial reward, acting as the instrument of an illegal organization, such as the Mafia. Professionals are seldom caught. Others will set fires deliberately as a means of obtaining large sums of money from the insurance on the property and its contents. These offences are sometimes indulged in by offenders whose businesses are failing and where there is a need to obtain large sums of money. This form of arson is often executed with a great deal of skill and is very difficult to distinguish from accidental ignition. (See Macdonald 1977.)

(2) Arson as a cover for another crime

From time to time, offenders may set fire to a building in order to cover up another crime, such as burglary or even homicide.

(3) Politically motivated arson

This form of arson is usually committed by political fanatics. They will seek to destroy places of worship or property used by religious and ethnic minorities. Others may be motivated by anarchistic beliefs and attack government buildings or the private homes of ministers or state officials. A further politically motivated group utilize arson as part of their terrorist activities —as, for example, when the IRA set fires in Northern Ireland and, less frequently, on the mainland. It has been suggested that some of these arsonists may be psychiatrically disturbed and not motivated solely by political belief. (For further information on these aspects, see the suggestions for further reading listed at the end of Chapter 4—*on hostage-taking, sieges, terrorist activity, etc.*)

(4) The politically motivated self-immolator

These are not arsonists in the conventional sense of the term but I have included them here in order to try to provide as complete a picture as possible. Epidemics of this type of behaviour appear from time to time; the last major outbreak occurred in the late 1960s and early 1970s. Such activity seems to have a 'copy-cat' effect and many of those who engage in it are probably very highly disturbed emotionally. For this reason, they are considered again in point 6 below.

(5) Arson committed for mixed and unclear motives

Anyone experienced in dealing with arsonists will acknowledge how very difficult it is to ascribe a single motive for the crime. More often than not, the motives appear to be mixed. In the research referred to earlier, my colleagues and I analysed a sample of 113 male arsonists who were eligible for consideration for parole. We found a number of cases in which it proved difficult to attribute single specific motives. We were forced to subdivide the group as follows. A small number of cases in which the offender appeared to have been suffering from a mild (reactive) degree of depression at the time of the offence. Such depression is not infrequently also associated with anger (at a spouse or other partner) so that there may also be an element of revenge (see point 7 below). In other cases, the arson appeared to be a disguised plea for help. There were one or two cases in our sample where the offender had engaged in such behaviour following a sudden separation or unanticipated bereavement. There were a number of other cases in which arson had been committed under the influence of alcohol. The ingestion of alcohol features very significantly in cases of arson (see Inciardi 1970 and Hurley and Monahan 1969). The offender states very frequently that he or she had been drinking very heavily at the time and cannot recall what happened. Such lack of recall may be due, in rare cases, to genuine alcoholic amnesia, but is more likely to be due to a 'befuddled' state caused by intoxication. It is possible that such fires may also be set accidentally as a result of intoxication. In my experience, however, such 'accidental' fires are rare. The following case illustrates very usefully the frequency with which one comes across a mixture of apparent motives.

Case 1[1]   This concerned a man in his middle thirties. He had a history of past disturbed behaviour, including setting fire to the parental home on one occasion and making numerous 'false alarm' calls to the police and fire services. Following a period of compulsory detention in hospital on a court order for one of his fire-raising episodes, he had been discharged to a psychiatric after-care facility. He did not get on at all well with the staff and considered they were 'picking on him'; during a depressive phase, in which he had also been drinking quite heavily, he set fire to the hostel, causing several thousand pounds' worth of damage.

(6) Arson associated with the presence of formal mental disorder or other illness

Such forms of arson may be subdivided into the following categories:

(a) *Severe affective disorder*: In Chapter 4 we saw how severe affective disorder occasionally might be associated with serious offending and violence. Such offenders may set fires as a result of this group of illnesses. One of the most famous cases of a psychotic arsonist is probably that of Jonathan Martin, the nineteenth-century incendiarist who fired York Minster. During the course of his illness (probably of a manic-depressive variety), he experienced severe religious delusions in which he considered it was his mission to burn down the Minster. It is of great interest that his illness was of long standing though intermittent; with hindsight, it is possible to see that he gave a number of warnings of his intentions (see Scott 1974). For the arsonist suffering from severe depression, it is possible that the setting of fires may not only satisfy the need for the purgation of guilt through a 'fiery furnace' but also serve as a means of purification. Occasionally, depressive arsonists may engage in their crimes as a means of getting back indirectly at the real objects of their depression. I know of one offender/patient who became severely depressed because his wife had left him; whilst in a state of great emotional upheaval, he set fire to the block of offices in which she had once worked. Somewhat more rarely, a hypomanic individual may engage in arson. In these cases, there is likely to be marked irrationality of thinking associated with the kind of delusional and hallucinatory symptoms described in Chapter 4.

(b) *Schizophrenic disorders*: A number of arsonists, particularly those detained in the Special Hospitals, suffer from a clear schizophrenic disorder (Fry and le Couteur 1966). A number of them have set fire to dwellings as a result of their hallucinatory experiences. One such offender/patient said to me, 'I set fire to the house to get rid of the evil in it'. Others will allege that they have seen the image of God and heard Him directing them to set fires. Occasionally, the schizoid or overtly schizophrenic vagrant may set fire to a building in the course of his or her confused wanderings. Schizophrenics may occasionally set fire to themselves. Some schizophrenic arsonists do not in fact set fire to occupied dwellings or other buildings but set fire to such objects as telegraph poles, fences, etc. (Virkunnen 1974).

(c) *'Organic' disorders*: Very occasionally, arson may be commit-ted by a person who is suffering from some organic disorder (brain tumour, injury, epilepsy, dementia, and disturbances of metabolism). Epilepsy is not commonly associated with arson, but one should always be on the look-out for the case in which arson has been committed when the person concerned was not in a state of clear consciousness. In their study of fifty arsonists detained in Grendon Underwood Psychiatric Prison, Hurley and Monahan (1969) found that 20 per cent had a history of head injury with loss of consciousness but without other neuro-logical sequelae. More rarely, we come across cases of arson committed by persons suffering from early senile dementia, chronic alcohol poisoning, or GPI. Much more frequently, however, we find arson associated with mental impairment of varying degrees of severity.

(d) *Mental impairment*: A history of mental impairment (retardation, handicap, subnormality) seems to occur quite frequently in those persons who have committed arson on more than one occasion. McKerracher and Dacre (1966) studied one such group of arsonists detained in Rampton (Special) Hospital (which at that time catered almost exclusively for dangerous sub-normal offenders/patients). They considered that the arsonists were more emotionally labile than other Rampton patients and displayed a wider range of psychiatric symptoms than did other residents. Very often, mentally impaired arsonists suffer from a variety of social and other handicaps as well. The following cases illustrate some of these difficulties.

Case 2 This was a woman in her late twenties, formally diagnosed as mildly mentally subnormal (impaired), who came from a highly disturbed background. Her parents had fought for years before finally divorcing. A number of her siblings had been before the courts on numerous occasions. Much of her behaviour was of the attention-seeking variety and over the years she had set fire to a number of establishments in which she had been detained. The offence for which she had received a sentence of life imprisonment (later made the subject of a Transfer Direction (see Chapter 3)) consisted of setting fire to bedding and furniture in a local hospital. Had it not been for the prompt intervention of the nursing staff a serious tragedy might have occurred involving the deaths of many patients and staff.

Case 3 This concerned a man aged fifty, detained in a Special Hospital. He had suffered brain damage as a child, which had resulted in quite severe mental impairment. From a very early age he had exhibited aggressive behaviour towards his own family and others—particularly towards children. His fire-raising activities had started early in life and these had been interspersed with sexual offences and crimes of violence. He claimed that the sight of fire excited him sexually (see point 9 below). His problems were compounded by the fact that in his early forties he had developed a concurrent psychotic illness, in which he heard voices telling him to set fires. The incident that brought him before the court on the occasion that resulted in his admission to a Special Hospital was an attempt to burn down a psychiatric hospital, to which he had been admitted informally.

Case 4 This concerned a man in his late thirties, diagnosed as suffering from mental impairment. He had set fire to a store-room containing highly flammable materials. The fire spread quickly to a building next door, where a number of people were working. He had a long history of fire-raising activities and making 'hoax' telephone calls to the police and fire services. He also suffered from concurrent physical disabilities—a severe speech impediment and a limp—which greatly lowered his self-esteem. His main interest in life was in raising fires and he was regarded as highly dangerous by the hospital authorities. When mental impairment is accompanied by severe physical disability or disfigurement, it presents greater problems be-cause the offender has to cope with two or more very real handicaps. In such cases, arson is often a way of drawing attention to oneself and one's plight (see Woolf 1977).

The case of Bruce Lee Such attention-seeking behaviour may present other hazards too. It is apparent that Bruce Lee—a self-confessed homicidal arsonist—had a very real need to draw attention to himself. Lee, aged about twenty at the time of his trial, was said to be of low intelligence. He also suffered from spasticity and was said to be epileptic; a sad assemblage of handicaps. He was also said to have been vengeful. He was originally charged with, and convicted of, a very large number of fires and killings but was cleared in the Court of Appeal of one of these fires, in which eleven elderly men had died. In this latter case, the Court of Appeal considered that his conviction was unsafe, giving as its main reason 'the unsatisfactory nature of the forensic evidence' (*The Times* 3 December, 1983). However, Lee is still detained in a Special Hospital for ten other fires which killed fifteen people. His case, which was investigated for a year by *The Sunday Times* Insight Team (*The Sunday Times* 14 March, 1982), highlights two important issues in relation to arson committed by those who may be of limited intelligence. In the first place, there may be such an overwhelming desire to seek attention that false confessions may be made. Second, in such cases, it is all too easy for pressure to be applied so that false confessions may occur. I made reference earlier in this book to the need for those suspected of such offences to be accompanied by a family member, solicitor, or social worker during police interrogation.

(e) *Pathological self-immolation*: This form of behaviour has already been referred to briefly. Topp (1973) has drawn attention to the extent to which self-destruction by fire has been occurring, infrequently but with some regularity, in penal establishments in recent years. He suggests that such individuals, who choose an obviously very painful method of death, are likely to be those who have some capacity for splitting off feelings from consciousness. It seems possible that some of these individuals may be schizoid or schizophrenic; more rarely, they may be epileptics in a disturbed state of consciousness. People vary considerably in their pain thresholds. Some would succumb very quickly to such an agonizing method of self-destruction. Shock and asphyxiation would probably occur within a short space of time, so that the severe pain caused by the burning of vital tissues would not have to be endured for long. Such may have been the fate of martyrs and others burned at the stake. Newton (1976) has described an unusual case of suicide by fire, which seems to cross the political/pathological boundaries mentioned earlier.

(7) *The revenge motive in arson*

Such motives may take two forms. First, arson may be used as a means of wreaking revenge against specific individuals. Second, it may be an expression of a more general vengeful feeling towards society. It is a motive that seems to cut across many of the others already described. It may be said to be the most common of all motives, though this is not always obvious on first inspection of the case. Very careful and persistent exploration may be required before it emerges. In our survey of imprisoned arsonists, to which I referred earlier, we found that motives of revenge predominated—in 38 cases out of the total of 113; the next highest category was that of the dull and subnormal arsonist (18 cases), followed by arson as a disguised cry for help (12 cases). In the accounts of the case of Bruce Lee, it is suggested that he indulged in arson in order to get back at those he felt had been harassing him or who had received the advantages of the happy home life he felt he had been denied. In more general terms, a feeling of revenge may be directed against the social order. Some politically motivated arson and terrorist activity could well come within this category (see Macdonald 1977). Arson is not uncommon as a form of more personal revenge expressed against employers. Considerable damage may be caused to property by those who are seeking to redress some real or imagined wrong such as unfair dismissal or reprimand. Some of this activity will, of course, take on political undertones, as in the cases of arson committed during the recent miners' strike. At the other end of the spectrum, school children may engage in vengeful activities and cause damage to school buildings and contents worth many thousands of pounds. Sometimes, such offending seems to occur 'out of the blue', though *past* animosity towards teaching staff can often be elicited. In these cases, the arson may often be associated with other demonstrations of aggression and anti-social conduct. There is also a further, more generally vengeful, group which may include those who have a fairly well encapsulated near-delusional system; their motives will be akin to the more psychotically motivated arson already described.

The revenge motive in arson is not a new phenomenon. Thomas, in his fascinating book *Religion and the Decline of Magic* (1984), draws interesting parallels between arson and the practice of witchcraft.

'In the seventeenth century, as at other times, it was a common means of revenge for those who felt themselves injured by their neighbours. Arson required no great physical strength or financial resources and could easily be concealed. It was an indiscriminate means of vengeance, however, for a fire once started, was likely to spread. As such, it perhaps appealed especially to those whose hatred for their neighbours was all-embracing.' (Thomas 1984: 634)

In drawing these parallels, Thomas likens witches to arsonists, since 'the witch like the arsonist assumed that the hardships of life were to be attributed to the personal failings of other people rather than to impersonal social cause' (1984: 636). Thomas also suggests that arson was not uncommon in the seventeenth century amongst low-paid and misused workers, who took their revenge on their employers. It is also of interest to note that in the fifteenth century one of the grounds for the compulsory detention of those thought to be mad was that they were thought

likely to set a house on fire; 'it was lawful to imprison ...
(someone) ... if he were mad and you believed that he
was going to do some mischief like burning down a house'
(Allderidge 1979: 325). The vengeful arsonist can be a very
dangerous person indeed, particularly if, as is sometimes the
case, he or she is intellectually able.

Case 5 A man aged about thirty had developed a passionate
and quite unshakable belief that a young female was in love with
him. His passions were not reciprocated; in fact, they were
actively resisted on several occasions. So obsessive were this
man's amorous interests that they had some of the delusional
qualities to which I referred earlier. As a means of gaining
attention to his plight and of getting back at the young woman
concerned, he placed an incendiary device in her home with the
avowed intention of killing her and her family. Fortunately, a
family member spotted the device and dealt with it before the
fire took too great hold. Many years after this event, the offender
(detained without limit of time) still harboured vengeful feelings and seemed quite without insight into what he had done or
compassion for his intended victims. It is important to stress
here that the vengeful arsonist is like to harbour his destructive
desires over a long period. In their twenty-year cohort survey of
arsonists convicted in 1951, Soothill and Pope (1973) found that
although the vast majority who had been convicted and sentenced for this offence were not reconvicted, the few who *were*
reconvicted tended to be those who did it for personal revenge or
as a more general response to conflict with authority.

(8) Arson motivated by 'heroics'

This form of arson is akin to that described in point 5, above, but
in the type of case now to be described the arsonist appears to
gain an explicit satisfaction from the fire itself. These are the
offenders who need to be at the centre of things and who demand
attention. They set fires in order to derive satisfaction from the
arrival of the fire brigade and the excitement and commotion
that accompanies this. These are the arsonists who, having set
the fire, will often inform the fire brigade of the conflagration,
busy themselves at the scene, and offer their unsolicited services
to the firemen. The volunteer or auxiliary fireman may perhaps

be one of these arsonists. In their well-known study, Lewis and Yarnell (1951) found fifty-one cases of volunteer firemen who had set fires on their own and a further forty-one instances where groups of men belonging to a volunteer fire department had been arrested for deliberately setting fires. It has also been suggested that, where volunteer firemen have been paid for each occasion on which they have had to attend a fire, there may have been an inducement to set fires deliberately in order to reap the financial rewards. Nevertheless, it is certainly true that a powerful element of attention-seeking behaviour pervades the lifestyles and histories of many arsonists. A large number of them are social isolates and are inapt in personal and social relationships. As with the revenge motive, this type of behaviour tends to cut across other classifications.

(9) Sexually motivated arson

Much of the earlier writing on arson stressed the relationship between sexual activity and fire-raising behaviour; this was most notable in the work of nineteenth-century German medical writers on the subject (see Harris and Rice 1984). Such views received further impetus through the work of Freud and, in particular, his analysis of the myth of Prometheus. This investigation led Freud to postulate that 'for primitive man to control and possess fire he had to learn to renounce his homosexually based desire to put fire out by urination' (Heath, Gayton, and Hardesty 1976: 229). Freud's one-time follower, Jung, proffered a wider interpretation, suggesting that fire-setting was a symbolic and archetypal outlet for sexual impulses (see Simmel 1949). Although such views are not given much credence today, it is still worth pondering over the mystical and ancient associations between fire, virility, and procreation. However, most modern writers tend to take a more comprehensive view of possible sexual motivation, in which sexual factors are only part of the picture (see Virkunnen 1974, Fras 1983). Instances of specific sexual satisfaction from fire-raising activities would seem to be rare; for example, we did not find a single specific example of a direct relationship in our series of imprisoned arsonists (Prins, Tennent, and Trick 1985). It is, however, likely that had we been examining a Special

Hospital population the picture might have been rather different.

Case 6 This man, in his thirties, suffered from both mental impairment and psychopathic disorder. He had a long history of arson offences, some of them quite serious. He claimed to have obtained sexual satisfaction (erection and occasional orgasm) from watching the fires he set. Perhaps of even greater significance, however, was his additional predilection for the mutilation of the corpses of both sexes. Such cases indicate not only gross psychopathology but also indicate the overlap between different categories of offences (see, for example, the discussion of necrophilic activity in Chapter 6).

There would certainly appear to be indications of sexual *difficulties* of various kinds in the histories of many arsonists. Sixty years ago, Stekel (1924) observed that impotence was not uncommon in the histories of some arsonists and I have come across some cases where this seemed to be an important element in the offender's background. In the study carried out by Hurley and Monahan (1969) referred to earlier, 54 per cent of the men had clear psychosexual and marital problems and 60 per cent described difficulties in social relationships with women. In a later study by Sapsford, Banks, and Smith (1978), a group of arsonists serving *life sentences* for arson were compared with a group who were serving *eighteen months or less*. They found that the life sentence group included a proportion of men who showed a compulsive element in their offending and that this appeared to have been predominantly sexually motivated; their histories showed a preponderance of sexual disorders as compared with the determinate sentence men.

(10) Arson committed by children and young adults

Many of the reports of research into arson committed by young people fail to distinguish adequately between arson committed by children and arson committed by adolescents and young adults. As we shall see, there are significant differences and I have attempted a two-part classification.

(a) *Arson committed by children*: Children below the age of criminal responsibility (at present, aged ten and under) would not, of course, be charged with arson and even above that age there are procedures that limit the circumstances in which they can be charged with such an offence. None the less, because fire-raising activity from a very young age seems to occur so frequently in the lives of adult arsonists, it seems useful to describe some aspects of its early occurrence here. The literature on children who set fires has recently been fully reviewed by Kafry. She investigated fire behaviour and knowledge in a sample of ninety-nine boys under ten years of age in California. She found an almost universal interest in fire and that '"fire play" was performed by 54 per cent of the boys studied' (1980: 47). Her research confirmed the much earlier contention of Lewis and Yarnell that 'the incidence of children who play with fire is far greater than any statistics show' (1951: 285). She also found that interest in fire begins at a very early age (18 per cent of the fires set in Kafry's study were set before the age of three). She also found that, although the parents of the children were well aware of the risks of fires, a large percentage of them did not give adequate instruction and warning to their children. Those who played with matches and set fires in Kafry's study seemed to be more mischievous, aggressive, exhibitionistic, and impulsive than those who expressed no interest. These findings deserve consideration because not only do they confirm the findings of many earlier studies but they also indicate that these are the characteristics that seem to dominate the adult arsonist— particularly the phenomena of aggression and impulsiveness. As far as family backgrounds were concerned, Kafry found that the homes of those boys who played with fire tended to be characterized by a greater degree of emotional and social deprivation; fathers played a less important rôle and the mother was often left to cope with rearing the children. The fathers were often perceived as having a negative relationship with their sons. It will be obvious to many readers that these are the same characteristics that are so often found in the backgrounds of other anti-social and delinquent children. Some confirmation of Kafry's findings can be found in a study carried out by Stewart and Culver (1982). They examined forty-six children who had set at least one fire and had been admitted to a psychiatric ward. The children were followed up after one to five years. Seven of the children, all boys and all less than thirteen years of age, were still setting fires but they were held to be less serious than the ones they had set before treatment. The authors considered that the persistent fire-setters seemed to come from the less stable homes and to be more generally anti-social on follow-up than the children who no longer set fires. On the other hand, as they readily admit, their study did not enable them to predict with any degree of certainty which children would continue to set fires. (See also Strachan 1981.) It would appear that fire-setting activities in *children* can be either a developmental, experimental phase or part of a more serious disturbed behaviour pattern. In the latter cases, the home backgrounds are often characterized by severe parental stress and parental psychopathology; the children have shown behaviour disturbances of one kind or another from an early age. These disturbances include abnormal aggressiveness, persistent truancy, absconding from home, enuresis, neurotic fears, and nightmares. We do not know to what extent such phenomena are exclusive to fire-setting or are merely part of a multi-faceted phenomenon of disturbance. Heath, Gayton, and Hardesty make a clear statement of what is required when they say that

'a comprehensive epidemiological study of childhood fire-setters which would provide data regarding incidence and prevalence, as well as clarify the relationship between child-hood fire-setting and such demographic variables as sex, age, socio-economic status, race and family size is definitely needed.'   (Heath, Gayton, and Hardesty 1976:235)

(b) *Arson committed by adolescents and young adults*: The back-grounds and motivations of adolescent and young adult arson-ists appear to be somewhat different from those characterizing children who set fires. The adolescents and younger adults we looked at in our sample seemed to be motivated more specifi-cally by boredom and to engage in the behaviour for 'kicks'. In some cases, there was also an accompanying element of getting back at a society that did not appear to care about them. Unlike their younger counterparts, their backgrounds seemed less socially and psychologically disturbed. It is also important to note that the arson offences committed by this age group are often closely associated with the ingestion of alcohol. The following case shows how some of these elements may be combined.

Case 7 A group of five unemployed older teenagers (ages ranging from sixteen to nineteen) had been to a disco, where they had imbibed a fair amount of alcohol, though they were not drunk. They had waited for a considerable time for the last bus home only to find they had missed it. They had been whiling away their time at the bus stop indulging in horseplay. As they became more impatient, their horseplay escalated into more aggressive activity. They smashed the windows of a large outfitters' shop nearby, entered it, and began damaging the contents. In the course of this activity, one of them lit some waste paper while the others looked on, encouraging him. A fire soon took hold, engulfing the premises and rapidly destroying the shop and its contents.

Management

The classification outlined above will, I hope, provide a starting point for more effective management; it should help us to distinguish between those arsonists who are clearly vengeful, those who are psychiatrically disturbed, and those for whom arson is only one aspect of a much more general disorder. The classification is still rather crude; for example, much of it attempts to suggest *motives* but some elements rely inevitably upon a description of *mental states*, which may merely *affect* motivation. It is possible, however, to give some general indications for management, whilst acknowledging that arson is still a much under-researched phenomenon and that very little work has been done on differential management techniques.

Those arsonists who engage in their activities because of serious psychiatric disorder may respond to treatment for their underlying illness. Medication, if taken regularly, may help to keep their most acute and intrusive hallucinations or delusions at bay. One of the problems that arises is that it is often difficult to anticipate the degree to which such offenders will continue to take their medication once they are in the community. The type of surveillance, supervision, and good team work advocated in Chapters 3 and 4 are essential in these cases.

For child and early adolescent arsonists, it may be necessary to keep them in residential care for a fairly prolonged period so that self-controls can be strengthened and supported. For younger children, family therapy modes of treatment aimed at exploring and modifying defective family attitudes and relationships may well be helpful. A useful example of what can be achieved is to be found in Chapter 11 of Minuchin's book *Families and Family Therapy* (1977). In other childhood cases, it is claimed that a behaviourally orientated approach has met with some success. Holland (1969) described the case of a boy aged seven, in which, as part of the treatment, he was rewarded financially for not striking matches. The fire-setting behaviour was eliminated with no recurrence at an eight-month follow-up. Welsh (1971) used a satiation technique on two seven-year-old boys. They spent their therapeutic sessions (lasting over an hour and a half) lighting matches under controlled conditions. It is important to point out that there was also a highly aversive component in the treatment: in one case, the child was required to hold the match until the heat could be felt on his finger-tips; in the other, the child was required to hold the lighted match at arm's length until fatigue intervened. Follow-up revealed that there was no recurrence at six months. In both these examples, follow-up was short and some readers may consider the methods used somewhat Draconian. In Los Angeles, some experimental work has been undertaken in providing counselling sessions for youthful arsonists and their families. Much emphasis has been placed on education in the appropriate use of fire (Vreeland and Levin 1980).

The management of the adult non-psychotic arsonist presents more difficulty and there is an absence of large-scale clinical data in this area. McKerracher and Dacre (1966) report upon a modest attempt to apply behaviour modification techniques in a Special Hospital setting. If we accept the fact that many arsonists commit their offences because they feel wronged or misunderstood (in other words, that they are 'malicious because they are miserable') then attempts to help them to explore and understand these alleged wrongs may be useful. Attempts can then be made to help them to find ways in which they may achieve more satisfaction from life's experiences. Since we also know that many adult arsonists are socially inept and that they set fires in order to draw attention to themselves, techniques aimed at improving their self-regard, self-image, and social competence should help to minimize the risk of future offending. This may be achieved by specific social skills training, such as the development of legitimate forms of social assertion, and by the development of skills in establishing initial relationships with others, as a prelude to longer-term relationships. It is well known that 'arson is often an aggressive act committed by an under-assertive individual' (Harris and Rice 1984: 32). Harris and Rice go on to emphasize the important but often overlooked point that arson is 'one of the few dangerous offences that can occur without face-to-face contact between offender and victim' (1984: 32).

Conclusions

Arson is one of the most dangerous of all offences. This danger arises for a number of reasons. First, as we have seen, it is not an easily detected crime and many cases of arson go undetected; even when the fire is thought to have been deliberately set, the arsonist often goes undetected. Second, it is an offence that can be committed with comparative ease and at one removed from the victim. Third, even if a single victim is intended for attack, there is always the strong possibility that others will be injured in the ensuing conflagration. Fourth, motivation is often obscure and it is all too easy to be misled by superficial explanations for the crime. Fifth, the assessment of the risk of repetition is extremely difficult and for this reason hospital and penal authorities and their appropriate review boards are very conscious of the dangers of early release of detained arsonists, particularly those who have repeated the offence. Sixth, although there is an abundance of anecdotal material (much of it rather dated and mainly psychoanalytic), there are very few large-scale studies of motives and characteristics that help us to distinguish between the arsonist who is likely to be a social nuisance and the arsonist who is potentially a social menace. Within the present 'state of the art', we can only try to make a judgement based upon a detailed and careful evaluation of the individual case, whilst bearing in mind the seventeenth-century proverb that 'Fire is a good servant but a bad master'.

References

Allderidge, P. (1979) Hospitals, Madhouses and Asylums: Cycles in the Care of the Insane. *British Journal of Psychiatry* **134**: 321–24.

Clisby, C. (1980) Experiencing Fires. In D. Canter (ed.) *Fires and Human Behaviour*. Chichester: Wiley.

Faulk, M. (1982) The Assessment of Dangerousness in Arsonists. In J.R. Hamilton and H. Freeman (eds) *Dangerousness: Psychiatric Assessment and Management*. London: Gaskell. (For Royal College of Psychiatrists.)

Foust, L. (1979) The Legal Significance of Clinical Formulations of Firesetting Behaviour. *International Journal of Law and Psychiatry* **2**: 371–87.

Fras, I. (1983) Fire-Setting (Pyromania) and its Relationship to Sexuality. In L.B. Schlesinger and E. Revitch (eds) *Sexual Dynamics of Anti-Social Behaviour*. Illinois: Charles C Thomas.

Fry, J.F. and le Couteur, N.B. (1966) Arson. *Medico-Legal Journal* **XXIV**: 108–21.

Harris, G.T. and Rice, M.E. (1984) Mentally Disordered Firesetters: Psychodynamic versus Empirical Approaches. *International Journal of Law and Psychiatry* **7**: 19–34.

Heath, G.A., Gayton, W.F., and Hardesty, V.A. (1976) Childhood Firesetting. *Canadian Psychiatric Association Journal* **21**: 229–37.

Holland, C.J. (1969) Elimination of Firesetting in a Seven-year-old Boy. *Behaviour Research and Therapy* **7**: 135–37.

Home Office (1982) *Criminal Statistics, England and Wales: Supplementary Tables, 1982 (Volume 4)*. London: HMSO.

—— (1983) *Fire Statistics: United Kingdom, 1982*. London: Home Office.

—— (1984) *Criminal Statistics, England and Wales: Statistics Relating to Crime and Criminal Proceedings for the Year 1983*. Cmnd. 9349. London: HMSO.

Hurley, W. and Monahan, T.M. (1969) Arson: The Criminal and the Crime. *British Journal of Criminology* **9**: 4–21.

Inciardi, J.A. (1970) The Adult Firesetter: A Typology. *Criminology* **8**: 145–55.

Kafry, D. (1980) Playing With Matches: Children and Fire. In D. Canter (ed.) *Fires and Human Behaviour*. Chichester: Wiley.

Lewis, N.D.C. and Yarnell, H. (1951) *Pathological Firesetting (Pyromania)*. Nervous and Mental Disease Monographs No. 82. New York.

Macdonald, J.M. (1977) *Bombers and Firesetters*. Illinois: Charles C Thomas.

McKerracher, D.W. and Dacre, A.J.I. (1966) A Study of Arsonists in a Special Security Hospital. *British Journal of Psychiatry* **112**: 1151–154.

234   *Dangerous Behaviour, the Law, and Mental Disorder*

Marchant, E.W. (1980) Modelling Fire Safety and Risk. In D. Canter (ed.) *Fires and Human Behaviour*. Chichester: Wiley.

Minuchin, S. (1977) *Families and Family Therapy*. London: Tavistock.

Newton, J. (1976) Suicide by Fire. *Medicine, Science and the Law* **16**: 177–79.

Prins, H. (1980) *Offenders, Deviants, or Patients? An Introduction to the Study of Socio-Forensic Problems*. London: Tavistock.

Prins, H., Tennent, G., and Trick, K. (1985) Motives for Arson (Fire Raising). *Medicine, Science and the Law* **25**: 275–78.

Sapsford, R.J., Banks, C., and Smith, D.D. (1978) Arsonists in Prison. *Medicine, Science and the Law* **18**: 247–54.

Scott, D. (1974) *Fire and Fire-Raisers*. London: Duckworth.

Simmel, G. (1949) Incendiarism. In K.R. Eissler (ed.) *Searchlights on Delinquency*. London: Imago.

Smith, J.C. and Hogan, B. (1983) *Criminal Law* (fifth edition). London: Butterworths.

Soothill, K.L. and Pope, P.J. (1973) Arson: A Twenty-Year Cohort Study. *Medicine, Science and the Law* **13**: 127–38.

Stekel, W. (1924) *Peculiarities of Behaviour*. New York: Liveright.

Stewart, M.A. and Culver, K.W. (1982) Children Who Set Fires: The Clinical Picture and a Follow-Up. *British Journal of Psychiatry* **140**: 357–63.

Strachan, J.G. (1981) Conspicuous Firesetting in Children. *British Journal of Psychiatry* **138**: 26–9.

Thomas, K. (1984) *Religion and the Decline of Magic*. Harmondsworth: Penguin.

Topp, D.O. (1973) Fire as a Symbol and as a Weapon of Death. *Medicine, Science and the Law* **13**: 79–86.

Virkunnen, M. (1974) On Arson Committed by Schizophrenics. *Acta Psychiatrica Scandinavica* **50**: 152–54.

Vreeland, R.G. and Levin, B.M. (1980) Psychological Aspects of Firesetting. In D. Canter (ed.) *Fires and Human Behaviour*. Chichester: Wiley.

Welsh, R.S. (1971) The Use of Stimulus Satiation in the Elimination of Juvenile Firesetting Behaviour. In A.M. Graziano (ed.) *Behaviour Therapy With Children*. Chicago: Aldine.

Woolf, P.G. (1977) Arson and Moebius' Syndrome—A Case Study of Stigmatization. *Medicine, Science and the Law* **17**: 68–70.

FURTHER READING

Both these works provide a very useful selection of further references to all aspects of the subject, including such matters as fire prevention.

Boudreau, J., Kwan, Q.Y., Faragher, W.E., and Denault, G.C. (1977)

Arson and Arson Investigation: Survey and Assessment. Washington: National Institute of Law Enforcement and Criminal Justice.

Duncan, J.T.S., Caplan, M., and Kravitz, M. (1979) *Arson—A Selected Bibliography.* Washington: National Institute of Law Enforcement and Criminal Justice.

Note

1 In this and subsequent case illustrations in this chapter, essential identifying details have been altered in order to preserve anonymity.

CHAPTER NINE
Training issues and concluding comments

'Piece out our imperfections with your thoughts.'

SHAKESPEARE
Henry V Prologue

In this book, I have tried to identify and bring together a range of materials that will prove useful to those who have to deal with those dangerous and high-risk offenders who pose a serious threat to the personal safety of others. I began by outlining the legal status of some of these offenders, the arguments over issues of criminal responsibility, and the problematic border-line between sickness and sin. I followed this with a discussion of the main systems of disposal of such offenders or offenders/patients and the problems faced by those who have to deal with them in the community. In subsequent chapters, I dealt with some of these high-risk categories in more detail. In this final chapter, I shall return to some of the issues raised in Chapter 4, in particular to the training needs of those charged with the difficult and anxiety-provoking task of working with such people. I make no claim for great originality of thinking in this book; I have tried to assemble and synthesize information that will be helpful to a wide range of readers. In undertaking such a task, one always stands in danger of being charged with compiling statements from the work of others. To quote Montaigne, 'It might well be said of me that I have merely made up a bunch of other men's flowers, and provided nothing of my own but the string to tie them together' (*Essays* 3(12)). As every good professional florist knows, however, there is a good deal of skill required in the selection of the most appropriate material and in its arrangement!

Although it is hoped that the *information* provided in this book will be helpful in its own right, information (knowledge) alone is insufficient. In this difficult and demanding area of work, opportunities must be allowed and taken for workers to examine their *feelings and attitudes*. It has been suggested recently in the media that social work and the allied services have become dangerous occupations; indeed, as I write this chapter, there have been a number of instances in which social workers have met their deaths in the course of their work. One instance involves a youth who has been charged with stabbing a social worker to death in a train. The assault appears to have been a frenzied attack, though whether the encounter and subsequent assault was work-related is not yet known. On 2 April, 1985, it was reported that a social worker in the London Borough of Haringey 'was savagely murdered whilst visiting a client' in the course of making a mental health assessment (*Guardian* 16 April, 1985). Only three days later, Walter Schwarz—a *Guardian* columnist—described how his cousin, a social worker at a psychiatric hospital, was stabbed to death by a former inmate with a known history of violence (*Guardian* 17 April, 1985).

In Chapter 4, I made a number of suggestions for reducing the likelihood of attacks by clients or patients on professional workers or on others but it is worth emphasizing that with all the best precautions in the world and with the highest skills available, it is quite impossible to anticipate and prevent the unpredictable and unexpected attack, for such attacks often come 'out of the blue'. Some offenders give no clues as to their intentions; subsequent examination of the events leading up to the attack often fail to reveal anything of significance. However, for those who have shown a *history* of violence in the past and a *continuing propensity* to behave in this way, some of the precautionary steps I suggested in Chapter 4 may prove helpful. (Some further useful measures are to be found in Owens and Ashcroft 1985, particularly Chapters 7 and 9.)

It is difficult to assess with any degree of accuracy statements that assaults on the staff of the caring and allied professions have been on the increase in recent years. Detailed statistics do not appear to be available and a well-publicized tragedy may lead to a distorted picture. It is doubtful whether probation officers and local authority social workers are assaulted more often than police officers, nurses, casualty officers, psychologists, prison staff, or DHSS officials. Even if we allow for the inadequacy of the figures and the consequent lack of precise information, however, it does *appear* that there has been an increase in the numbers of assaults taking place on a wide range of social service and allied staffs. Such an increase is not altogether surprising, if we consider that there are increasing numbers of people liable to suffer frustration as a result of long-term unemployment and the hopelessness and loss of self-esteem that this engenders. In a society that is felt not to care, the phenomenon of the 'short fuse' is a very understandable one. Moreover, this 'short fuse' phenomenon seems to be occurring in all areas of our social life—from the ranks of the frustrated unemployed to the increasing degree of bad temper and irascible behaviour shown by politicians in such institutions as the House of Commons. Certainly one has the *feeling* that we live in a much more confrontational and abrasive society these days.

It is also likely that a larger number of assaults occur on professionals than are ever actually reported to employers or other authorities. Many workers are reluctant to report even fairly serious assaults, since they tend to see an attack on themselves as an indication of some failure on their part. They fear, quite erroneously in most cases, that they may be thought to have mishandled a situation, so rather than lay themselves open to possible (though often groundless) criticism, they keep quiet about the incident. This is sad for two reasons. First, a calm examination of what actually happened may well be a useful learning experience. Second, by keeping quiet, workers are denying themselves the opportunity of help and sympathetic support from colleagues. Such support is not only vitally important in cases where workers have themselves been attacked; it is equally important in cases where a client or patient under supervision has seriously injured others. In such instances, workers will frequently experience, and to some extent express, feelings of guilt and inadequacy. 'I feel I could have prevented it . . . if only . . .', 'I could have done better . . .'. If such feelings are dammed up and not given free expression, this is harmful and may well prevent effective work in other cases. If workers can accustom themselves to 'off-loading' in the way I have indicated and are used to being afforded support and encouragement, then, when things do go badly wrong (as they sometimes will), it will be that much easier to react undefensively. *If* we can be reasonably confident that we have acted in our best professional manner and *if* we have sought and implemented the best advice we can in highly problematic situations, we should not then feel too defensive when the inevitable tragedy occurs. For occur it will; this is the price the community has to pay for allowing potentially dangerous people their liberty. The other alternative is to 'throw away the key' on a number of people who should be given a chance to prove they can survive non-dangerously in the community.

I have always felt that the public at large is not as critical of social workers, psychiatrists, and allied professionals when occasionally things go wrong as the media sometimes seeks to suggest. I consider that thinking members of the public have a pretty fair idea of the difficult decisions that have to be made; if asked, they would be prepared to admit that they have respect for those who are charged with caring for, or controlling, some of society's more worrying misfits. It is understandable, though, that members of the public will show anxiety when things go wrong. There is probably nothing more frightening to contemplate than the notion that potentially violent people can lose control of themselves and, when in this state, commit horrendous acts. This being the case, those who care for and exercise control over those adjudged to be at high risk and dangerous have to undertake an additional and important task of public relations. The rôle of the worker in all such cases can only be effective if he or she is in as much command of the situation as possible. The worker must not only be armed with knowledge but also have a sense of order and priority about its use. Smale (1984) likens such a process to that encountered by the navigator.

> 'Any sailor is seriously handicapped without a chart to tell him what is under the surface as well as where the land lies. But he also needs to look at what else is actually moving around him, ideally using radar to inform him of events beyond his natural sight.'   (Smale 1984: 432)

For our purposes, we may substitute for radar the acquisition of insight developed through training. With this analogy in mind I come to a brief consideration of some issues related to specific training for work in this field.

An approach to training

In the last few years, a handful of courses have been developed with the purpose of enhancing understanding and practice in work with high-risk and dangerous offenders. Some of these courses have been workshop based and have aimed at offering specific help in dealing with clients or patients who show violence *towards the worker*. Fewer courses have been devoted to work with offenders who have behaved dangerously, or have a propensity to behave dangerously, towards others in their immediate environments—such as partners, other relatives, or complete strangers. It is also true that hardly any basic professional social work and other training courses cover this area in any depth; in fact, most barely mention it. On the MA course offered in my former department at Leicester University, we did make special provision for those students who wished to learn more about mentally abnormal offenders and, in particular, those who might show dangerous propensities; however, such special provision is still fairly rare. The two accounts of special provision that follow are offered as illustrations of what can be achieved. They appear to have been highly successful in meeting their aims and those who have attended have expressed almost unanimous satisfaction with them. It is possible that others may be providing similar courses elsewhere but I have no knowledge of them.

TWO SHORT COURSES

Course 1

Since 1981, I have tutored an annual three-part course for experienced probation officers, which is run under the auspices of the Probation Service Regional Staff Development Office for the North of England. *Part I*, which is residential, provides four days' teaching and discussion of theory and practice. In *Part II*, the officers return to their areas and work on case material chosen by them in Part I. In this second phase, they try to apply some of the ideas and attitudes they have acquired in Part I. *Part III*—also residential and lasting four days—follows about three months later. This part provides officers with the chance to feed back their experiences from Part II and to take their knowledge and understanding further.

The primary aim of the course is the development of the knowledge, attitudes, and skills of probation officers engaged in work with high-risk and violent clients. The course focuses on two main categories of offenders:

(1) those who have committed very serious offences against the person and where there is a fear that they will commit a similar offence, and,

(2) those offenders who show a general continuing propensity towards violent behaviour.

The formal content of Part I consists of lecture inputs consisting of the presentation of the following range of material:

(a) Ways of empathizing with those who are seriously disturbed and dangerous. In this session, considerable use is made of great literature and the arts to demonstrate ways in which empathic imagination may be enhanced. Particular emphasis is placed upon the use of Shakespeare as an aid to understanding in this area. (Readers will doubtless have noted quite a large number of such illustrations at various points in this book.) In my view, we do not make enough use of such material on courses that educate and train people for dealing with the human predicament in all its many forms.

(b) The relationship between mental disorder and criminality.

(c) Various aspects of violence.

In addition to these formal inputs, officers are enabled to react more generally to the material (some of it highly emotive) in small group discussions led by experienced members of the probation service. These small groups provide opportunity not only for the clarification of those aspects of the course that appear puzzling or confusing but also offer a unique opportunity for officers to explore their personal styles of working with dangerous offenders and to share anxieties. To further facilitate this process, course members also take part in a range of exercises which have an experiential basis. I now describe some of these.

Exercise I   The aim of this exercise, which takes place at the first session of the course, is to identify and share incidents and situations which course members have found created fear or anxiety. For this exercise, the course (normally of some thirty members) is divided into six groups. Participants are asked to think themselves back into an anxiety-provoking situation. This should take about five minutes. Each member is then asked in turn to discuss this with the small group and to identify the elements that made the situation anxiety-provoking or particularly difficult. (Time allowance about fifteen minutes per person.) The findings of the small groups are then collated and written up on 'flip' charts, so that they may be shared by all concerned. This is always a very productive exercise. It enables course participants to begin to work quickly for themselves, it encourages sharing of anxieties, and it enables the presenter to incorporate the course members' own material into subsequent teaching.

Exercise II   In order to complement the formal lecture inputs on violence and for some of the feelings that such material arouses to be worked with, we have shown course participants a series of video rôle-played interviews with a range of violent clients. These have been produced by a colleague—Jean Merchant —with the help of her office colleagues. One of these 'vignettes' depicts a first interview with a quietly menacing parole licensee just released from a long prison sentence for rape. The offender (rôle played by a probation officer) gives a compelling presentation of a man full of menacing attitudes towards women. Course participants are asked to divide into small groups for discussion of this and the other case illustrations. The manner in which these are handled by the various officers has always produced very profitable discussion.

In Part III of the course, I present further material on the prediction, assessment, and management of dangerous behaviour. There are also sessions about dealing with serious sex offenders and the rôle of probation officers, in relation to their dual concerns as protectors both of the individual offender and of society. This aspect is given a good deal of attention. The final formal session is devoted to the need for officers to have the benefit of effective and supportive supervision in this difficult area of work. In this third part of the course, the small group discussions are used primarily to enable officers to discuss and share the cases they have been working on in Part II. As in Part I, a number of exercises are used to facilitate the learning experience; the following is an illustration.

Exercise III The purpose of this exercise (originally devised by my colleague Jean Merchant) is an attempt to look at and share the anxieties experienced by probation officers when dealing with serious sex offenders. Officers are given the real (but carefully disguised) case of a man aged thirty-seven, who had sexually assaulted and killed, in a highly sadistic fashion, a girl aged eleven. He had a record of some seven previous convictions, including two cases of indecent assault on females, arson, theft, and making false telephone calls to the police (bomb hoaxes). He had been sentenced to life imprisonment for the current offence. Course participants are asked to engage in a rôle-play situation in which they are undertaking the task of preparing a post-sentence social enquiry report for the Home Office. For the purpose of the exercise, it is assumed that they will be meeting this offender for the first time and that the interview will be the starting point for longer-term contact. One officer has the task of rôle-playing the offender. This officer has to try to imagine his or her way into the mind and attitudes of a man described as a cold, callous killer. He is alleged to have said, in a statement to the police, that he thought the victim was seductive but contemptuous of him. He did not remember what he did but does remember feeling 'out of control'. He is said to have 'come to' when walking away from the scene of the crime and 'feeling good'. 'She got what she deserved.' Currently, he is fearful for his safety in prison. A second officer has to play the part of the probation officer meeting this inmate for the first time. The officer assuming this rôle has in his or her possession the basic facts about the case, including a detailed account of the horrifying injuries inflicted on the child before and after death. A third officer is assigned the task of acting as an observer of this first meeting between offender and probation officer. The object of the exercise is to concentrate upon the probation officer's task. Twenty-five minutes are allowed for the encounter and fifteen for feedback from the observer and for discussion. At the end of the session, the main task of the observer is to help the worker to disentangle the difficult emotional aspects that have accompanied this task; for example, the officer's anxieties about trying to get the offender to begin to realize what he has done, frustration at the offender's apparent defensiveness, and his or her own anger and revulsion at the man's behaviour. We have found that such an exercise provides a rich learning experience and although it is productive of stress, this can be contained and worked through. In the brief account I have given of this particular course, I do not intend to suggest that it should in any sense be a prototype. It is merely meant to exemplify one team's approach to a difficult educational task. In my view, it is the type of course that could, with suitable modifications, be reproduced for use in other settings.

Course 2

With the implementation of the Mental Health Act of 1983, local authorities are required to provide specific training for those social workers who are to be designated as 'approved' under the new legislation. Local authorities have approached the task of providing training in a variety of ways. Our own authority (Leicestershire) has taken the matter very seriously and implemented a seven-week programme, which includes both theoretical and practical elements. Since the inception of the training courses some two years ago, I have provided a two-day input on working with the mentally disordered and high-risk offender/patient in the community. This input contains, in highly condensed form, some of the material described in the probation course above. Although the time allowed is comparatively short and there is a very real need to provide a sound knowledge base, it has also been possible to provide an experiential element, as will be seen from the following examples.

Exercise I   The use of the following exercise, modified from the probation course described above, has been found to be particularly useful at a very early stage in the two-day sequence, since it enables the presenter to engage quickly with course members' experiences and anxieties. The time allowed for it is about fifty minutes. The course membership (usually about fifteen to twenty) is divided into groups of three. The purpose is to bring into the course incidents and/or situations that participants have found to have caused fear, or anxiety, or a sense of impending danger. Course members are asked for five minutes to think themselves back into a situation, incident, or case that created special anxiety for them. Each member of the trio is then asked to try to identify the elements that made the situation particularly traumatic (about ten to fifteen minutes is allowed per person). The trio are then asked to summarize each person's experience (under single-line headings) on a 'flip' chart, so that the information can be shared with the rest of the course membership.

Exercise II The following exercise, originally devised by my colleague Tony Walker, for use on the probation course referred to above, has been found to highlight most successfully the need for effective supervision felt by workers when handling high-risk and dangerous cases. The exercise in question has been used on courses for senior social workers who have the task of supervising the career grade staff who handle such potentially dangerous clients. The time allowed for this exercise is about forty minutes. The senior social workers are asked to 'imagine themselves' into the following situation.[1] 'You are members of an area group of *Local Authority Senior Social Workers*. Your Area Director has received a letter from an experienced social worker, which indicates dissatisfaction with the supervision afforded by the worker's senior in relation to a mentally disordered and dangerous client. The Area Director asks that appropriate supervision be provided for colleagues who have to work with such cases and to this end suggests that you address yourselves to the following remit:

(a) Identify the special elements in working with such cases and which are felt to necessitate different patterns of staff supervision being provided in such work.
(b) Indicate how a special pattern of supervision relating to such cases might operate in practice and show how staff at

each level might be involved (i.e. consider the resource implications).

(c) Whether or not the group favours a special pattern, you should indicate ways in which staff supervision in such cases might be made more purposeful for all concerned.

Summarize your findings on a "flip" chart and be ready to speak to them.'

This exercise has always provoked a good deal of thought and discussion. The nature of the task not only involves identifying the nature of the problems for workers in dealing with such cases but also makes the senior social workers examine their own responsibilities for encouraging good social work practice and reminds them of their wider responsibilities to the public. It also enables discussion of the rôle of senior management and the allocation of time and resources. Although this particular task has been designed for use in the training of social work staff, there is no reason why it could not be modified quite simply for use by other professional groups.

The question of public accountability is a very important issue for social services staffs, particularly those in senior management. As part of the training for 'approved social work', our own local authority mounted a week's course for area directors and other senior line management staff. I was asked to make a half-day contribution on the management implications of dealing with mentally disturbed and potentially dangerous offenders/patients in the community. Following a highly compressed account of the nature of the relationship between mental disorder and dangerous behaviour (supplemented by handout material), I presented the senior management staff with the following exercise.

Exercise III 'You are a group of area directors of social services and have been called to a meeting by the Director following the commission of an offence of homicide by an offender/patient already on conditional release and under supervision by your department for a similar offence. The Director has received a number of communications from various quarters (including local councillors and an MP), implying that the degree of supervision afforded to the worker in charge of the case was inadequate. There is no question of disciplinary proceedings or a public or other enquiry. The Director has asked you to address yourselves to the following two issues:

(a) Identify the special elements that may be involved in work with such cases and that may help to reduce the risk to the public.
(b) Identify the key considerations for line management in the provision of effective support for basic grade staff.

You are allowed forty minutes for this task and are asked to summarize your findings on a "flip" chart and to be prepared to speak to them.'

This exercise has many elements in common with Exercise II but includes the additional element of public accountability at a higher level of management structure. There is also the issue of responsibility to elected representatives at both local and central level. As with the previous exercise, it could be modified for use by a variety of professional groups.

Concluding comments

The common element in all the courses with which I have been associated in recent years is the need for good inter-professional communication and co-operation. Such co-operation can best be taught by example. One such course, concerned with the management of the mentally abnormal offender, is mounted each year by the Adult Education Department of Leicester University. On this course, a psychiatrist colleague and I take a joint share in the ten weekly lecture presentations. In these, we are able to demonstrate that professional workers can sometimes choose to disagree quite strongly but without rancour or loss of face. It is much easier to *demonstrate* professional co-operation in this way than merely to talk about its advantages. Good professional co-operation, particularly between the medical and other professions, requires the build-up of confidence and a capacity to 'let down one's hair'; this can only really take place after many weeks or months of preliminary 'fencing' and 'skirmishing'. Wilson and Wilson (1985), writing about the relationships between community psychiatry and general practice, have provided some graphic illustrations of the manner in which defensive ploys may be engaged so as to maintain autonomy and status. They suggest that in order to overcome such defensive manoeuvres, one must take account of some of the unconscious motivations that may stand in the way of progress. In this book, I have attempted to view the problems presented by dangerous and high-risk offenders as requiring an interdisciplinary approach. In Chapter 1, I suggested that the 'central aims . . . (of this book) . . . are to enhance under-standing, to improve communication between disciplines and agencies, and to encourage the development of good practice'. I hope I have achieved a modest degree of success in my endeavours.

References

Owens, R.G. and Ashcroft, J.B. (1985) *Violence: A Guide For the Caring Professions*. London: Croom Helm.

Smale, G.G. (1984) Self-fulfilling Prophecies, Self-Defeating Strategies and Change. *British Journal of Social Work* **14**: 419–33.

Wilson, S. and Wilson, K. (1985) Close Encounters in General Prac-tice: Experiences of a Psychotherapy Liaison Team. *British Journal of Psychiatry* **146**: 277–81.

Note

1 With a small course, it is possible for the whole group to engage in the exercise. If the course numbers more than twelve persons, I usually divide participants into two groups.

Name Index

Subject Index